LIVING BY THE PEN

LIVING BY THE PEN

Women writers in the eighteenth century

Cheryl Turner

London and New York

First published 1992
Paperback edition published 1994
by Routledge
11 New Fetter Lane, London EC4P 4EE

Simultaneously published in the USA and Canada
by Routledge
29 West 35th Street, New York, NY 10001

Typeset in 10 on 12 point Garamond by
Florencetype Ltd, Kewstoke, Avon
Printed in Great Britain by
T.J. Press (Padstow) Ltd, Padstow, Cornwall.

A catalogue record for this book is available from the British Library

Library of Congress Cataloging in Publication Data
Turner, Cheryl
   Living by the pen : women writers in the eighteenth century /
by Cheryl Turner.
      p.   cm.
   Includes bibliographical references and index.
   1. English fiction—Women authors—History and criticism.
2. Women and literature—Great Britain–History—18th century.
3. Authors and publishers—Great Britain—History—18th
century.   4. Women—Great Britain–Books and reading—
History—18th century.   5. English fiction—18th century—
History and criticism.   6. Women novelists. English—18th
century—Biography.   7. Authorship—Sex differences.   I. Title.
PR858.W6T8   1992
823´.5099287—dc20   91–45967

ISBN 0–415–04411–1 (hbk)
ISBN 0–415–11196–X (pbk)

For my parents, Betty and Bruce Turner

CONTENTS

FIGURES

ACKNOWLEDGEMENTS

This study has been achieved through the co-operation and goodwill of many people. In particular, I would like to thank Professor Bob Coats for the support he gave me as supervisor of my Ph.D. and for his interest in my subsequent work, and Dr Alan Rodway, Dr Helen Meller, Nick Ryan, and Dan Smith for their help with the original thesis. I am also very grateful to Elaine Hobby and Jane Spencer for their comments on various drafts of the book, and to Helena Reckitt, Talia Rodgers, and Julia Hall at Routledge for their patience and encouragement.

Thanks are due to the staff at various libraries who have dealt promptly with many enquiries, particularly at the British Library, the Bodleian, the National Library of Wales, and the libraries at Birmingham, Keele, Nottingham, and Sheffield Universities and at North Staffordshire Polytechnic. I am indebted to the Social Science Research Council for the grant which made the initial research possible, and to the Workers' Educational Association (East Midland District) for the extended leave which helped me to complete the manuscript of the book.

I should like to express my appreciation of the encouragement and ideas given to me over the years by my students, whose enthusiasm for women's writing in the eighteenth century has been a joy to share. Finally, my special thanks goes to Mike Attwell, who has seen me through all the stages and given me unstinting support throughout; his generosity has made this possible. Needless to say, the errors are all my own.

INTRODUCTION

The eighteenth-century literary landscape was rich in prose. Books, period-icals, newspapers, pamphlets, broadsheets, and chapbooks offered quantities of fiction and non-fiction to an expanding reading public whose tastes encouraged the growth of an increasingly sophisticated and commercial market. New genres emerged, grew, and obtained important positions within the contemporary popular culture, and none more so than the novel.

Many years ago, Ian Watt (1957) outlined a convincing role for the novel in the rise of middle-class cultural priorities. Identifying such elements as realism, individualism, and a puritan sexual code (which idealized marriage and advo-cated sexual continence) within the work of Defoe, Richardson, and Fielding, Watt helped to locate the emergent form within a wider social historical context and to establish its significance therein. Recently, Michael McKeon (1988) has offered a revision of this view, perceiving 'the novel' and 'the middle class' during the eighteenth century as simple abstractions whose 'origins' during the early modern period were founded upon a considerable pre-existence.

Thus, as both contributor to and reflector of changes in Georgian (and earlier) society, the novel has received a wealth of attention. There is, however, one element of its development that has been relatively neglected and misinterpreted, namely the contribution of women writers. Why should this be? In the past, some historians have advanced an evolutionary answer to that question: the fittest will survive (like Shakespeare or Milton) and the unworthy will disappear or be preserved as literary curiosities. *Ergo*, women's fiction is relatively unknown because it deserves to be. Yet clearly, we are not dealing with an immutable process of natural selection. On the contrary, decisions are made and selections are obtained by historians and critics on the basis of certain criteria of aesthetic value which, until recently, have largely excluded women's material. Moral considerations are part of the web of ideas underlying such assessments of literary worth and these have been used by some historians to support their rejection of women's fiction – particularly their early eighteenth-century fiction – on the grounds that it is lubricious. Sustained disapproval or indifference to women's writing, for aesthetic or moral reasons, has contributed to a high level of ignorance about

1

the scope and scale of women's involvement in the literature market which embraces all genres and which applies particularly to their pre-nineteenth-century material.

Fortunately, however, this situation is changing. Since the 1960s, feminist literary historians and critics have made considerable advances in identifying 'lost' works and in establishing their value by debating and redefining the criteria by which this is judged. The impact of their research has been felt across the spectrum of critical opinion and this is reflected in the inclusion of more female authors, and recently more pre-nineteenth-century authors, in the critical canon. This is not merely a process of literary excavation intended to uncover a few major writers in a female 'Great Tradition' or the lost doyennes of pulp fiction. Feminist critics have set out to 'map the territory of the female imagination' with a view to establishing a context for the analysis of individual works and to identify the links and continuity between them (Showalter 1986: 6).

Accompanying the increased attention paid to women's literature has been an equally significant growth of historical interest in women's lives. This is reflected both in the scope of recent social historical studies, which have taken greater account of matters relating to the status of women, and in the emergence of 'new women's history'. The latter has philosophical and methodological roots in both social history and feminism and, in ways similar to the advances made within literary scholarship, its historians have uncovered a mass of information about women's past activities, whilst engaging in a debate about the conceptual models employed in historical analyses.

Interdisciplinary thinking has been integral to the epistemology of both fields. As Selma Leydesdorff has explained in relation to women's history, it has operated at a number of levels: 'first of all at the level of exchange between the different branches of historical scholarship, secondly at the level of exchange with other scholarly subjects, and thirdly at that brought about by the theoretical questions put forward by feminism' (1989: 13). Women's historians have turned to the contents of women's literature in order to find insights into the social, economic, and ideological movements that concern them. Equally, in their search for a distinctively female subculture, feminist literary historians have recognized the need to examine the social and intellectual forces at work upon the writers they study.

By embracing both fields, the purview of this study lies within that area of interdisciplinary exchange. The foci are primarily literary – the rise of women's prose fiction and the emergence of female literary professionalism – but understanding of these phenomena is sought within an extra-literary context. This is in part a response to the literary critical emphasis of previous analyses, and in part a reflection of a belief which underpins this study: that significant changes in cultural patterns can be understood better in such broad-based terms, than through the perspectives of a single discipline.

Exclusivity is central to the theoretical basis of studies such as this which choose to concentrate upon women only. Therefore, although such a selection is no longer unusual, closer scrutiny of the reasoning behind it is still necessary and can be revealing.

Fundamental to the work of critics and historians of women's writing is the contention that their focus helps to redress the overwhelming imbalance found in previous analyses which have misjudged and mislaid 'good' material by female authors. In a further development of the argument, it has been suggested that women's novels merit particular attention because they were (and are) intrinsically different from men's. By asserting that the sexes have a different relationship with language and by emphasizing the 'differences between traditional female preoccupations and roles and male ones' (Spacks 1975: 7), some critics have proposed the existence of a 'feminine' literary style. The subjects of women's writing and the forms of expression they employ are, it has been argued, part of an 'imaginative continuum, [involving] the recurrence of certain patterns, themes, problems, and images from generation to generation' (Showalter 1977: 11). Thus, the idea of a distinctive 'female imagination' is fundamental to a female literary tradition which was identified initially as emerging in the late eighteenth century (Moers 1978: 125) and which has subsequently been located many decades earlier (Spender 1986).

Although they have proved immensely valuable, I have reservations about some aspects of gender-based interpretations of the creative imagination; they can come perilously close to a notion of feminine sensibility which echoes the most prescriptive eighteenth-century didacticism. On the other hand, strenuous social, cultural, and economic forces were undoubtedly at work upon women writers and it is these forces and their effects that I am seeking to understand. Women are considered as a group in this study, therefore, because their sex had a profound influence upon their place within the patriarchal power structures of eighteenth-century society. Their behaviour was guided, judged, and controlled by contemporary notions of femininity and this affected not only what they wrote but why and how they put pen to paper. Certain barriers and inspirations were held in common.

There is another reason. The rise of women's fiction during the eighteenth century was a cardinal phase in women's increasing involvement in our written culture. As such it warrants detailed attention. The investigative method chosen by most previous studies has been to dissect the development, to look in depth at individual writers and to induce more general conclusions from their lives and achievements. On the other hand, we can try to analyse the phenomenon as a whole, an approach that is facilitated by the fact that the overwhelming majority of the authors concerned came from amongst the middle ranks of the population. By viewing these women as a group (rather than as individual subjects for biographical scrutiny) this study will address questions about their behaviour and milieux that have remained either unanswered or answered only partially. For example: What circumstances (if any) external to the contents of the novel facilitated the growth of their work? How many of these writers were professional and how did they manoeuvre and survive in a competitive market? How did the publishing trades respond to these women? How did they and others regard writing as a female occupation? What were the social and economic backgrounds of these women? And did the palpable changes in the contents of their fiction either reflect or cause significant changes in their authorship?

Finding answers to these questions will deepen our understanding of eighteenth-century reading tastes and the mechanisms of production and distribution at work in the literature market. Furthermore, it will add to the ever-expanding narrative about the condition and contribution of women in the past. In turn, I hope that this will strengthen the complementary process of reviewing and challenging the evaluation of women's achievements within our own society.

> When you, most generous Heroine! stood forth,
> And show'd your Sex's *Aptitude* and *Worth*.
> Were it no more! yet you bright *Maid* alone,
> Might for a World of *Vanity* atone!
> Redeem the coming Age! and set us free
> From the false Brand of *Incapacity*.
> (Elizabeth Thomas, 'To Almystrea, *on her* Divine Works', 1722: 219)

1

EARLIER INTERPRETATIONS OF THE DEVELOPMENT OF EIGHTEENTH-CENTURY WOMEN'S FICTION

To account for the complete lack not only of good women writers but also of bad women writers I can conceive no reason unless it be that there was some external restraint upon their powers. . . . Why, unless they were forcibly prohibited, did they not express these gifts in writing, music, or painting?

(Virginia Woolf, 16 October 1920)

OLD ROOTS, NEW SHOOTS: THE BACKGROUND FOR CHANGE

Those interested in eighteenth-century women's fiction who turn to the secondary sources for the first time will probably be struck by the way in which (with conspicuous exceptions) these novelists have been squeezed into the margins and corners of our literary heritage. Although this emphasis is changing as recent studies have undertaken to bring more women writers to the fore, in the past, large tracts have been devoted to a relatively few male writers from this period and the principal guides have normally taken us from one monumental critical construction to another. Thus, the casual traveller *en route* between Defoe, Fielding, Richardson, Sterne, and Smollett could be forgiven for unwittingly bypassing their female contemporaries.

Whilst such observations are true in general terms, it is important to note also that even amongst earlier literary historians there were those who did not subscribe to contemporary approaches which marginalized the significance of individual seventeenth- and particularly eighteenth-century female authors. In the 1950s Walter Allen (1958) identified Aphra Behn as the best of the early professional fiction writers and prior to this, Summers (1915), Sackville-West (1927), and Woodcock (1948) had argued for her prominence amongst contemporary authors. More recently there has been an escalation of interest in Behn (particularly since she was identified erroneously as the first professional woman writer) and Link (1968), Duffy (1977), Goreau (1980), and Hobby (1988), amongst others, have added substantially to our understanding of her contribution and significance.

5

Behn has been selected relatively frequently for special consideration but she was by no means the sole recipient of early biographical and critical attention. Studies of lesser-known writers like Mary Mitchell Collyer (Hughes 1917), Charlotte Lennox (Small 1935), and Mary Davys (McBurney 1959) are amongst a handful of detailed accounts which contributed to an intriguing but highly fragmented picture of individual achievement during the eighteenth century.[1] A few women besides Behn attained positions of relative prominence in that picture. Fanny Burney's spectacular initial success as a novelist and the wealth of social historical detail in her journals, Ann Radcliffe's conspicuous contribution to the popular romantic Gothic novel, and Mary Wollstonecraft's philosophical challenge to contemporary concepts of womanhood, have secured comparatively frequent analyses of their lives and works. Beasley (1978) and, more recently, Ferguson and Todd (1984), and Chard (1986) have demonstrated that they continue to do so.

Over the last three decades our understanding of eighteenth-century women novelists has enlarged and become more detailed. Obscured writers like Elizabeth Elstob and Sarah Robinson Scott have been brought forward for consideration whilst others, such as Delarivière Manley, Charlotte Lennox, and Maria Edgeworth, have been the subject of further reappraisal. To an extent, mounting interest in these writers has been stimulated by (and has stimulated) a growing number of reprints of their material. This publishing market development has extended the range of recent editions beyond works by Behn, Burney, Edgeworth, Radcliffe, and Wollstonecraft, to include lesser-known authors like Ferrier, Fenwick, Hamilton, Hays, Fielding, Sheridan, the Lees, and Scott. This is an invaluable resource. Surely, there can be no better way of initiating interest in the work of these women writers; however far we may wander in this field, most of us begin with the text.

In terms of the women writers they include, the general literary histories of the period and histories of the novel have had similar foci to the biographers. Radcliffe and particularly Burney emerge from even the earliest of these studies as significant figures, in Burney's case as the vital link in 'one of the important lines of English literary history' (Leavis 1960: 4), between Richardson and Austen. Furthermore, from the *Cambridge History* (1913 and 1914) onwards, a range of other female authors, including Smith, Inchbald, Edgeworth, and Reeve, have been discussed, often in terms of the writers' contribution to the evolution of particular types of fiction such as the Gothic, Regional, and Jacobin novel.

These schools of writing belong to a period in the novel's development which has been viewed as interesting for a number of reasons (for experimentation in the form; the revival of a moral dialogue; and for its expanding readership), but also as something of a literary lull between the storming talents of Smollett and Austen. Thus, these 'types' are often assigned a rather minor position in our panorama of eighteenth-century literature and this has had a reductive effect upon the writers' literary status.

Despite this, studies focusing upon particular species of fiction are a fruitful source of information about the female novelists who made use of them. For example, Morgan's (1911) study of the novel of manners, Singer's (1933) examination of the growth of epistolary fiction, and Tompkins's (1932) exploration of the late eighteenth-century popular novel all make extensive references to women writers. These include obscure authors whose works have, until recently, failed to appear in the standard checklists of the period.[2] This unusual weight of numbers is sufficient to introduce the reader to the notion that women authors were certainly more productive and probably more significant than we would gather from most accounts of the eighteenth-century novel.

This conclusion is confirmed by textual analyses which assign prominent positions to women. Gary Kelly (1976), in his examination of the late eighteenth-century Jacobin novel, identified Elizabeth Inchbald as particularly influential in this form, whilst John Richetti's (1969) study of popular fiction before Richardson considers the particular contribution of Manley, Haywood, Barker, Aubin, and Rowe. His observations upon the impact of individual writers (for example, Rowe's successful welding of entertainment with didacticism as a redemptive influence upon the image of 'She-Wits') have found an echo in the conclusions of the latest studies of these literary women.

It is clear from this brief survey that there has been, and there is still, an informative body of material about certain eighteenth-century women authors which lies within the 'mainstream' of the literary history and criticism of this period. In proportionate terms it is small, which is a reflection of aesthetic and moral judgements and not of the number of women writers, but it is growing. Additionally, from at least the early decades of this century we have been able to garner substantial insights into the lives and works of individual figures from literary biographies.

After reading these sources we could begin to pose a few general questions about the rise of women's fiction: for example, were these few authors so extraordinary or were there other women writers about whom we know even less? If so, how many others were there and did they share the same motivations, aspirations, and difficulties? Having raised these questions we find ourselves facing one more: what or whom do we consult in order to find our answers?

A cursory glance at even the earliest literary histories would begin to solve the first issue at least. We are told of an escalation in the numbers of women writers at the end of the eighteenth century which is linked with the concurrent popularity of romantic fiction. Even with only this hint of a development to focus upon, it is still puzzling that it has taken us so long to outline and investigate the growth more fully. There is no simple solution to that conundrum and instead I offer two contributory factors.

7

Traditionally, the period between *Pamela* (1740) and *Humphrey Clinker* (1771) has been seen as one of artistic efflorescence in the novel as the work of Richardson, Fielding, Sterne, and Smollett helped to define and elevate the new genre. With the disappearance of the great quartet, the novel is characterized by 'its popularity as a form of entertainment and its inferiority as a form of art' (Tompkins 1932 [1962]: 1). It is viewed within the context of the ascendancy of commerce over artistic priorities and the consequent undermining of the writer's status. The emergence (even, it is alleged, predominance) of female novelists is noted as a contributory factor in these regressive developments. Tompkins, who has helped to chart this literary hinterland, outlines the argument:

> The establishment of circulating libraries, which catered especially for their [i.e. women's] leisure, conspired with the failure in the succession of male novelists of power and seriousness to push back the novel from the position which Fielding had claimed for it and to debase it into a form of female recreation. Women, to complete the link in the argument, liked to read what women had written, to meet in books with a reflection of their own interests and point of view; it was a new pleasure, and gave such plentiful occupation to 'your female novel-writers, your spinning-jennies'.
>
> (ibid.: 120)

If we set aside for the moment the assumptions and bias in the schema, the reasoning is straightforward: why should a critic or historian be interested in looking more deeply at the yarns spun by such literary workhorses, and therefore, why should it matter that there were apparently so many of them doing it?

In addition to the impact of the criteria employed in the pursuit of literary excellence, there has also been a lack of knowledge about the actual numbers of novels written by women during the eighteenth century. Until recently, the main bibliographical sources for their fiction were check-lists of particular decades or types of fiction, catalogues of library collections (from the vast reserves of the National Libraries to the smaller, private collections typified by Hardy's (*c*.1982) listing), specialized studies such as those by Singer and Tompkins, histories of the novel, for example Stevenson's (1960) chronological survey, or biographical and critical studies of women novelists.

Careful sifting and amalgamation are necessary if these sources are to provide a coherent impression of growth for the whole period. This is due to the limitations of the scope of each study, and because (with the exception of those focusing on women) relevant details are mixed either alphabetically or chronologically with information about male and anonymous writers.[3] These difficulties do not negate their value for those willing to trawl and indeed, in combination, they have been a major source for the catalogue appended to this study.

A broad understanding of the proportions of the rise of eighteenth-century women's fiction has been made considerably easier in recent years by the bibliographies supplied by Séjourné (1966), Larson (1981), and Spender (1986) in their analyses of women's fiction, by Todd's invaluable *Dictionary* (1987), and by information in *The Feminist Companion* (1990) by Blain *et al*. A brief glance at these sources would be sufficient to confirm previous claims that a substantial expansion in women's fiction took place during this period. Unfortunately, more detailed questions of scale, of escalation or recession, must remain unanswered. This is because of the primarily alphabetical rather than chronological arrangement of the listings,[4] and because there has been no co-ordination over the criteria for the selection of material. This is essential for a consistent policy on the treatment of, for example, translations or multiple-novel volumes.

Since a prerequisite of this study is an understanding of the overall scale and pattern of the development of eighteenth-century women's fiction, I have compiled a new catalogue of their works (Appendix A). As a resource for a broader analysis, it is not intended to be exhaustive, but it does extend the information offered in the most recent listing by Dale Spender (1986: 119–37) by adding further novelists and novels, and by supplying details of publication. It should also be emphasized that the information for Appendix A was gathered with an awareness of the key problem of definition affecting bibliographies of this period, namely, how to distinguish between embellished autobiographies and fictional accounts purporting to be fact. The criteria for selection are outlined in chapter 3, preceding the analysis.

More general questions about the writers themselves, their motivations, achievements, and difficulties (which have been stimulated by our gradual appreciation of their substantial output, and by re-evaluations of its literary merit) may find answers in the critical biographies noted previously and in those studies that have addressed eighteenth-century women novelists as a group.

Since the publication of Kavanagh's *English Women of Letters* (1862), there has been a tributary academic interest in early female authors. In recent years this has surged forward as part of the rise of the international women's movement and it now embraces a multiplicity of genres including drama, poetry, polemical works, private writings, instructive material, journalism, and prose fiction. Elaine Showalter located this process as a second phase in the evolution of feminist criticism, describing it as 'a massive recovery and rereading of literature by women from all nations and historical periods' (1986: 6). Initially at least, the focus of 'gynocriticism' (Showalter 1979: 25) was primarily upon nineteenth-century writers. Recently, however, the work of scholars like Beilin (1987) and Hobby (1988), who have built upon the conclusions of early pioneers like Whitmore (1910), Reynolds (1920), and Gagen (1954), has introduced us to the rich heritage of women's writing that survives from at least the English Renaissance.

Interest in the women novelists of the eighteenth century has run a parallel course, from the laudatory cameos presented in Thackeray's *A Book of Sybils* (1883), through the extensive range of MacCarthy's (1944, 1947) two studies, to Spencer (1986), Spender (1986), and Todd's (1989) comprehensive analyses. Amongst the earlier approaches, Joyce Horner's (1929–30) exploration of the connection between women's fiction and the growth of feminism between 1688 and 1797 has proved particularly enduring. Within her analysis, Horner argued that the controversial triumvirate of Behn, Manley, and Haywood gave way to a new type of writer, a gentlewoman or 'Lady Novelist', who took her literary and moral direction from Samuel Richardson. She interwove this development with the emergence of erudite and celebrated women (epitomized by the Bluestockings) and with the rise of large numbers of female novelists.

This key change in the public's perception of the female novelist has continued to play a significant part in the analyses of most later critics. Richardson is frequently allocated a critical role in this process of 'feminization' on the basis that *Pamela* initiated a current in English fiction that was distinctly feminine (by comparison with the 'masculine' picaresque of writers like Fielding) in its milieu, morality, and emotional outlook. As Janet Todd has explored recently, Richardson's eponymous heroines were fictional models for the 'cult of sensibility [which] stressed those qualities considered feminine in the sexual psychology of the time: intuitive sympathy, susceptibility, emotionalism and passivity' (1986: 110). Women novelists employed this increasingly popular sentimental style in large numbers with, it is argued, a resulting impact upon their public persona.

Critics of women's writing differ over how this development should be interpreted. Katharine Rogers has argued that the glorification of 'tender and delicate feelings' enabled women to 'articulate the emotions and sanction the values that were important to them as women' (1982: 3) and therefore, to invest almost everything they wrote with 'feminist feeling' (1982: 4). However, there are difficulties with the theoretical basis of this approach as it seems to imply the existence of previously suppressed, essentially feminine values which were released by sensibility, rather than fashioned by it. Furthermore, crucial questions of definition are raised when the expression of those values is equated with feminism.

Dale Spender has taken the argument one step further, contending that the very existence of women's material in the face of such formidable difficulties was a feminist achievement:

For women who had no rights, no individual existence or identity, the very act of writing – particularly for a public audience – was in essence an assertion of individuality and autonomy, and often an act of defiance. To write was to be; it was to create and to exist. It was to construct and control a world view without interference from the 'masters'.

(1986: 3)

Again, this argument appears to imply a direct correlation between the rise of women's writing and the emergence of an autonomous and subversive perspective amongst women writers. On the other hand, whilst appreciating the impressive scale of the achievement which underpinned the emergence of women's fiction, which has been so clearly outlined for us by Spender, amongst others, can we argue that greater visibility in the popular culture necessarily constituted and strengthened a challenge to the status quo? As Jane Spencer has suggested: 'the underlying assumption that women's writing *must* have a feminist meaning, must in all cases be a gain for feminism, needs to be questioned' (1986: xi). A key issue for critics of this material must be how that 'world view' should be interpreted. Was it truly 'without interference from the "masters" ', or could women's writing gain in stature whilst strengthening rather than undermining a restrictive definition of womanhood? That question is considered later in this study when changes in the image of female writers are discussed in relation to the growth of their fiction and professionalism.

An awareness that the duality of oppression and resistance can be an insufficient framework for criticism, and may in fact leave interesting aspects of women's achievements still hidden, unexplained, or misunderstood, has permeated recent debates within women's history. Since its earliest years, this field has sustained a vigorous discussion about the theoretical basis for historical analysis. Its initial subsumption within the broader field of 'new social history' produced a fruitful exchange of methodology and information. As Carroll Smith-Rosenburg explained:

Without the growing methodological sophistication of contemporary social history [for example, demography], the New Women's History could not be written. . . . But the path between . . . is not a oneway street; the history of women has significantly expanded the concerns of contemporary social history.

(1975: 188)

However, as women's history matured, the link between the two was questioned and Davin (1972), Lerner (1975), Davin and Alexander (1976), and Kanner (1979), amongst others, set about defining their field as an identifiable branch of historiography. Their approaches were informed by historical and interdisciplinary perspectives and methodologies, newly formed categories of analysis, the achievements of the pioneers of women's history like Clark (1919), Pinchbeck (1930), and Stenton (1957), and the issues and literature of the women's movement since the mid-1960s. Thus, these scholars drew a distinction between older historical studies of women,

11

notably descriptive, biographical depictions of 'female worthies', and their own work which was influenced 'unavoidably (but self-consciously)' (Kanner 1979: 10) by contemporary feminism.

The debate about historical models has continued as some feminist historians have advanced the importance of focusing upon gender as a category of analysis rather than upon women alone. Recently, Showalter has located this discourse within a broader change occurring across the humanities:

> Gender theory began to develop during the 1980s in feminist thought in the fields of history, anthropology, philosophy, psychology, and natural science, marking a shift from the women-centered investigations of the 1970s, such as women's history, gynocriticism, and psychology of women, to the study of gender relations involving both women and men.
>
> (1989: 2)

Leydesdorff has identified another recent change in perspective amongst those women's historians who have shifted the emphasis of their analyses away from the issue of resistance. Without rejecting such concerns, which were rooted in a desire to establish the longevity of current beliefs and struggles, she has argued that 'we should realise and acknowledge that there are many women historians today who wish to concern themselves also with women with whom they cannot immediately identify' (1989: 16).

Clearly, important changes are taking place in the theoretical perspectives of both women's history and women's literature, giving rise to new and vigorous debates about the definition and usage of such categories as gender, class, sexuality, and race, and about the role of language, and historical and social processes in their construction. To some extent these reflect an accommodation of more general issues: the degree to which our own cultural framework predetermines what we look for in our investigation of literature or the past; and the way in which it affects our interpretation of what we find. People can read *against* the grain and are not necessarily persuaded in the way that we assume;[5] and incomplete information and vested theories can lead to incorrect imputations of newness or significance.

They demonstrate also that these fields are dynamic. Traditional paradigms have been challenged and sometimes rejected, and new paradigms created which are subjected to the same questioning. Such theoretical developments which validate the study of seemingly 'non-resisting' and economically privileged women from the middle ranks have contributed to the framework of this study. Echoing the observations of Spencer and Leydesdorff in their respective fields, I am not seeking proto-feminist heroines or attempting to isolate the great writers and wranglers who triumphed in the publishing world (although I am delighted to find them).

My focus includes the whole range of women who turned to novel writing for money, and their strategies for making their efforts successful. The fact that some failed commercially as well as aesthetically, that some were only temporary travellers on the 'common hackney turn-pike road' (Lloyd 1774: 172), and that to succeed some may have added weight to contemporary constraints upon other women, is all part of the fascinating picture that waits to be uncovered.

THE SOCIAL AND ECONOMIC CONTEXT OF THE EMERGING NOVEL

The public authority that late eighteenth-century women had begun to acquire in particular areas has been identified by both literary and social historians: the rise of a confident didactic tone in women's writing ran parallel with the entrance of women into the public arena of organized philanthropy. These developments are independently intriguing but to understand them fully we need to take account of them both. Inter-disciplinary thinking is essential to such an understanding and to this study.

Between them, social and literary historians have identified a number of key threads in the interaction between the eighteenth-century novel as an emerging genre and aspects of the broader environment. These are the warp and weft upon which more detailed pictures can be created. A brief description of the fundamental elements will help to provide a foundation for many of the later arguments of this study.

The position of writers was changing during the eighteenth century. Alterations in the law of copyright, the decline of aristocratic patronage, and the rise to power of influential publishers, all contributed to more commercial relations between authors and booksellers. In turn, this stimulated the growth of alternative ways of structuring publications, for example in the form of fascicles, and of financing books, notably through subscription. These developments were part of an expansion in the book trades in London and provincial centres that was sustained by the growth of newspapers and other ephemeral material, and facilitated by improvements in communications and travel. Thus prose fiction was part of an expanding secular culture which, within the restrictions of literacy, location, and income levels, percolated through the social hierarchy. Increasingly, parts of the literature market were linked with the growth of a leisure industry, enriching the pursuit of pleasure which was gaining credence as a legitimate human ambition. Allegations that the writer's craft was thus reduced to a labour-intensive industry were counterbalanced by increasing publishing opportunities and growing demand. These were prerequisites for a redefinition and consolidation of literary professionalism. 'Literature had arrived as a "fourth estate" ' (Saunders 1964: 146).

Changes in the composition of the readership were critical to this process but accurate investigation of the potential demand is problematic. Such literacy statistics as do exist for the period are subject to methodological and interpretive caveats; the ability to read, which is the skill at issue here, cannot be monitored accurately through evidence from signatures. Interest in the social spread of the reading habit (and not simply the extent of literacy) during the eighteenth century has been shared by authoritative accounts from Collins (1927) onwards and most recently by Vincent in his examination of *Literacy and Popular Culture* (1989). On the basis of evidence from the spread of education, corroborative observations made by interested contemporaries, the publication of novels, the growth of circulating libraries, the extensive circulation of newspapers and magazines, and the rise of 'number' publications, such studies have inferred that a significant expansion in reading took place during this period.

Historians have associated the greater social spread of this activity with a gradual alteration in the 'centre of gravity' of the reading public (Watt 1957 [1972]: 53). Until recently the prevailing view saw literature as belonging increasingly during the eighteenth century to a 'trading-manufacturing society governed by an oligarchy' (Dobrée 1959: 9–10). It was argued that the gradual ascendancy of the values of that society was a major stimulus to the contemporary growth of print culture and that the emergence of the novel in particular symbolized the drive of the middle class towards cultural hegemony. The genre, it was argued, gave a new and authoritative expression to the interests of the widening middle ranks of merchants, traders, shopkeepers, manufacturers, professionals, craftworkers, and farmers: Perkin's 'long, diverse but unbroken chains' between the landowner and the labouring poor (1969: 22).

Recently, this interpretation has been challenged by Michael McKeon (1988), whose schema places the 'origins' of the novel, like those of the 'rising' middle class, at the end of a long history of 'preexistence'. He argues that the growing acceptance of 'the novel' as a canonic term during the eighteenth century was forged by far-reaching dialectical relationships, a process of conflict for questions of truth and virtue that occurred in stages and which included countercritiques that harked back to the original refuted postures of 'romance idealism' and 'aristocratic ideology'. This process, McKeon suggests, explains apparent inconsistencies in the genre such as its capacity to accommodate simultaneously both formal realism and features of the romance tradition, and to mediate opposing approaches to questions of virtue and truth.

Recent debates about the cultural location of the emergent novel are a continuation of a discussion begun in the earliest years of the genre. From Congreve's *Incognita* (1692) to Reeve's *Progress of Romance* (1785), the form was distinguished from previous prose fiction (i.e. the 'aristocratic' heroic romance) by its social realism; its presentation of events that were 'not such as are wholly unusual or unprecedented' (Congreve 1692 [1971]:

ii–iii).[6] Thus, a classical education, which was a prerogative of the male aristocracy and gentry, was not regarded as necessary in order to write or read the novel and therefore the genre had a potentially wide constituency. It is in this context that most historians have identified a central role for women.

Middle- and upper-class women (mainly from London and fashionable provincial centres like Bath) have been viewed as an important part of the growing readership which was cultivated assiduously by the increasing 'tribe' of novelists. This development is attributed to an increase in female leisure arising from the impact of industrial production on domestic tasks and from the employment of more servants. This was itself a result of growing affluence and social aspirations within the middle ranks. Women from this stratum, it is argued, were consigned by their narrow social and economic role to inactive lives filled with voracious novel reading. Improvements in education produced literate but inadequately educated young women for whom the novel was a potent mixture of romantic escapism and moral guidance. Recently, we have become more aware of the fact that this set of circumstances also produced lives that were shaped by vulnerability. Once financial stability receded, economic dependence became threatening; limited training had to be used and abundant social restrictions negotiated in order to keep body and soul together, and preferably 'in figure'. These were circumstances that led women to take up the pen for money.

Domestic servants, who as a group were particularly exposed to the influence of their middle- and upper-class employers, are seen as another important element in the new broad-based demand for fiction. The fact that very early in the debate Watt noted that novel prices were 'far beyond the means of any except the comfortably off' (1957; [1972]: 46) has not presented problems. The solution has been found in the growing number of circulating libraries. These establishments, which spread through the country during the eighteenth century, are commonly held to have provided a plentiful supply of low-quality romantic fiction which could be borrowed for a fraction of the retail price. Indeed, novels are regarded as the libraries' chief attraction and it is suggested that they appealed particularly to female subscribers and domestic servants. In this schema, therefore, the novel as a genre, women as readers, and circulating libraries as distribution centres are regarded as critical to the development of popular romantic fiction.

THE ROLE OF WOMEN WRITERS?

Why has this general outline failed to expose the role of women novelists? This is not because their existence has been ignored entirely, although there are scholars, like Watt, who managed to eliminate them from their accounts. As we have seen, even the selective vision that prevailed amongst historians before the 1970s

15

encompassed some individual women novelists in its scope and there has been a long-standing association between the domestic sentimentality of contemporary romances and the domestic orientation of the women who wrote as well as read them. It is more a matter of historical perspectives and priorities. As writers, women's contribution to the upward trajectory of the novel has been widely regarded as marginal (with specific exceptions). On the other hand, there is a broad consensus that women readers were central to the expansion of popular literature (including but not confined to the novel) and the cultural flexing of the middle ranks. Therefore, there has been a strong reason for focusing upon the latter role but not upon the former. However, interest in the social and economic forces at work upon women authors requires a further stimulus beyond the relocation of their work in our critical canon. It entails a belief in the proposition that the extra-literary experiences of women as writers were sufficiently different from those of men for them to warrant investigation and eventual assimilation into our broader historical picture.

This applies particularly to the previous coverage of women's literary professionalism. The appearance of a blatantly commercial approach amongst women writers attracted contemporary interest and the conspicuous part played by certain authors excited some extreme responses: from encomiums to the best of the 'Fair Sex' to embittered allegations of indecency in both their literary and personal activities. Our own historical interest in these women has been somewhat less intense and indeed it is only recently that literary historians have begun to look at their professionalism in detail.

The combative world of the eighteenth-century professional writer has been the subject of a few specialist studies which provide between them an overview of the occupation, from Grub Street hacks like Oldmixon to the exceptional polymath, Dr Johnson. Rogers's (1972) foray into the topography of 'Dulness' locates Haywood within the literal and metaphorical world of Grub Street and in the company of a certain type of 'Suburban Muse' who reaches the pages of our literary histories only rarely. Unfortunately, other key studies in the field, by Collins (1927) and Saunders (1964), whilst offering useful information about the impact upon authorship of various publishing market developments, discuss these matters almost entirely in relation to male writers. This is not surprising, as until recently professionalism was hardly acknowledged as a significant aspect of early women's writing and any references to such authors tended to focus upon exceptional cases where notably large payments were secured for material.

Subsequent advances in our knowledge of the women writers of this period have now placed their professionalism on the agenda for proper consideration. Biographical studies of individuals like Manley, Haywood, Scott, and Smith have revealed much about the social, economic, and legal plight of such women,[7] whilst general studies of the novelists of the period have also ranged over such factors as the composition of the readership and the financial rewards of publication (e.g. Spencer 1986: 8–11). More recently, Shevelow (1989) and Todd (1989) have both made substantial progress in confuting previous misconceptions about women's early professionalism, exploring the authors' strategies for success, their work, and their attitudes towards it. Between them they have demonstrated what an extraordinarily rich and complex area we are beginning to understand.

This study hopes to contribute to that investigation by tracing the prevalence of this phenomenon amongst women novelists as a whole rather than viewing it as a significant feature of the work of particular individuals. It will argue that eighteenth-century women writers were aware of and responsive to each other's work; and that professionalism was common amongst these women, who were, by and large, competent to deal with its requirements, and in some cases very astute in exploiting its possibilities. In other words, without proposing that one should shift the locus of discussions about nineteenth-century female novelists several decades backwards in time, one may argue that aspects of women's writing and of its context that have been identified most frequently with the 1800s were in fact evident in their work at least a century earlier.[8]

Recent critics of eighteenth-century women's fiction have engaged to differing extents in a discussion of that environment and of the contemporary condition of women. Between them they have identified several major factors: the changing role and status of women within public ideology; the effect of this upon familial relations; the impact of limited employment opportunities in the context of economic dependence for women from the middle stratum; increasing access to education for certain women; and the character of the curriculum.

The historical movements that are reflected in these changes and their impact upon women have been explored more fully by social and women's historians who have now given us a much clearer idea of what the lives of middle-class women were like and how they were changing. The conclusions of these scholars will be discussed and amplified in the remaining chapters of this study as the context of women's fiction writing and literary professionalism is explored.

2

SEVENTEENTH-CENTURY FOUNDATIONS

Remember, I pray you, the famous Women of former Ages, the *Orinda's* of late, and the more Modern D'acier and others.

(Astell 1694: 10)

In a sense, historical analyses impose an artificial segmentation upon past developments: it is always possible to delve further backwards to identify roots that are buried still more deeply. This applies to the continuum that we describe as the growth of women's writing. Each 'phase' can reward close examination and has its own distinctive contribution to make, and equally, each one provides a foundation for the ensuing chapters in the story.

As a result of recent work in the field, we are acquiring a fuller appreciation of the ways in which the pattern of women's writing in the eighteenth century provided a context for the work of their better-known Victorian successors. Equally, significant aspects of women's authorship in the 1700s can be traced from at least the period of the 1650s onwards. These features include: a broadening of the social and economic base amongst these writers and an increase in the numbers who published their material; a growing tendency to use writing as a means of exploring and commenting upon the contemporary social and ideological environment and the position of women within it; a rise in the number of female authors who addressed themselves to a female readership; and the emergence of women's literary professionalism.

Poetry accounts for a large proportion of women's writing before the eighteenth century and for some of their most interesting, skilful, and subversive work (Hobby 1988: 128–64). The range of their poetic styles encompasses the satire and sensuality of Aphra Behn, Anne Finch's evocative descriptions of nature, Katherine Philips's celebration of friendship and love, and the ingenious conceits of the Duchess of Newcastle. The form was also useful to women's early literary professionalism through verses written to attract patronage, and, as I shall demonstrate in chapter 6, it continued to be a source of income for women writers in the eighteenth century. However, the genre will not be considered in any greater detail in this

18

chapter as the main objective of the ensuing discussion is to identify any common or similar aspects between women's fiction writing in the 1700s and their seventeenth-century authorship. These can be perceived more clearly in relation to other literary forms.

PRIVATE WRITING

Before reviewing women's published non-fictive prose, drama, and prose fiction, I shall turn first to the evidence offered by their private diaries and autobiographies. Matthews (1950; 1955) has produced annotated bibliographies for both forms which cover this period. He lists seventeen women's diaries for the whole of the century, ten of which belong to the second half, and we can add at least two further examples to his total.[1] He includes eight autobiographies by seventeenth-century women, all of which fall within the second half of the period and again we can add at least two examples to his list.[2] As Matthews, and more recently Graham et al. (1989) have demonstrated, this material offers us an insight into women's activities and thoughts on a great variety of topics: domestic work, familial relations, spiritual matters, love and marriage, travel, business, women's independence, and major national issues such as the plague, the Great Fire, and the Civil War.

Matthews reveals a general growth of such material during the seventeenth century, a trend which continued throughout the eighteenth century. Spiritual matters were, according to his notes, a major preoccupation but subordinate in men's writings to military and public affairs. Religious observance as a theme appears to have been more dominant amongst the texts by women, perhaps reflecting the way in which writing could function as a valuable private resource, a rare outlet for self-expression, and an opportunity to examine complex and sometimes troubling matters.

These diaries and autobiographies were produced by women from diverse social and economic backgrounds. The writers include the Countess of Warwick, the Viscountess of County Down, the wife of a sea captain, the daughter of a minister, a London midwife, the wife of a country gentleman from Yorkshire, and a Huguenot refugee in York.[3] Allowing for the erratic survival and uncovering of this type of material, it none the less suggests a social base amongst writing women that had broadened beyond the upper reaches of the gentry and aristocracy. This is borne out by other extant private material such as prayers and notes on reading, and by activity mentioned in contemporary accounts. John Evelyn's diary, for example, reveals the continuous literary output of Margaret Blagge (Mrs Godolphin). Glimpses of secret scribbling are also afforded by titles listed in the Stationers' Company's records, witness: *The experiences of God's gracious dealing with Mrs Elizabeth White, late Wife of Mr. Tho. White, of Coldecot in the County of Bucks; as they were written under her own hand, and found in her Closet after her decease: she dying in Childbed, December 5th 1669* which was entered for Easter 1671 (*Term Catalogues* 1903: 70).

This development is understandable when viewed in the context of the turbulent intellectual climate which gave rise to the philosophical and political ideas of such radical thinkers as Bacon, Hobbes, and Locke. The divine precepts of God were equated with equally immutable but rationally explicable scientific laws, and Nature was likened to a machine that could be understood and even controlled through method and knowledge. Mediation by the clergy in their role as interpreters of the sacred texts was challenged and the basis of popular religion undermined through theological disputation conducted via the increasingly available printed word. It is important to note in this context that women's contribution to this process was of a crucially different nature in that it was primarily inspirational rather than rationalistic.

From the Calvinistic determinism of some Puritans, to the mystical pantheism of ranterism, dissenting theology proposed a direct responsibility to God for each individual. Axiomatically, spiritual introspection was essential for all, regardless of gender, and it was therefore incumbent upon women as well as men to examine their moral well-being. Private writing by educated women from the aristocracy through to the middle ranks of society was one expression of a need for careful self-awareness.

WRITING FOR A READERSHIP

There is an important distinction to be drawn between those women who wrote on such issues for their own enlightenment or that of their immediate family and friends, and those who wrote for a general and unknown readership. Significantly, there was a notable increase in the middle of the century in the number of women who wrote for publication. Elaine Hobby (1988) has shown that a substantial amount of this material consisted of prophecies by female members of the radical sects that emerged before and during the Civil War. These writers presented themselves as inspired by God and it has been argued (Hobby 1988: 26) that contemporary notions of womanhood confirmed women as particularly suitable conduits for inspiration: their humble social status and perceived absence of independent-mindedness made them more receptive to divine messages and less likely to distort their meaning through personal interpretations. Thus, women were enjoined to make a claim upon public attention, albeit with the most profound humility. The urgency and inexorable nature of their task led them to undertake extraordinary missions, petitioning Parliament, bearing witness against the views of others, debating doctrinal matters, castigating the apostasy of former allies, and travelling and preaching at home and abroad on behalf of their faith. We can glimpse, through the numerous letters written by the Nottinghamshire Quaker Elizabeth Hooton, the level of antagonism they encountered *en route*. Elizabeth described her confrontation with the magistrates in Cambridge, Massachusetts, who, having already committed her to jail without bread or water,

> made a Warrant to whip me for a wandring vagabond Quaker at 3 townes 10 stripes at whipping poast in Cambridg & 10 at Watertowne & 10 stripes at Deddam at ye Carts tayle wth a 3 corded whip 3 knotts at end, & a handfull of willow rods at Watertown on a cold frosty morning. . . .

> > (*c.* 1662, Manners 1914: 41)

Divine authority also gave women a licence or vocation to address the major religio-political issues of the day through their writing. Their challenge, through this medium, to both the ecclesiastical hierarchies and their relationship with the secular powers were seen as highly subversive, provoking similarly outraged responses. Women were imprisoned, in some cases repeatedly, they were accused of madness and committed to Bedlam, they faced allegations of devilry and therefore the possibility of being burnt for witchcraft, and their beliefs and actions were castigated in print. The response of some sectaries to these attacks was to seize the offensive by publishing their own repudiation of their protagonists' opinions, demonstrating through their willingness to enter into public disputation the authority with which they held their views.[4] Thus, although some writings by these women were probably spontaneous and ecstatic outpourings of religious fervour, others, although sometimes dismissed in that fashion, were in fact carefully reasoned doctrinal presentations interwoven closely with apposite biblical references. Furthermore, as Hobby has shown, at times these women addressed their messages specifically to their own sex (1988: 43).

In general, however, this level of activity amongst women, including their polemical writing, was not sustained after the Restoration. Dissenting sects, like the Quakers and some Baptists who had proposed radical alternative roles for women, were either crushed, or withdrew and reorganized. Although the influence of their beliefs continued, women were denied the inspiration, opportunities, and support that they had gained from membership of these groups. Quaker women, who had been prominent amongst the prophets, did not lose their new areas of activity immediately, but the combined effects of intermittent persecution of the sects between 1662 and 1689, the restoration of the authority of the Anglican gentry in the countryside (with the exception of rural industrial areas like the West Riding), and the gradual absorption of dissenters into commerce, industry, and education, undermined the radicalism that had been conducive to women's published polemical literature. Quaker women continued to write in support of the role of 'Women's Speaking' but their tone became more measured. Eventually they retreated or were withdrawn from their promi-

21

nent position in the public ministry to Women's Meetings which were concerned largely with more conventionally feminine matters such as philanthropy (Hobby 1988: 45–7).

As will be seen later, this process of exclusion and the apparent ascendancy of a more passive role for female Quakers contains within it an interesting parallel with changes in the persona of the eighteenth-century woman novelist. In both cases, an expansion in women's writing was facilitated by the authors' negotiation of existing constructs of femininity and not by an outright challenge to them: in the seventeenth century women were the weak-willed, susceptible projectors not of their own words and ideas, but of God's; in the eighteenth century, women writers became more feminine, and therefore more acceptable, as the purveyors of didacticism – the family guide and mentor became the public guide and mentor.[5] In both cases this process had a restricting influence, but equally in both cases it contained within it the opportunity for women to discover a new potential and new challenges to their social and economic position.

The growth of women's writing before the Restoration accentuated several important developments which were to have an enduring impact upon their later work. Most obviously, the printed word was recognized as a medium (perhaps *the* medium) for their public commentary upon the wider social and intellectual climate. The expansion of the social origins of women writers was confirmed and the earlier pattern of a highly selected, often personally acquainted readership for women's material was broken. Substantial numbers of women had directed their work towards a general public and in some cases towards female readers in particular.

Many of these women had written with a strong sense of vocation, which had enabled them to overcome their fears about entering into print. Of equal interest to this study, however, are the few examples of early writers whose motivations were more commercial, for example, the two seventeenth-century women who are known to have produced astrological almanacs. Almanacs were annual astrological calendars or diaries costing only a few pence each and containing basic information about planetary movements and their astrological implications. They provided advice about all manner of human activities, from planting crops to sexual relations, a mass of practical information, and in a few cases, political and religious commentary and satire. Thus, they were a combination of utilitarian manuals and escapist literature. Bernard Capp (1979), in his study of the genre, has argued that the authors of almanacs were often astrologers or medical practitioners for whom such publications were a means of obtaining prestige in their occupations, of advertising wares and services, and of criticizing other physicians and astrologers who had used the genre for similar purposes. Mary Holden, for example, published almanacs for women in 1688 and 1689 and claimed that she was a midwife and physician who specialized in women's diseases.

Sarah Jinner, who described herself as a student of astrology and 'physick', published almanacs in 1658, 1659, 1660, and 1664 and was one of the few astrologers and almanac writers to act as a political critic. In addition to her predictions and medical notes, she included social observations and political commentary from an anti-authoritarian perspective. Although Hobby states that Jinner was not a radical sectary (1988: 182), Capp has described her basic theme as the misrule of governments (1979: 87). Unusually, Jinner used this generally mysogynistic genre to defend women and to make fun of the behaviour of men. There was nothing diffident about the manner in which she expressed her views; she used a cheap and very popular medium which publicized them widely.

The work of these writers adds further weight to the contention that literate women from the lower social strata wrote for publication seeking a wide readership for their material before the eighteenth century. More particularly, they had a professional motivation behind their writing which was similar to that of some eighteenth-century female novelists who combined writing with other complementary paid activities such as teaching and publishing. Jinner and Holden used their literary skills to enhance the commercial success of their other work, almost undoubtedly they wrote for money, and they chose a popular genre for this purpose. Finally, they addressed themselves to a female readership, offering information and advice on health, conception, pregnancy and children, and prescriptions for sexual satisfaction and restraint.

ADDRESSING FEMALE READERS

An emerging orientation towards female readers is present in a range of other works appearing from the early seventeenth century onwards. These may be grouped together loosely on the basis of their common interest in women's social and familial duties and their ability to fulfil them. Elaine Beilin (1987), in her study of the women writers of the English Renaissance, has identified five early seventeenth-century authors of 'mothers' advice books', four of whom presented their works as a legacy to their young and unborn children. The intention was to provide their families with spiritual guidance in the event of their own deaths, but the material also became popular with a more general public, for example Elizabeth Jocelin's *The Mothers Legacie to her unborn Childe* (1624) reached a third edition by 1625, and was still being reprinted two hundred years later. They inspired similar works during the second half of the seventeenth century, such as Lady Anne Halkett's *The Mother's Will to an Unborn Child* (1656). According to Beilin:

> As mothers, these writers acknowledge their primary identity in a uniquely feminine role, and recognize that this places them in the private sphere and under the jurisdiction of men. But each recognizes

23

that to write, ostensibly for the eyes of her own children, brings her to public notice, particularly as she assumes the authority of a preacher. [Elizabeth] Jocelin, [Dorothy] Leigh, and the Countess of Lincoln express their anxiety over this infringement, but find various means to rationalize it and do not let it prevent them from writing down their motherly advice. . . . In their defence . . . these writers identify themselves as possessors of spiritual worth, impelled by their calling as Christian women into the role of writer. In the process, three of these mothers attain a more general ministry for the salvation of souls.

(1987: 266–7)

The sense of duty which enabled these women to surmount their doubts and self-deprecation is similar to that of the female sectaries who were to follow, and of eighteenth-century writers like Elizabeth Bonhote (particularly her early children's books),[6] and Hannah More and Sarah Trimmer, whose didactic material was part of their crusade against, as Trimmer described it, a 'torrent of infidelity' (*The Guardian of Education* 1802: 15) and Jacobinical thinking. Their preoccupations reflect also the growing importance being attached to familial intimacy and affection, which accentuated the role of mothers as spiritual and social guides to their young children (male and female) and companions to their older daughters. The late seventeenth-century tracts which recommended such attitudes are typified by Richard Allestree's *The Ladies Calling*, which advocated for mothers:

The being as much with them [children] as you can, and taking the personal Inspection of them; not to turn them off wholly to Servants, no nor yet Governesses, but frequently themselves to examine how they proceed in the speculative part of knowledge. . . .
But if this be useful in childhood, 'tis no less than necessary in the next period, of their time, when they arrive neer the growth and age of woman, then indeed the mother should not only make them her companions, but her friends, allow them such a kind yet modest, freedom, that they may have a complacence in her company.

(1673: 194, 197)

It is not surprising, therefore, that the practical aspects of women's domestic role received increasing attention during the seventeenth century. The breadth of the potential demand is indicated by the appearance of texts addressed to female servants and young women contemplating service, for example, *The complete servant maid, directing young maidens how they may fitt and qualify themselves for any of these employmts waiting woeman, house keeper, chamber maid, cooke maid, under cook maid, nursery maid, daiery maid, laundrey maid, house maid & scullery maid composed for the greate benefitt of all young maidens* (1677) (London Stationers' Company

24

1913–14: vol. 3, 32). Suzanne Hull (1982) has demonstrated that before the mid-seventeenth century most of the books in this potentially lucrative market were actually written by men. This situation changed significantly in the second half of the period.

The first woman to make her mark in this field was the professional author Hannah Wolley. Hobby has shown how Wolley gradually acquired a thorough understanding of her market and became ambitious to address a wide female readership (1988: 166–75). She was very successful, acquiring a considerable reputation over the course of five publications, most of which achieved more than one edition. Along with her contemporary Sarah Jinner, and those, like Elizabeth Raffald, who followed a similar path to publication in the 1700s, she showed that she was adept at using skills acquired in another area (in this case domestic service) to inform her writing, and at using her writing to advertise her extra-literary accomplishments as a consultant and instructor.[7]

By the end of the century few areas of women's lives remained outside the close attention of female writers, witness: the *Midwives' book, or The whole Art of Midwifery discovered, directing Child-bearing Women how to behave themselves in their Conception, Breeding, Bearing and Nursing, of Children: in Six Books. By Mrs. Jane Sharp. Practitioner in the Art of Midwifery above thirty years* (1671) (*Term Catalogues* 1903: 71). Sharp and her contemporary Elizabeth Cellier (a royal midwife and campaigning pamphleteer) used publication as a means of informing women about matters that were of vital concern to them, but they also had a polemical intention behind their work.[8] These writers were antagonistic to the gradual erosion of the authority of women in a traditionally female trade and they used publication as a means of defending midwives and of advocating (and contributing to) an improvement in their skills as practitioners. Like the female sectaries, these women recognized that they could advance their cause through the medium of print. This understanding was to inform the approaches of later polemicists (including novelists) who followed them into the publishing market in the 1700s.

Other seventeenth-century women used this means to enter the contemporary controversy about the educational opportunities available to their sex. The charge was put succinctly at the turn of the century by Lady Mary Chudleigh in *The Ladies Defence* (1701), her response to a wedding sermon preached in 1699 by the Nonconformist minister Mr Sprint, who advocated the complete subjugation of wives. In her reply, Chudleigh asserted that, amongst other things, women were

> Debarred from knowledge, banished from the schools,
> And with the utmost industry bred fools.

> (1709: 19)

Bathsua Makin and Mary Astell, both of whom were demonstrably well educated, undertook to confute contemporary arguments against women's learning by encouraging their female readers to take up the challenge of serious study. They addressed themselves to the situation of gentlewomen rather than their sex as a whole, and accompanying Makin's *Essay to Revive the Antient Education of Gentlewomen in Religion, Manners, Arts, and Tongues, with an Answer to the Objections against this Way of Education* (1673) was a prospectus for her new school in Tottenham High Cross which was designed for precisely such students. Again, we find evidence here of writing being used in a way that was complementary to the author's other activities. Furthermore, in this case, Makin's use of her pedagogical skills (obtained as a royal tutor) in writing her *Essay* anticipated those eighteenth-century professional women authors whose experience of teaching informed their didactic fiction for children and educational texts.

Astell's *Serious Proposal to the Ladies for the Advancement of their true and greatest interest* was only part of the output of this highly respected and influential prose writer who inspired other contemporary female intellectuals including Lady Chudleigh, Lady Mary Wortley Montagu, and the Anglo-Saxon scholar, Elizabeth Elstob. Astell's *Proposal* was for a 'Monastry', a place of *'Religious Retirement'* for upper- and middle-class women, where they could 'quit the Chat of insignificant people, for an ingenious Conversation; the froth of flashy wit for real wisdom; idle tales for instructive discourses' (1694: 60, 61, and 64). As is discussed in chapter 4, the issue of the availability and quality of girls' education resurfaced in women's writing a number of times during the following century, and Astell's particular solution, although not actually achieved, was explored in general terms by Sarah Scott in her novel *Millenium Hall* (1762), and was advocated explicitly by Priscilla Wakefield in *Reflections on the Present Condition of the Female Sex* (1798). Furthermore, her argument for the moral necessity of improved education on the grounds that 'Ignorance is the cause of most Feminine Vices' (ibid.: 31) was repeated throughout the 1700s, most notably (as I discuss later) in the work of 'Sophia' and Mary Wollstonecraft.

This range of instructive material written by women for a female readership antedates the didacticism and feminine orientation of women's journalism and prose fiction during the eighteenth century. In the later period, the novel added an imaginative dimension to women's fulfilment of their evolving responsibility to guide the conduct and opinions of their own sex and the young. Together with the expanding periodical press, the new genre increased their opportunities to do so.

THE EMERGENCE OF PROFESSIONALISM

As we have seen, women's literary professionalism emerged during the seventeenth century in association with their non-fictive prose such as almanacs and domestic manuals. However, most historians have linked its appearance with women's drama, largely due to the work of the Restoration playwright Aphra Behn.

Although there is evidence to show that under the Commonwealth women were interested in and experimenting with the dramatic form, it was the reopening of the theatres after the Restoration which gave them access to this masculine world.[9] Availing themselves of the new opportunities, actresses like Nell Gwynn and Mrs Bracegirdle swiftly established their presence as favourites of the theatre-going public and, at the same time, women also began to write for the stage.

Probably the first woman dramatist to secure a London performance of her material was Katherine Philips, whose translation of Corneille's *Pompey* was produced early in 1663, followed by a version of *Horace* in 1669. A year later Aphra Behn began her professional career with a production of *The Forced Marriage; or, The Jealous Bridegroom* (1671) and she went on to write a further eighteen plays. All of these were performed and published, many were very successful, and a few, such as the celebrated *Rover* (1677) and *The Emperor of the Moon* (1687), were performed well into the eighteenth century. Her witty, well-crafted comedies were the mainstay of her professional career, and they have sustained her ranking amongst the important literary figures of the period.

Other women, including Frances Boothby, Jane Wiseman, and 'Ariadne', wrote for the Restoration theatre and attained London performances for their material, but Behn's key successors were Delarivière Manley, Mary Pix, Catharine Trotter, and Susanna Centlivre.[10] With the exception of Manley, these dramatists apparently originated from within the broad reaches of the middle ranks, and they all displayed a professional approach to their writing. They obtained patrons and remunerative dedications for their material, and negotiated their way successfully within the competitive world of the theatre.

Our estimatation of their achievements in this field should take account not only of the pioneering nature of their involvement, but also of the effects of contemporary hostility towards conspicuously educated and literary women. This found expression in satirical attacks, such as *The Female Wits*, a comedy which targetted Manley, Pix, and Trotter. Perhaps more seriously, it created a pressure upon these writers to deny their own successes.[11] As Catharine Trotter complained in her plea to Queen Caroline for her support and favour for women writers:

Learning deny'd us, we at random tread
Unbeaten paths, that late to knowledge lead;
By secret steps break thro' th' obstructed way,
Nor dare acquirements gain'd by stealth display.

If some advent'rous genius rare arise,

27

Who on exalted themes her talents tries,
She fears to give the work (tho' prais'd) a name,
And flies not more from infamy, than fame.

(*Gentleman's Magazine* 1737: vol. 7, 308)

Ridicule or even public calumny were not the only possible drawbacks to acknowledging authorship for, as we shall see later, there was also a risk of lost income from disrupted and unsuccessful performances. Disguised identity, as happened with some of Centlivre's material, was a means of circumventing the problem.[12] On the other hand, professionalism could entail the sense of authorial autonomy expressed by Behn in the 'Preface' to *The Lucky Chance; or, An Alderman's Bargain* (1687 [1915]: vol. 3, 185–7) in which she defended her right to artistic freedom and her entitlement to the fame. Equally, mutual praise and publicity could be a resilient response to criticisms. Centlivre, Manley, Trotter, and Pix were enthusiastic in their praise of the work of their predecessors Behn and Philips, and they were equally effusive towards each other (although Manley later turned against Trotter in *The New Atlantis*), heralding their work as continuing an illustrious inheritance from Sappho onwards. Manley's comparison of Trotter with Philips and Behn was included in the publication of Trotters's *Agnes de Castro* (1696), whilst her own *The Royal Mischief* (1696) was published with eulogies by both Pix and Trotter, although the latter was careful at the same time to mention her own status as the author of *Agnes de Castro*.

The theatre continued to play a significant role in the careers of eighteenth-century women writers, offering a route, often via acting, into the literary profession, and giving access to a potentially lucrative genre for the successful. However, the significance of drama within the repertoire of female writers was superseded in the early 1700s by prose fiction. This is reflected in the fate of Manley, whose first work of fiction appeared in 1696, the year *The Royal Mischief* was produced. Although the publication of her *Letters* was unauthorized and indeed opposed by her, the prose medium itself was to become the mainstay of Manley's subsequent career.

Within the range of women's non-fictive prose, the epistolary form has perhaps the clearest links with the later novels. The seventeenth-century vogue for published letters encouraged their use for public utterances on many themes, including debates on religious, scientific, economic, and political issues, and travelogues. It stimulated a demand for the published correspondence of major literary figures such as Dryden, Rochester, and Otway, and some letters by women were circulated in the public arena, for example, those of Aphra Behn, and those exchanged by Mary Astell and Damaris Cudsworth with John Norris and John Locke. However, these were exceptional and overall, letters were a private medium for women during this period.

In a sense, letter writing spanned the gap between the fugitive diary or autobiography and work written for publication. Although it was a highly personalized form, it developed general stylistic conventions and critical standards. Publications that were designed to instruct the novice and to provide exemplars became available, some of which were aimed specifically at female readers, for example, Henry Care's *The Female Secretary, or Choice new Letters, wherin each degree of Women may be accomodated with variety of presidents for expressing themselves aptly and handsomly on any occasion proper to their Sex. With pertinent rules for inditing and directing letters in general* (1671) (*Term Catalogues* 1903: 88). The letter, therefore, allowed women to assess and cultivate their formal prose-writing skills without requiring them to face a readership larger than one. Furthermore, as the exuberant and observant letters of Dorothy Osborne (1928) demonstrate, the form permitted a freedom and informality of expression that might elude those seeking publication when 'a self-conscious straining after wit' (Sutherland 1969: 231) or an awareness of social mores could inhibit natural talent.

Although Osborne's protracted correspondence with her suitor William Temple was a purely private exchange, it is possible that another notable contemporary letter writer, the poet and dramatist Katherine Philips, was conscious of the public appeal of her work. Her most quoted letter is one addressed to Poliarchus (Sir Charles Cotterell), which prefaces the posthumous edition of her *Poems*. This asserts her shock and dismay at the earlier unofficial publication of her poetry, which until then had circulated only in manuscript. Whilst the letter is presented to the reader as a purely private communication between friends, an examination of the collected *Letters to Poliarchus* (1705) has revealed that it was written deliberately so that it could be shown to anyone who might suspect that Philips had been immodest enough to connive secretly at the publication (Hobby 1988: 132). Thereafter, as a poet, literary personality, and exponent of the virtues of friendship, this writer was eulogized by contemporaries. The self-deprecation that characterized the public presentation of her writing contributed to her reputation as the exemplar of discreet female genius, and she remained a standard by which other women writers were judged throughout the eighteenth century.

Interest in published correspondence, and particularly in letters detailing the vicissitudes of friendship, courtship, and marriage, continued through the 1700s. For example, Elizabeth Griffith and her husband Richard raised desperately needed income through a subscription publication of their courtship correspondence, the popularity of which helped to launch Elizabeth's literary career. She also published three novels in this style. A cursory glance through the titles in Appendix A will confirm that she was amongst many women authors who found that 'A Series of Letters' suited their skills and intentions. For some writers, like Mrs Courtney, the letter was perhaps their most familiar form of writing and therefore it was the natural choice for their only (known) novelistic venture, whilst for others, like Mrs Cartwright, it remained a tried and tested framework for most of their fiction. The enduring popularity of this type of prose is highlighted by the remarkable success of Fanny Burney's first epistolary novel *Evelina*, published in the late 1770s.[13]

Amongst the seventeenth-century semi-fictional works that contributed to the development of this type of novel are a number of interesting pieces by women. The Duchess of Newcastle's *CCXI Sociable Letters* (1664) could be viewed as an early prototype on the basis of the imaginary scenes and conversations that are included in the mixture of non-fictive critiques and letters to real people. On the other hand, Aphra Behn demonstrated the kind of commercial acumen which was to play a significant part in the development of women's fiction when she successfully exploited the fashionable preoccupation with intrigue and the popularity of real or fictitious love letters in her *Love Letters Between a Nobleman and His Sister* (1683–7).[14]

However, Behn's achievements in the field of prose fiction were greater than her *Love Letters* alone would suggest. In the second half of the seventeenth century the market for prose was dominated by translations and imitations of continental originals. The heroic romances of the Scudérys and Gomberville, amongst others, passed through many editions and they were joined by the *nouvelles* and *chroniques scandaleuses* of such authors as Marie-Catherine Desjardins, Charlotte de la Force, and Bussy-Rabutin. Few English writers could compete with their popularity and fewer still produced material of literary importance. Historians have ranked Behn amongst the latter. These claims are based largely on her most famous work of prose fiction, *Oroonoko: or, The Royal Slave* (1688). Although there are similarities between this and her other prose works, she departs from the common path by successfully combining the heroic romance idiom with a high degree of verisimilitude. The latter has long been regarded as a distinguishing feature of the early novel.

Behn's appearance in the literature market was a significant moment in the development of women's writing. Her career consolidated several important tendencies that were already perceptible in their work: a professional approach; the desire for a wide readership; a background from within the middle ranks; and a reflection in their material of the contemporary social and economic environment and their opinion of the position of women within it. Her writing helped to confirm a commercial as well as literary role for women in the development of prose fiction and only a century after the posthumous publication of her *Collected Histories and Novels* (1696), women had become firmly established in the market as popular novelists, many were writing for a living, and a few had earned small fortunes through their pen. It is these extraordinary developments that the remainder of this study seeks to understand.

3

THE GROWTH OF EIGHTEENTH-CENTURY WOMEN'S FICTION

Of the various species of composition that in course come before us, there are none in which *our* writers of the male sex have less excelled, since the days of Richardson and Fielding, than in the arrangement of a novel. Ladies seem to appropriate to themselves an exclusive privilege of this kind of writing; witness the numerous productions of romantic tales to which female authors have given birth.

(*Monthly Review* 1790)

DESCRIBING THE DEVELOPMENT

The success of writers like Aphra Behn, Delarivière Manley, and Eliza Haywood ensured that women were relatively conspicuous in the fiction market from the beginning of the eighteenth century. By the later 1700s, contemporaries had identified another reason for the prominence of women novelists: the sheer quantity of their published work. Reviewers implied that there was a seemingly limitless flow of material from the female pen, complaining that 'This branch of the literary *trade* appears, now, to be almost entirely engrossed by the Ladies' (*Monthly Review* 1773: vol. 48, 154). The absolute accuracy of such statements can be refuted by reference to the review magazines and secondary check-lists of the period, but the extremity of the language employed suggests that these market observers were indeed responding to a substantial incursion by women writers.

The first task of this chapter, therefore, is to expose the scale and pattern of that development before discussing the possible causes of any notable periods of expansion or recession in the growth. In order to achieve this a new bibliography of women's fiction has been compiled which covers the period between 1696 and 1796. Although in one sense these dates are arbitrary, they serve to encapsulate a century of change and consolidation. Furthermore, they represent in themselves the highest levels of skill within women's prose fiction writing during that period: 1696 was the publication date of Aphra Behn's *Histories and Novels*, and 1796 was a central year in

31

Jane Austen's first great creative period, when she began *First Impressions*, later published as *Pride and Prejudice*.

The information is presented in the form of two appendices. The first of these, Appendix A, comprises an alphabetical list of women authors (including the alternative names by which they were known, such as maiden, married, or colloquial names, and pseudonyms), an indication of their professional status, their novel titles in chronological order with the first edition dates (unless otherwise stated), the number of volumes for each work, and details of the publisher(s) and place of publication. Appendix B is a chronological listing of these authors from 1696 to 1796, providing annual publication totals for those who published more than one novel in any given year, and indicating those women who wrote collaboratively.

Appendix A is confined to prose fiction published in book form and material has been selected for inclusion on the basis of certain criteria. The most important of these concerns the type of prose to be defined within this study as fiction. In the majority of cases the classifications of the secondary sources have been accepted, but an exception has been made with seemingly autobiographical material.

During the eighteenth century elements of autobiography were incorporated into the evolving novel and, as Cynthia Pomerleau (1980: 31-6) has demonstrated in relation to women's autobiographies and contemporary fiction, writers of both genres shared common themes and catered to a similar market.[1] Thus, Mary Carleton's criminal autobiography *Historicall Narrative* (1663), and Francis Kirkman's semi-fictional account of Carleton's life *The Counterfeit Lady Unveiled* (1673), Defoe's novel *Moll Flanders* (1722), and Manley's embellished autobiography *The Adventures of Rivella* (1714), all catered to the contemporary taste for romanticized accounts of the lives, and particularly the sexual adventures, of real or fictitious men and women. Out of the thirty examples of women's autobiographies from the eighteenth century recorded and described by Matthews (1955), nine purport to chronicle the author's sexual intrigues and he suggests that at least one of these, *The History of Biddy Farmer* (1760), might be fictitious (1955: 98).

The impact upon writers of the fashion for verisimilitude can be gauged from the many published 'Lives' and 'Genuine Memoirs' that we find listed in the 'Novel' sections of contemporary circulating library catalogues. These are additional to those recorded separately under 'Autobiographies', 'Histories', and 'Miscellanies', reflecting the fact that 'Authentick Memoirs' were also a successful form of fiction. Such confusions have been acknowledged since the eighteenth century. The anonymous 'Oxford Scholar' who was hired to write a comparison of the memoirs of Laetitia Pilkington and Constantia Phillips, felt it was necessary to qualify his conclusion that, on the whole, such works were not corrupting, by remarking:

When I say this, I confine it to real Memoirs, for a wrong-headed

Author may dress up his own Fictions, contrary to all the Laws of Writing and of Nature. These Books of Amusement, therefore, may be, and certainly are pernicious, of which a Multitude of Instances might be given, . . . I will, however, take the Liberty of adding, that many grave Histories are as dangerous, in this respect, as the most absurd Fictions; because the Writers study to misrepresent Facts, and labour to deceive, under Pretence of informing their Readers.

(1748: 24)

I have taken a direct path through these complications, excluding books with titles suggesting an autobiographical basis, such as 'Lives' and 'Memoirs', unless further information has argued otherwise. As a result I may have eliminated some fictional material, or semi-autobiographical accounts that were largely read as fiction, but equally, a more liberal response could have included a number of factual accounts, thus extending, without method or thoroughness, the range of the sample into another genre. The other criteria employed in the selection of information are specified in the introduction to Appendix A. In combination they mean that to be included a work must be prose fiction, published in book form, and written by a British woman who worked either alone or with female collaborators whose names are known.

As this study is concerned with women's prose fiction in general, and not exclusively with the novel, Appendix A contains works (for example, emphatically didactic tales written for the instruction of children and the literate poor) that might reasonably be excluded from a bibliography of the genre. I shall argue later that this type of fiction is a valuable guide to important changes in the status and role of women writers, and that it had thematic links with their novels.

The initial decision to limit the scope of this bibliography to fiction published in book form was made in response to the focus of previous studies which implied that, with rare exceptions, this was the way in which women's fiction appeared in the eighteenth century. It soon became clear, however, that this was an inadequate assessment of the amount of material by women that was available and an over-simplification of the way in which it was distributed. Research revealed that not only had historians seriously underestimated the number of novelists and books, they had also overlooked the considerable amount of women's fiction, including serialized novels, that was published in magazines. Knowledge of the existence of so much additional material has informed the arguments and conclusions of this study and women's magazine fiction receives attention in chapters 6 and 7.

It is worth noting that even as regards fiction published in book form, the totals in Appendix A are an underestimate of the actual numbers of female novelists and their novels. This is due partly to the limitations of this survey, and more importantly, to our inability to attribute the many anonymous novels that were published during this period. We know that a number of the authors recorded in Appendix A chose this discreet path to publication and it is reasonable to assume that more eighteenth-century women novelists continue to elude public notice. Appendix A therefore exposes only a part of women's output of fiction during the eighteenth century.

None the less, the bibliography lists 174 authors and 446 works,[2] which is sufficient to demonstrate that a substantial quantity of women's fiction was published in book form. However, these figures alone, although intriguing, do not reveal the nature of the growth in either the number of women writers or their material during that period. We might conclude from statements in previous studies that there was 'a great influx of women writers' (MacCarthy 1947: 39) into the market after 1750, but this gives us little idea of the scale and significance of this increase relative to the level of entry and output in the earlier part of the century. A detailed understanding of the statistical pattern of the development of women's fiction throughout the century is clearly desirable, and to obtain this it is necessary to look at the variations in the number of authors and in the number of novels produced.

A statistical analysis of the development: the method

Figure 1 shows the annual fluctuations in the number of prose-fiction publications produced by women between 1696 and 1796. These fluctuations result from two factors: first, despite the entrepreneurial initiative of publishers like the Noble brothers and Lane, novels were not mass-produced goods and therefore output was erratic whatever the overall market tendency; second, until the final decades of the century, the number of publications in any one year was small, making a minor absolute difference appear striking in proportionate terms. To smooth out these short-term variations and to emphasize overall trends in the pattern of development, a five-year moving average has been calculated, the results of which are presented in Figure 2.[3]

It is inappropriate to adopt this approach to the information about the novelists. In particular, to present simply the number of women who published in each year would produce a highly erratic profile which would obscure the overall trends.[4] Furthermore, it would imply that a woman was writing only during the year in which she published, an assumption that is particularly suspect in the case of professional authors like Eliza Haywood and Charlotte Smith, who were certainly writing during some of the intervening periods. Unfortunately, the biographical information which might establish the precise length of each woman's literary career is often either deficient or entirely absent. Therefore, two criteria have been devised in order to use the publication dates in the appendices to obtain an indication of overall trends in the number of women writing.

First, a woman has been regarded as a writer for the period between (and including) the dates of her first and last publications, and the total number of authors calculated for each year between 1696 and 1796.[5] The results are presented in Figure 3. The major drawback to this approach is that the graph reflects primarily the variations in the number of women who produced more than one publication. This is due to the assumption that a multiple producer was writing throughout the time between her publications, whilst single producers are represented for one year only. Additionally, in certain cases, biographical information suggests that protracted gaps between novels

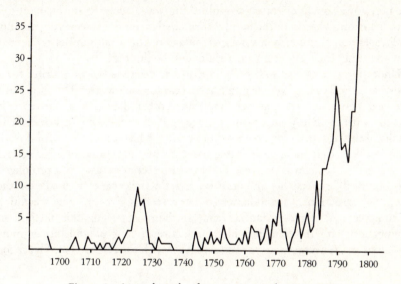

Figure 1   Annual totals of women's novels 1696–1796

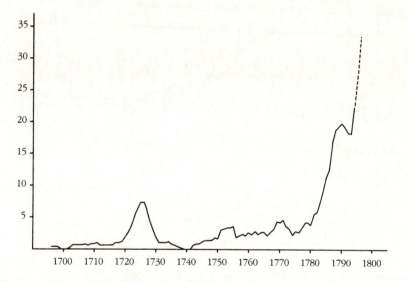

Figure 2   Five-year moving average of annual totals of women's novels 1696–1796

occurred because these women had in fact temporarily ceased to write. For example, after Fanny Burney published *Cecilia; or Memoirs of an Heiress* (1782), there was a gap of fourteen years before she produced her next novel *Camilla; or, A Picture of Youth* (1796). During these years she wrote only occasionally (four tragedies and a pamphlet) as her time was dominated by employment in the Queen's service (1786 to 1791), and then by marriage and the birth of a son. Her return to publishing was largely to supplement her royal pension, which was the family's principal income. However, providing such cases constitute only a small percentage of the total number writing at any one time, their effect on the results will be limited.

Under the second method, each woman has been viewed as a writer for a five-year period centred on the publication year for each work.[6] The choice of a five-year period has no especial significance other than that it corresponds broadly with the five-year moving average applied to the data for novels. The results of this approach are presented in Figure 4 which covers the period from 1696 to 1794.[7] Like Figure 3, this graph depicts overall trends but it has several advantages. A woman is not regarded as writing continuously if a prolonged gap occurred between her publications and thus allowance is made for the temporary cessation or abandonment of her career. It gives an equal weighting to multiple and single producers and, furthermore, using this method in conjunction with the data provided in Figure 2, it is possible to examine variations in the average rate of production through the century (see Figure 5).

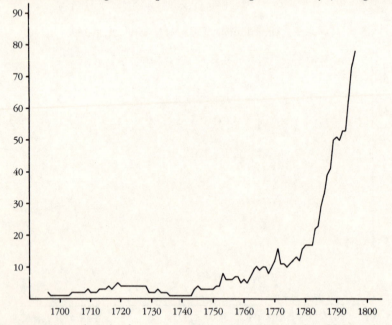

Figure 3 Annual totals of women novelists (1696–1796) produced by viewing a woman as a novelist for the period between her first and last publications

36

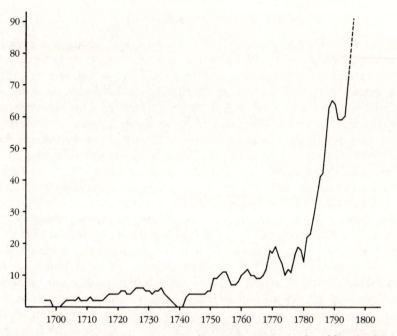

Figure 4 Annual totals of women novelists (1696–1796) produced by viewing a woman as a novelist for five-year periods centred on the dates of her publications

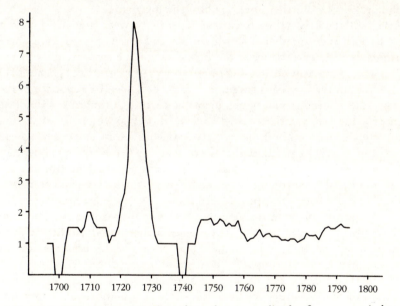

Figure 5 Mean average number of novels per novelist for five-year periods centred on each year between 1696 and 1796

37

The Results of the Analysis

Figures 1 and 2 demonstrate that there was not a simple, continuous growth in women's fiction during the eighteenth century. Rather, there were two distinct 'phases' of development: a steady, rapid rise in output reaching a peak around 1725, followed by an equally substantial decline to a slump around 1740; then a gradual increase in production from the mid-century onwards until the mid-1780s, followed by an abrupt upward surge during the next decade. Figures 3 and 4 show that the pattern of increase in the number of authors ran broadly parallel with the growth in their publications, with the same two broad 'phases' in the development.

The distinctness of these 'phases' is emphasized by the number of women whose literary activities (according to the first method) spanned 1740. Of the fifteen women in Appendix A who were writing at the beginning of the century, only one continued to publish beyond the slump around 1740 and this was the indefatigable Eliza Haywood. This implies that, in terms of the writers involved, women's fiction published before 1740 was quite separate from that of the rest of the century, although clearly this does not preclude its influence upon the work and social and literary status of later authors. In contrast, the second major turning point in the development – the rapid acceleration in production in the mid-1780s – was indistinguishable from the preceding period in terms of the authors involved. The appendices reveal that 46 per cent of the women who published fiction in the decade up to and including 1785 had further novels published after that date.

Although there is a broad correspondence between the development patterns both of the number of female authors and of their prose fiction, there is a notable difference between the behaviour of the two variables in the 1720s, when the rise in the number of novels was proportionally greater than the increase in the number of writers. This is explained by reference to the average rate of production, which increases sharply during this period (see Figure 5), due to the work of a single author, Eliza Haywood.[8] The level and consistency of her output in the 1720s was unequalled by any other woman throughout the century, although it is worth noting that many of Haywood's works consisted of 100 pages or less, whilst a typical late eighteenth-century novel comprised three volumes of about 200 pages each. Haywood published fiction in almost every year of the third decade (with the exceptions of 1720 and 1721), producing at least thirty-five novels or approximately 70 per cent of the total output (in Appendix A) by women in that period. Additionally, in most of those years she published more than one novel; for example, in 1725 (the peak year for novel output in the decade) she produced ten.

The marked fluctuations in the rate of production which occur through the first half of the century are the result of the low number of authors, and in this context Haywood's influence is proportionally greater than if she had written after 1760. None the less, the scale and continuity of the rapid increase between 1716 and 1724 and the subsequent decline are quite remarkable. After 1760 there is a smoother growth curve displaying a slight but steady rise in the rate of production. This is due partly to a modest increase in the proportion of women who wrote more than one novel, particularly from the mid-1780s onwards, and partly to a slight increase in the productivity of the multiple producers.[9]

In summary, therefore, the preceding statistical analysis has demonstrated that the growth in women's fiction during the 1700s was neither exponential nor continuous. Rather, it fell into two distinct periods: a growth and then rapid decline before 1740, during which time Haywood was unassailably dominant in quantitative terms at least; followed by a very gradual increase (in output and authorship), culminating in a dramatic, unparalleled surge in the 1780s which incorporated not only an increase in the number of authors but also, proportionally, a rise in their rate of production. This accords broadly with the more restrained conclusions of those previous studies which have recognized that a considerable expansion in women's fiction took place in the late 1700s.[10] Interestingly, there is also a degree of correlation between the pattern identified here and the observations of the eighteenth-century bookseller, James Lackington. This shrewd but not entirely disinterested market commentator remarked in his *Memoirs* that 'the sale of books in general has increased prodigiously within the last twenty years' (1792: 386), and he later went on to state that 'the most rapid increase in the sale of books has been since the termination of the late war' (ibid.: 387). In other words, Lackington identified an acceleration in growth after the end of hostilities with America in 1783.[11]

Previous comparisons of this increase with earlier levels of women's output have been very generalized and often inaccurate, and although references to the 'single spies' (Tompkins 1932 [1962]: 118–19) who appeared before the advancing battalions of the mid-century have now been overturned by the information in recent bibliographies, a greater understanding of the overall growth is obtainable only through an analysis which addresses the century as a whole. In attempting this, the preceding discussion has highlighted marked variations in the pace of growth at different times, raising the possibility that certain literary and extra-literary factors were particularly influential at specific moments or watersheds in the development.

THE PATTERN OF THE DEVELOPMENT CONSIDERED

Even without a thorough survey of men's novels, it is reasonable to suggest that the escalation in women's novels in the late 1700s was part of a concurrent, overall expansion in the publication of fiction. Robert Mayo has observed such a development in the periodical press, noting a 'marked increase after 1770' in the number of magazines that attempted to 'satisfy the growing appetite for "tales" and "histories" ' (1962: 2). Within this context, the contribution of William Lane is of notable importance. His biographer, Dorothy Blakey, tells us that by 1784, Lane was advertising for novels to publish and had probably established his own press (1939: 9). Rapid expansion followed, to the extent that by the end of the eighteenth century he could no longer manage his business alone. His success after 1790 was based almost exclusively upon his investment in the novel and this increased substantially during that period. Lane's production totals for successive five-yearly periods from 1779 to 1804 are 18, 74, 93, 121, and 166. These demonstrate that his output of novels mirrors the growth pattern identified in women's fiction, with a leap forward in the second half of the 1780s, followed by a continued increase into the early 1800s. The activities of this entrepreneur undoubtedly contributed to a general growth in the demand for fiction, but of more particular interest is the fact that he was responsible for a substantial number of the later eighteenth-century novels by women. His central role in the post-1780s surge in their fiction is explored later.

Changes in the law controlling copyright may also help to explain an escalation in the production of novels during the 1780s. As was noted in chapter 1, the introduction in 1709 of a statutory right to literary property in the author's favour was a critical new element in publishing market relations. The measure was controversial, not least because it failed to clarify the status of the author's (and therefore the bookseller's) common law right to perpetual copyright. According to Johnson:

> Notwithstanding that the statute secures only fourteen years of exclusive right, it has always been understood by *the trade*, that he, who buys the copyright of a book from the authour [*sic*], obtains a perpetual property; and upon that belief, numberless bargains are made to transfer that property after the expiration of the statutory term.
>
> (As quoted in Boswell 1799 [1927]: vol. 1, 292)

Under the Act's provisions, groups of copies began to fall free from control after either fourteen or twenty-one years and some booksellers were quick to exploit the opportunity to produce cheap editions of popular texts. Efforts were made to consolidate the customary position. There was an unsuccessful attempt to present a Bill in 1735 and court cases were fought at regular intervals throughout the century. Booksellers managed to obtain injunctions against 'pirated' editions at first, but in *Donaldson* v *Beckett* (1774), a dispute between two publishers over Thomson's *The Seasons*, the judges decided that perpetual copyright no longer existed. It survived in three vestigial forms only, and although the booksellers tried by mutual compact to preserve their traditional rights, the way was now clear for a new growth in cheap literature, stimulating further expansion in the reading public.

Contemporary reaction to Donaldson was mixed. There were those who argued, like Dempster (in conversation with Johnson), that 'Donaldson, Sir, is anxious for the encouragement of literature. He reduces, the price of books, so that poor students may buy them' (as quoted in Boswell 1799 [1927]: vol. 1, 293). On the other hand, critics of the decision feared that it would squeeze out the talented writer whose work, with limited market appeal, was a long-term investment for the publisher who would have to surrender the right eventually to all the trade. In *A Modest Plea for the Property of Copyright*, Catherine Macaulay argued that the decision would increase the market tendency to produce 'trifling wretched compositions as please the vulgar; compositions which disgrace the press, yet are best calculated for general sale' (1774: 34). These could include that 'drug', 'trash', and 'lumber' of the literary world, the commercial novel, designed for a quick financial return.

If Macaulay's interpretation was correct, the 1774 decision shifted the interests of the publishers closer to those of the novelists, creating a market atmosphere that was conducive to a substantial growth in their numbers in the final decades of the century. Her fear that an increased emphasis upon short-term investments would undermine manuscript prices was of little concern to producers of fiction, which, with notable exceptions such as material by Fanny Burney, Henry Fielding, and Ann Radcliffe, was rarely bought with perpetuity in mind. On the contrary, the secret of a successful trade in novels was novelty.

The image of the woman writer: constructing femininity

Thus far, I have argued that the rapid increase in women's novels at the end of the eighteenth century can be seen as part of a general and not exclusively female trend. However, there were a number of variables that had a bearing upon the rate at which women in particular entered the fiction market and, critical amongst these, was the public's image of the female writer. Fundamental to our understanding of the impact of this factor is an appreciation of contemporary notions of femininity. These were themselves subjected to changing social and economic pressures, and therefore to constant questioning and redefinition. In such confusing waters one small piece of *terra firma* is the fact that (as I discuss in chapter 4) the women we are concerned with here were largely from the middle ranks.

Although recent studies in the fields of social history and women's history have increased our knowledge of the lives of such women, Ivy Pinchbeck's (1930) account remains one of the authoritative texts on the subject. Building upon the information presented a few years earlier by M. Dorothy George

(1925), her chapter on 'Craftswomen and Business Women' was an early revelation of women's extensive involvement in the economy in the early years of the industrial revolution. Both scholars noted, however, that, although women from the middle classes were expected to contribute to the family income, this active, economic partnership was under pressure to change.

George, in explaining the apparent freedom from work amongst married women noted by foreign observers, pointed to a level of metropolitan industrial development which had subsumed certain domestic tasks undertaken previously by housewives, such as brewing, weaving, baking, and candle making. Pinchbeck identified two other pressures. First, a gradual rise in capital costs attendant upon the development of larger scale businesses, she argued, made it increasingly difficult for women to fund their enterprises. Second, she perceived an incipient separation occurring amongst the middle ranks between the locations of economic and domestic work. This theme has been explored recently by Davidoff and Hall (1987) for the period 1750 to 1850 and, like their predecessors, they argue that the bifurcation of familial activity, moving commercial and industrial enterprise away from the home, helped to confirm and confine women's influence within the domestic sphere.

The variety of industrial and commercial arrangements during this period (in particular the persistence of the domestic system of manufacture well into the nineteenth century) means that we are talking here about factors that contributed through the century to the definition of an ideal, and one that pertained to the middle ranks upwards, rather than an immediate economic reality.[12] We are charting the emergence of the Conspicuously Leisured Wife as a totem of the middle classes and although the 'foolishly vain' tradesman who would have his wife 'sit above the parlour, receive visits, drink Tea' and know nothing about his business affairs, was viewed with concern by Defoe (1727 [1969]: vol. 1, 292), he and his spouse were probably more a feature of the later Georgian period.

Coercive economic pressures ran parallel with complementary movements in public ideology. In his second *Treatise* (1690), John Locke described a 'state of nature' within which people were free to order their actions and to dispose of themselves and of their property in accordance with the 'law of nature', which preserved liberty but which did not permit licence. The institution of some kind of civil government was necessary in order to create a higher mediatory authority and this was achievable by means of a social contract. Underpinning this process was the existence of the body politic, which was itself dependent upon a set of relations subsisting between individuals on the basis of their common rationality and social nature, qualities which could and should be cultivated through education.

The senses at first let in *particular* ideas, and furnish the yet empty cabinet, and, the mind by degrees growing familiar with some of them,

42

they are lodged in the memory, and names got to them. Afterwards, the mind proceeding further abstracts them, and by degrees learns the use of names. In this manner the mind comes to be furnished with ideas and language, the materials about which to exercise its discursive faculty. And the use of reason becomes daily more visible, as these materials that give it employment increase.
(Locke, *An Essay Concerning Human Understanding* 1690 [1975]: 72)

The principles and methods for initiating and sustaining this progression were explored in *Some Thoughts Concerning Education* (1693), in which Locke stressed the utilitarian and moral purposes of teaching, and the importance of parental involvement in the character development of children. As these ideas gained credence in the following century, they provided a philosophical basis for an expansion in educational opportunities, particularly for middling-rank children, and for an increasingly secular orientation of the curriculum.

Whilst educational theorists, like Locke, emphasized the individuality of each child, on the whole, the subjects on offer at these establishments followed common patterns, reflecting widely held educational and social priorities. A number of historians, notably Gardiner (1929) and Kamm (1965), have demonstrated that for the daughters of the middle stratum, these priorities were primarily literacy, a patina of learning, and social accomplishments. This unambitious combination militated against their later involvement in business affairs and encouraged the idea that matrimony was their future career.

Theories of liberal individualism, whilst providing a rationale for the increasing importance attached to parental involvement in the upbringing of children, also laid particular emphasis upon the critical role of mothers in that process. Changes in the configuration of domestic life during the eighteenth century, described variously as the rise of the 'companionate' (Stone 1979) or 'sentimental' (Okin 1982) family, contributed to a perception of these relations as governed by 'natural' laws and as separate from the wider public and political world. Thus, as economic forces were nudging certain women towards the home, so enlightenment thinking was progressively confining them to that sphere whilst enhancing their moral status within it.

However, the delineation of women's major domestic responsibilities did not entail the concession of equal authority. Katherine Clinton has pointed out that even Locke's definition of marriage as a voluntary alliance between the sexes, with shared powers over children, allowed the 'ultimate prerogatives to the husband in view of his "natural" physical superiority' (1974–5: 292). Increasingly, 'natural' feminine attributes were identified (and idealized) as those of emotion, spontaneity, and intuition, as opposed to rationality and objectivity; the elements of sensibility were being assembled.

Inherent within this set of ideas was an emphasis upon the redeeming

43

capacities of women, whose responsibility for conjugal felicity was upheld as morally as well as socially imperative. Anticipating the arguments advanced by Mrs Beeton in her 'Philosophy of Housekeeping' (1865 [1984]: i–vii), the eighteenth-century professional writer Jean Marishall contended that: 'from domestic happiness, springs public tranquillity. That man who enjoys peace and contentment in his own family, will seldom or ever go abroad to stir up sedition and strife' (1789: vol. 1, 144–5). Yet how was this comfortable containment of male passion to be achieved? In her *Essays, Addressed To Young Married Women*, another professional writer, Elizabeth Griffith, outlined the formidable nature of the task ahead:

> A love of power and authority is natural to men; and wherever this inclination is most indulged, will be the situation of their choice. Every man ought to be the principal object of attention in his family; of course he should feel himself happier at home than in any other place. It is doubtless, the great business of a woman's life to render his home pleasing to her husband; he will then delight in her society, and not seek abroad for alien amusements. A husband may, possibly, in his daily excursions, see many women whom he thinks handsomer than his wife; but it is generally her fault if he meet with one that he thinks more amiable.
>
> (1782: 24–5)

Should a husband, despite these ministrations, fall prey to the 'natural depravity and inconstancy of his nature', Griffith's advice was that a wife should enter 'into a serious, strict, and impartial review of her own conduct, even to the minutiae of her dress and the expressions of her looks'. Should these survive her scrutiny, then 'let her steadily pursue the same behaviour she has hitherto practised; . . . For to resent, or to retaliate, neither her duty, nor her religion will permit' (27–8).

An unequal emphasis upon female fidelity and chastity, with its inherent 'double standard' of behaviour, was given an ideological framework by those who argued for an innate *moral* superiority amongst women.[13] Women were the possessors of 'that delicate sensibility which Heaven has placed in female minds as the out-guard of modesty' (Griffith 1782: 92). Johnson, whilst agreeing with this allocation of the blame for infidelity (male wantonness, female negligence), identified a more material reason for the importance of faithfulness in wives: 'Confusion of progeny constitutes the essence of the crime; and therefore a woman who breaks her marriage vows is much more criminal than a man who does it' (as quoted in Boswell 1799 [1927]: vol. 1, 372).

The elevation and idealization of the moral nature of woman, whether for economic or ideological reasons, was clearly not original to the eighteenth century. McKeon, by proposing its fundamental importance to the challenge of 'progressive ideology', identifies a significant transition in attitudes after the Reformation when 'the dominance of the Christian rationale [emphasizing continence and fidelity in both sexes] is moderated, and the genealogical rationale [emphasizing female chastity] comes more clearly into view' (1988: 157). However, as Marlene LeGates has argued, female chastity and sexual fidelity acquired a new currency during the 1700s through the expansion of print culture and particularly through prose fiction:

> This new literature, centering on the encounter between a sexually aggressive male and the innocent, superior female, was the traditional conduct book fictionalized; it succeeded in catching the imagination of the reading public in a way impossible with the pedantic tracts of the past.
>
> (1976–7: 27)

Depicting the process of innocence challenged, corrupted, or preserved, had a vigorous ideological basis and considerable market appeal. Patricia Meyer Spacks (1974–5) has highlighted how women writers were concerned to explore the ambiguities of innocence as both a *sine qua non* of femininity and (in terms of its ineffectualness against sexual corruption) a potential source of danger. As we are becoming increasingly aware, women writers were interested also in turning those ambiguities to account, by tapping the commercial potential of fiction that described and sensationalized the tensions between love and duty. The extent to which they were identified with ambiguity (the power of love) on the one hand, or moral certainty (the power of duty) on the other, had a direct bearing upon the way in which they and other female authors were viewed by the readership.

The 'wittily prophane' and the 'chaste in Wit'

As we saw in chapter 2, there were several dramatists and prose-fiction writers amongst the earliest female literary professionals. In view of the *mores* governing female behaviour, it was perhaps inevitable that these pioneers should attract hostility, and it is arguable that the character of their work intensified contemporary disapproval. Behn, Manley, Trotter, Pix, Centlivre, and Haywood worked in genres that were not yet established as suitable for the female pen and, in contrast to the successful seventeenth-century professional Hannah Wolley, their work was aimed at a mixed rather than female readership. Behn and Centlivre's tragi-comedies and comedies incorporated humorous and critical representations of the manners and priorities of fashionable society, the behaviour and intrigues of lovers, and marital and extramarital relations, all of which were popular with the theatre-going public. There were those, however, who found such material, or more specifically the fact that it was written by a woman's hand, offensive. Both dramatists defended themselves robustly against their critics, charging them with hypocrisy and asserting their entitlement to write: 'for since the Poet is born, why not a Woman as well as a Man?' (Centlivre 1707: A2).

It is true that such allegations should be viewed within the context of the 'new spirit of reformation' (Sutherland 1969: 140) spearheaded by Jeremy Collier and which was critical of the libertinism of both male and female writers. Furthermore, complaints about biased audiences can be seen as special pleading, or as a means of discounting other difficulties to do with the performance, such as clashes between the dramatist and the company.[14] On the other hand, the relevance of the sex of the writer to such hostility was sufficiently acknowledged by contemporaries for Centlivre's bookseller to hide her identity in order to protect his investment. In her Preface to *The Platonick Lady* the dramatist recorded:

> A story which my Bookseller, that printed my *Gamester*, told me, of a spark that had seen my *Gamester* three or four times, and lik'd it extremely: Having bought one of the Books, ask'd who the Author was; and being told, a Woman, threw down the Book, and put up his Money, saying, he had spent too much after it already, and was sure if the Town had known that, it wou'd never have run ten days. No doubt this was a Wit in his own Eyes. It is such as these that rob us of that which inspires the Poet, Praise. And it is such as these made him that Printed my Comedy call'd, *Love's Contrivance*; or, *Medincin* Malgre lui, put two Letters of a wrong Name to it; which tho' it was the height of Injustice to me, yet his imposing on the Town turn'd to account with him; and thus passing for a Man's, it has been play'd at least a hundred times.
>
> (1707: A2–A3)[15]

Although Delarivière Manley and Eliza Haywood were connected with the theatre at early stages in their careers, their reputations were built primarily upon their work in the prose-fiction market. Manley became famous as the author of very popular scandal chronicles which served a political function (on behalf of the Tory faction) by 'revealing' the intrigues of notable Whigs. The fact that her *New Atlantis* (1709) was reissued seven times, and long after the fall of the Whig ministry in 1710, suggests that her skill lay in depicting a world of corruption that had a sustainable imaginative as well as satirical dimension. The currency of the work is indicated in *The Rape of the Lock* (1714) by Pope's use of the claim, 'As long as Atlantis shall be read', as a measure of great endurance (1714 [1846]: 53).

Haywood's rise to prominence was based upon the popularity of her amatory novellas. With her first novel *Love in Excess* (which passed through six editions in five years), Haywood identified the formula that was to sustain her prolific output during the 1720s and she became highly effective at exploiting the possibilities of sexual conflict, of predatory male lust in pursuit of female innocence. Her breathless prose led the reader from one melodramatic tableau to another, in which emotional intensity was manufactured through eleventh-hour interruptions and successive denouement where the 'Power of Love' triumphed either by force (sexual assault) or through unknowing, even unconscious (and therefore innocent) female complicity.[16]

The elements of satire, sexual desire, and scandal to be found in the work of these two women, and the professionalism which characterized their approach, inspired praise, criticism, insults, and rivalry. Manley fell out publicly with Richard Steele, and they both used their publications (including several periodicals, pamphlets, and in Manley's case, fiction), to trade attacks before their eventual reconciliation in 1717.[17] Her arrest and temporary imprisonment in 1709 following the appearance of the *New Atlantis* made her even more notorious. The case against Manley was discharged a few months later, and her career in the depiction and exposure of political and social intrigue continued apparently unabated.

Haywood's problems really began after the publication of her second scandal chronicle, *Secret History of the Present Intrigues of the Court of Caramania* (1727), in which she attacked Mrs Henrietta Howard, a friend of Alexander Pope. It has been suggested that the poet was the true hand behind Richard Savage's 'Author to Let', an attack on Edmund Curll in which the writer commented that he was 'very deeply read in all pieces of scandal, obscenity, and profaness, particularly in the writings of Mrs Haywood, Henley, Welsted, Morley. . .' (1777: 267).[18] We can be confident, however, that Pope was responsible for the lines in *The Dunciad* (first published in 1728) in which Haywood was represented with 'Two babes of love close-clinging to her waist' (1743 [1846]: 453), and as the prize for a urinating competition between Curll and Osborne. This made a substantial contribution to the contemporary perception of Haywood as a reprobate, and it procured her an unenviable and distorted place in literary history.

Such vituperations aside, these women dramatists and prose writers were impressive as well as conspicuous figures. Their material enjoyed many repeat performances and editions, and such successes must have been encouraging for other women. Furthermore, they had their panegyrists like James Sterling, and even Clara Reeve later conceded 'strong marks of Genius' in Behn's material, and 'wit and ingenuity' in Haywood's (later) writings (1785 [1930]: 117, 122).[19] On the other hand, the calumny and criticisms they shared (disparaging their lives as well as their works) made them difficult and even undesirable models for women less willing to fly in the face of convention. The threat to the reputation of any woman tempted to follow their example was apparently considerable, and for many, the loss of this fragile and essential commodity must have seemed too high a price to pay. Virginia Woolf was not far from the truth when she wrote:

For now that Aphra Behn had done it, girls could go to their parents and say, You need not give me an allowance; I can make money by my pen. Of course the answer for many years to come was, Yes, by living the life of Aphra Behn! Death would be better!

(1929 [1977]: 61)

Our greater knowledge of women's late seventeenth- and early eighteenth-century writing means that we can be reassured that these literary pioneers did not confront the difficult (but grand) choice between death or dishonour. A more prosaic option was emerging in the form of a counter-current in the public persona of the female writer which offered commercial success without threat to the author's respectability.

Historians have identified the early stirrings of this tendency within the irreproachable public demeanour of the seventeenth-century poet and playwright Katherine Philips, and later, in the works of the celebrated Elizabeth Rowe, John Dunton's 'Pindarick Lady' and the 'Bright Wonder of her Sex' (1818: vol. 1, 185). Rowe became well known for her religious poetry, sacred pieces, private meditations and prayers, and for her imaginative prose in *Friendship in Death* (1728). Through the latter, she contributed to the development of prose fiction by employing 'the ornaments of romance in the decoration of religion', a design which was begun, according to Johnson, by Mr Boyle's *Martyrdom of Theodora*, and which was completed by Rowe. Johnson praised them both for being in the class of writers 'who please and do not corrupt, who instruct and do not weary' (as quoted in Boswell 1799 [1927]: vol. 1, 208). In the process, Rowe influenced the way in which women writers were viewed, partly counterbalancing the effect of her controversial contemporaries. After her death in 1737 she remained a standard by which other women authors could be judged; as Theophilus Cibber remarked: 'The conduct and behaviour of Mrs Rowe might put some of the present race of females to the blush, who rake the town for infamous adventures to amuse the public' (1753: vol. 4, 340).

Through her pen, prose fiction became a reforming force. The impact of Rowe's material was due to her particular vision and strength of faith, but also to the care that she took over her work. We are told that: 'The famous Mrs *Singer*, afterwards Mrs *Rowe*, burnt whole Quires of Poetry, which I dare say contributes no less to her Reputation than all she published' ([Anon] 1748: 21). This discriminating approach produced material which passed through many editions in both England and America.

For eighteenth-century women writers, Rowe was an exemplar of both accomplished and virtuous womanhood, and in praising her achievements, they distinguished between her works and those of other, less 'respectable' female authors. Rowe's friend and admirer, Penelope Aubin, distanced herself more than once through the prefaces to her novels from 'the other female Authors my Contemporaries, whose Lives and Writings have, I fear, too great a resemblance' (*The Life of Charlotta Du Pont* (1723) as repub. in *A Collection*, 1739: vol. 3, vi), and she took care to align herself with Rowe on

48

the side of the encouragers of virtue and exposers of vice. According to the anonymous author of the Preface to the posthumous publication of Aubin's *A Collection of Entertaining Histories and Novels* (1739), Aubin's particular niche lay in her successful blend of a 'very entertaining Variety of Incidents, which flow naturally from her Subjects, and keep the Mind attentive and delighted' with 'very instructive Observations and Reflections' (ibid.: 4–5). Indeed, the same author considered Aubin's work to be a fine example of the application of the 'Rules . . . for constituting a good Novel' (ibid.: 5). These rules, to be 'inviolably observed' (ibid.: 2), were:

> First, A Purity of Style and Manners, that nothing may be contained in them that has the least Tendency to pollute or corrupt the inexperienced Minds, for whose Diversion they are intended. Secondly, That the Subjects should be such as naturally recommend all the Duties of social Life, and inforce an universal Benevolence to Mankind. Thirdly, That when a guilty Character is introduced, it should in the Conclusion appear to be signally punished or distressed, that others may be deterred from the Pursuits of those Follies, or Mistakes, which have been the Occasion of its Misfortunes. Fourthly, That Virtue or Innocence, on the contrary, be not finally permitted to suffer; but that a Prospect at least should be opened, either here or hereafter, for its Reward, in order to encourage every one who reads it to Imitation. And, lastly, that the whole have, at least, an Air of Probability, that the Example may have the greater Force upon the minds it is intended to inform.
>
> (ibid.: 2–3)

The *reductio ad absurdum* of a great art? Or a step by step guide to the cultivation of a new market? Perhaps these 'Rules' represent both developments but their survival throughout the eighteenth century, and beyond, means that they cannot be discounted easily. On the contrary, like Congreve's frequently quoted remarks in his Preface to *Incognita* (1692), they read like an early map, outlining the contours of a newly discovered territory which had yet to be fully explored or claimed. Congreve's differentiation between the 'lofty Language, miraculous Contingences and impossible Performances' (1692 [1971]: ii–iii) of romances and the greater realism of the novel has a resonance in the above 'Rule' requiring 'Probability', and in the anonymous author's disparagement of the 'unnatural Flights and hyperbolical Flourishes' of other women's novels which have 'too romantick an Air for Probability' (1739: 4).[20] The striking difference between the two attempts at definition is that by the early eighteenth century (and before Richardson) the novel was clearly being viewed as a potential resource for the didacticist. Indeed, the requirement to instruct was presented as the guiding principle of the new genre; we can identify here the beginnings of LeGates's 'conduct book fictionalised' (1976–7: 27).

Aubin, although presented as upholding all these 'Rules' of 'good' novel writing, did not introduce herself to her readers so sententiously. Rather, she showed her understanding of such alternative attractions as masquerades, and even gaming, before offering her work modestly 'to pass away that time that must hang heavy on our Hands: And Books of Devotion being tedious, and out of Fashion, Novels and Stories will be welcome' (*Noble Slaves* in *A Collection* 1739: vol. 1, viii). This was the approach of a writer who had some understanding of her market and of how to cultivate her readers. In the Preface of her fifth novel *Charlotta Du Pont* (1723), she referred to the success of her earlier works as the reason for her writing. This would help to deflect any charges of unbecoming arrogance and give her the *cachet* of a successful, popular author. Furthermore, despite her claim not to be writing for 'Bread', her adherence to the advice of her booksellers not to employ her pen on more serious and learned works and to stay with a lighter style (although rejecting their recommendation to be rather more modish) was entirely professional; 'I shall forbear publishing any Works of greater Price and Value than these, till times mend, and Money again is plenty in England' (*Charlotta Du Pont* in *A Collection* 1739: vol. 3, vi).

The commercial strength of a 'moral' tone in fiction is demonstrated by Aubin's consistent success (most of her novels achieved a second edition in their first year),[21] and by the fact that the publisher Edmund Curll made more than one foray into this market. Although his name has become a synonym for scurrility, he was an astute interpreter of market trends who catered for a diverse demand. It is significant, therefore, that his choice for his first novelistic publication should be Jane Barker's *Love's Intrigues* (1713), which, despite its title, was free from any hint of scandal. The success of this novel and of her subsequent publications helps to explain Curll's persistent interest in the writings of this genteel and provincially educated woman who admired the exemplary Katherine Philips.

In the early years of the eighteenth century, therefore, an interesting juxtaposition of contrasting impressions of women writers emerged. The duality was portrayed succinctly by Jane Brereton:

Fair Modesty was once our Sex's Pride,
But some have thrown that bashful Grace aside:
The *Behns*, the *Manleys* head this motley Train,
Politely lewd and wittily prophane;
Their Wit, their fluent Style (which all must own)
Can never for their Levity atone:
But Heaven that still its Goodness to denote,
For every Poison gives an Antidote;
First, our *Orinda* [Philips], spotless in her Fame,
As chaste in Wit, rescu'd our Sex from Shame:
And now, when Heywood's soft seducing Style
Might heedless Youth and Innocence beguile,

Angelic Wit, and purest Thoughts agree,
In tuneful *Singer*, and great Winchelsea.
    ('Epistle *to Mrs* Anne Griffiths. *Written from* London, *in* 1718',
                                1744: 34–5)

The relative significance of the trends in women's fiction noted by Brereton altered considerably during the remainder of the century. This process is highlighted by the vicissitudes of Haywood's career. After she was attacked in *The Dunciad*, this formerly prolific novelist seems almost to have withdrawn from the fiction market. During the next two decades she published three translations, her periodical *The Female Spectator* (1744–6), the non-fictive *Present for a servant Maid* (1743), and a few pieces for the theatre; she returned to the stage, appearing in several plays at the Haymarket before its closure; she tried to launch herself into a new career as a bookseller; and, apparently, she produced only four works of prose fiction. It is possible that she wrote and indeed published more fiction during this period, but if so, she shielded her identity with unprecedented effectiveness.

It is tempting to argue that Pope's attack shattered her literary reputation and therefore the pattern of her career, forcing her to turn elsewhere for her income. It is possible also that the productivity of the 'Great Arbitress of Passion' through the 1720s had largely satisfied the demand for her works, and that the appetite for her particular style of fiction, commanding 'the throbbing Breast, and wat'ry Eye', was on the wane. McBurney, who has described Haywood as 'one of the last (and in the novel, the best) of the latter-day Restoration female rakes' (1964: xxiv), has pointed to the inspiration she gained from the *romans* and *nouvelles* of authors like Mlle de Scudéry and Mme D'Aulnoy, whose popularity was declining during this period. Simultaneously, the success of writers like Rowe, Aubin, and Barker demonstrated that there was a substantial demand for a type of fiction that was, in its presentation at least, radically different from her own.

According to Clara Reeve, writing towards the end of the eighteenth century:

> Mr *Pope* was severe in his castigations, but let us be just to merit of every kind. *Mrs Heywood* [*sic*] had the singular good fortune to recover a lost reputation, and yet greater honour to atone for her errors. – She devoted the remainder of her life and labours to the service of virtue.
>
>   (1785: 121)

Haywood's progress towards the moral high ground can be traced in her periodical *The Female Spectator* (1744–6) where we find her expounding upon the ill effects of irresponsible fiction:

> I can by no means approve of such Definitions of that Passion [love] as

we generally find in Romances, Novels, and Plays. In most of those Writings the Authors seem to layout all their Arts in rendering that Character most interesting, which most sets at Defiance all the Obligations, by the strict Observance of which Love can alone become a Virtue.

(1744: vol. 1, 9)

It is true, as Haywood acknowledged, that there were in fact 'Many little Histories . . . interspersed' in her periodical which described the unfortunate 'Consequences of Amour', but she caught the changing mood of her readership when she claimed that the main aim in publishing her monthly essays was didactic, 'to rectify some Errors, which, . . . if indulged, grow up into greater, till they at last become Vices' (ibid.: 1). This astute professional further confirmed her reformation when she excluded salacious detail from her later novels. *The History of Betsy Thoughtless* (1751) and *The History of Jenny and Jemmy Jessamy* (1753) were both suitably 'domestic' tales and they remained popular throughout the rest of the century.

Taken together, these factors suggest that the reduction in Haywood's output of novels after the 1720s is not attributable solely to a wounded reputation. Indeed, it could be interpreted as the response of a professional writer to the exhaustion of one lucrative fictional vein before another had appeared. In this context it is worth noting that her output of novels reached its peak in 1725 and that Pope's poem was published at a time when her productivity was following a downward rather than upward path. Therefore, as this was a period of transition not only for Haywood but for the novel market as a whole, it is not entirely surprising that there are no entries in Appendix A for the years between 1736 and 1744.

The ascendancy of respectability

When women writers reappeared in the novel market after 1744 they did so as the inheritors of Rowe. According to the *Gentleman's Magazine*, 'Mrs. Rowe, Mrs. Carter, Mrs. Fielding, Mrs. Lennox, Mrs. Griffith, Mrs. Brooke . . . are all sentimental – have all supported the cause of virtue' (1775: vol. 45, 536). Although it was still possible, as Charlotte Charke's autobiography demonstrates, for a woman to strengthen her own claim to 'Decency' by condemning earlier female writers and the imprudence 'which too often led 'em into Errors, [which] Reason and Modesty equally forbid' (1755: 12), it became less necessary to propitiate the guardians of public morality by disowning earlier excesses. Indeed, as the century progressed, women writers began to take on the mantle of censor themselves.

As was noted earlier, historians have described this change in image as the emergence of the 'Lady Novelist', assigning a major role in her ascendancy to Samuel Richardson. There are other factors that we can now identify which help to explain this process: the skills of writers like Rowe and Aubin, who caught the imagination of their readers and may have encouraged other women to take up the pen; larger economic and ideological factors which placed a growing emphasis upon the role of women within the home and the family; and, as I shall discuss later, the involvement of different publishers who shifted the locus of women's fiction away from the Grub Street milieu. Thus, the content of much of women's fiction was brought securely within the accepted realms of women's experience. Tompkins (1932 [1962]) has demonstrated how, through domestic scenes of love, courtship, marriage, and parenthood, these writers promoted a type of 'prudential morality' that focused on the need for filial obedience above inclination, on the privilege rather than duty of chastity, the grace and correctness of the generous submission of wives to their husbands, and on the virtues of delicacy and sensibility (ibid.: 141–71).

The growing expectation, even insistence, that didacticism should be a distinguishing feature of women's fiction is suggested by the emphasis of contemporary critics. The tone of numerous reviews of later women's novels is represented by the *Monthly Review*'s response to Mrs Bonhote's *Darnley Vale; or Emelia Fitzroy* (1789). After remarking that 'the volumes are pleasingly, and, with some few exceptions, very correctly written', the reviewer became enthusiastic about the 'Lessons in virtue and morality [which] do the greatest honour to the writer's heart. A beautiful picture of *female friendship* is likewise to be found in these pages. We recommend it to the attention of women of every degree' (1790: vol. 1, 223–4).

The reviewers' willingness to temper criticisms of stylistic failure when faced with an exemplary sentiment was, as I shall explore later in this chapter, a mixed blessing for female writers. Such indulgences were, however, quite irrelevant to the reception of the work of a significant number of women whose *literary* achievements were recognized and applauded by the critical community. Fielding, Lennox, Sheridan, and Brooke were regarded as skilled members of the literary profession, and this enhanced perception of women's contribution was confirmed by the later work of Burney, Radcliffe, Smith, and Reeve. The status accorded to these authors, coupled with their obvious commercial successes, must have been highly encouraging to an aspiring writer, only this time, no caveat about the threat of death or dishonour was necessary. As the reviewer of *Lumley-house; The first Attempt of a young Lady* (1787) lamented: 'Almost every female of sensibility (and we observe it with much regret) is apt to imagine herself a Burney, and to believe that she cannot be better employed than in *favouring the public with a pretty novel*' (*Monthly Review* 1787: vol. 77, 162). The cumulative effect of increasing numbers of women novelists entering the literature market without threat to their respectability underpinned their accelerated ingression from the mid-1780s; literature was becoming an easier target for feminine ambition.

The moral and social values projected in domestic, sentimental fiction were not without their critics however. Mary Wollstonecraft satirized such material in *Mary, A Fiction* (1788), associating it with the worst excesses of sensibility. The fashionable Eliza, mother of the eponymous heroine, had, 'to complete her delicacy, so relaxed her nerves, that she became a mere nothing' (1788 [1980]: 2). In addition to an adulterous husband and two lap dogs, this 'nought' of the 'female world' had recourse to novels to keep herself entertained:

> She [Eliza] was chaste, according to the vulgar acceptation of the word, that is, she did not make any actual *faux pas*; she feared the world, and was indolent; but then, to make amends for this seeming self-denial, she read all the sentimental novels, dwelt on the love-scenes, and, had she thought while she read, her mind would have been contaminated. . . .
>
> (ibid.: 3)[22]

Wollstonecraft's views on contemporary fiction were part of her wider critique of prevailing social, economic, and cultural forces. Her radical vision was shared by a number of other writers, artists, and intellectuals, including the novelists Thomas Holcroft and William Godwin, who were sympathetic to the ideals of the French Revolution. The critical spirit of these English Jacobins was shared to varying degrees by other fiction and non-fiction writers including Mary Hays, Elizabeth Inchbald, Helen Maria Williams, 'Perdita' Robinson, and Mary Ann Radcliffe. In particular, Wollstonecraft, Hays, and Radcliffe focused their thinking upon the condition of their own sex, and their advocacy of various kinds of emancipation (intellectual, economic, sexual, and social) was a continuation and development of what had become, by the 1790s, a persistent theme in women's writing.

Inevitably, the republicanism and nascent feminism of these writers inspired protagonists of equal energy and conviction with their own views on how moral values should be protected or changed. The novel was becoming a forum for a serious conflict of ideas, and once again, female writers attracted the hostility of parts of the readership. For example, Lonsdale (1989: xxxix) tells us how Richard Polwhele attacked Wollstonecraft, Barbauld, Robinson, Smith, Williams, and Yearsley in his poem *The Unsex'd Females* (1798) for their democratic tendencies and seeming rejection of 'natural' feminine behaviour, ranging against them such examplars of virtuous womanhood as Burney, Ann Radcliffe, and More. The latter had aligned herself with a number of 'anti-revolutionary' writers, including Isaac d'Israeli, George Walker, Elizabeth Hamilton, and Sarah Trimmer, who had taken up the challenge in their fiction and non-fiction. Central to their thinking was a perception of the important role of women in that struggle. There was a need, More, Hamilton, and Trimmer argued, for the privileged of their sex to divert surplus money and time into fruitful and morally uplifting projects. As well as fighting listlessness (which, like Wollstonecraft, they saw as a potential source of corruption), these actions would disseminate improving benevolence and counter the threat of atheism and republicanism. Along with the author Priscilla Wakefield, these women were themselves active in numerous philanthropic projects, including schools, savings schemes, and hospitals. Through a combination of their writings and other public activites, they became prominent figures, epitomizing benevolent womanhood.

The character of these achievements should be viewed in the context of a remarkable concurrent increase in institutional charities and, as F.K. Prochaska has demonstrated, a substantial rise in the involvement of women, whose interest was, she argues, an 'extremely important force behind the rapid extension of charity in the years 1790–1830' (1974: 431). Underlying both the literary and extra-literary developments was the growing strength, in the late eighteenth and early nineteenth century, of the Evangelical movement which appealed strongly to perceived feminine predilections. Women's response was a zealous advocation of voluntary, Christian benevolence which persisted throughout the 1800s and which became a hallmark of middle-class Victorian womanhood.

In the nineteenth century, a commitment to philanthropy led women to organize, question, and campaign in ways and about issues (such as female suffrage) which were sometimes at variance with the ideal of femininity that had underpinned their increasing involvement. The contradictions inherent in such militant femininity and its capacity to stretch and redefine the limits of acceptable female behaviour can be seen also in the careers of prominent late eighteenth-century women.[23] For example, to the readers of the *Lady's Monthly Museum*, Hannah More was upheld as an inspiring example of 'Female Worth', the first of a series of 'patterns of exquisite taste and talent' (1798: vol. 1, 2). As we shall see later, she was also a highly professional writer, whose zeal led her to investigate her chosen market thoroughly and whose ability to use that understanding made her wealthy as well as famous. Furthermore, she campaigned publicly against slavery and, for many years, she ardently promoted 'narrow' improvements in education for the poor (letter to Sir William Pepys 1821, in More 1925: 198). Despite her profound, orthodox faith and essentially conservative views, she was, none the less, a highly contentious figure to some contemporaries. In a letter to the Bishop of Bath and Wells she reported that

> In one of the principal pamphlets against me, it is asserted that my writings *ought to be burned by the hands of the common hangman*. In most of them it is affirmed, that my principles and actions are corrupt and mischievous in no common degree.
>
> (1801, in More 1925: 187)

Whatever degree of controversy attended their activities, More, Trimmer, Hamilton, and Wakefield, amongst others, provided proof of the unequivocal respectability of the woman writer, thus contributing to her emerging status as censor and guide of public morality. This role (similar to its domestic equivalent) was both profoundly influential and constraining. Its effects can be traced in More's writing, which, to an extent, became fashioned by didactic and polemical considerations. When she published *Village Politics*, which was written at the behest of the Bishop of London to counteract the present 'wild impression of liberty and equality', she changed her publisher to Rivington. This was done solely to protect her identity, and she later commented in a letter to Mrs Boscowen that the work 'is as vulgar as heart can wish; but it is only designed for the most vulgar class of readers. I heartily hope I shall not be discovered; as it is a sort of writing repugnant to my nature' (1793, in More 1925: 129). Relinquishing literary possibilities in favour of moral certainties may have produced flawed fiction, but it helped to confirm wider social and economic changes that were transforming the lives of women from the middle ranks upwards. In other words, something as seemingly 'unfeminine' as the rise of women's literary professionalism (as exemplified by More) may actually have reinforced more restrictive notions of 'femininity'.

Women's contribution to this paradoxical process was identified by Lynne Agress (1978) in her investigation of the 'feminine irony' of passive feminine stereotyping in the work of early nineteenth-century female novelists, and more recently it has been brought into sharp focus by Kathryn Shevelow (1989). Through her examination of Haywood's *Female Spectator*, Shevelow has demonstrated that some women editors and writers played a special role in the paradox. Not only did Haywood project the separate spheres of women's concerns that were already well established within the periodical press, but she used the femininity of her own persona to add a new kind of authority to her communications (ibid.: 167–74). The duality could not be represented more strongly: the idealization of domesticated femininity was utilized and projected by one of the most conspicuous professional female writers of the period.

The effect upon professionalism

The increasing emphasis during the eighteenth century upon the 'femininity' of women's fiction was rather like the curate's egg, good and bad in parts. On the one hand it undermined their authorial autonomy, confining the creative process within narrow boundaries and authorizing critical responses to their work which concentrated upon sentiment rather than literary skill. As More explained, the aspiring writer experienced the 'mortifying circumstance of having her sex always taken into account; . . . her highest exertions will probably be received with the qualified approbation, *that it is really extraordinary for a woman*' (1799: vol. 2, 12–13). Increasingly, women's writing was defined 'as a special category supposedly outside the political arena, with an influence on the world as indirect as women's was supposed to be' (Spencer 1986: xi).

On the other hand, as I have suggested earlier, the authority that some women acquired within these boundaries gave them considerably greater influence within the extra-literary and literary worlds than such general conclusions imply, and it allowed them to address the major religious, social, and political issues of their day. The outstanding success of More's material, for example, must rank her amongst the most socially influential writers of the period. Furthermore, if we look at the broader development of women's fiction during the 1700s, at the emergence of the woman novelist as a significant cultural figure, it is clear that this process was strengthened considerably during the final years of the century.

The consolidation of their respectability meant that more women could write, and, as we have seen, substantially more women did write. This signified more than an improvement in access to a medium for self-expression (however restricted). The legitimizing of women's voices in didactic literature facilitated a simultaneous expansion of their literary pro-fessionalism. It helped to define certain genres (such as children's books, educational texts, and of course the novel), in which they could hope to be successful and, importantly, earn money. The impoverished middle-class woman need struggle no longer between the Scylla of disgrace and the Charybdis of destitution.

The emergence of writing as an accessible career for middle-class women is signalled by Sarah Fielding's statement that

> Perhaps the best excuse that can be made for a woman's venturing to write at all, is that which really produced this book; Distress in her Circumstances, which she could not so well remove by any other means in her power.
>
> (*David Simple* 1744 [1987]: vol. 1, Preface)

This development was based to some extent upon the tempering of the image of female authors; virtue in distress could succeed with public sympathy where references to ambition or entitlement would probably fail. However, here again, the probable response to such an appeal made it a double-edged sword.

At the beginning of the century, as we have seen, adverse public reaction to 'Female Wits' meant that to secure a favourable reception for her plays, Centlivre's identity as a playwright was sometimes hidden. In contrast, according to the *Monthly Review*, the 'fair Authoress' of *The Runaway; a Comedy* (1776) argued in her Dedication to Garrick that it was the public's sympathetic reaction to her sex that had contributed to the successful performance of her play at the Theatre-Royal:

> I perceive how much of this applause I owe to my *Sex*. – The

RUNAWAY has a thousand faults, which, if written by a Man, would have incurred the severest lash of criticism – but the gallantry of the English nation is equal to its wisdom – they beheld a *Woman* tracing with feeble steps the borders of the Parnassian Mount – pitying her difficulties (for 'tis a thorny path) they gave their hands for her support, and placed her *high* above her head.

(*Monthly Review* 1776: vol. 54, 216)

Self-denigration and flattery were *pro forma* for a dedication, but the fact that she could cite audience indulgence towards a female dramatist as a plausible ingredient of this bid to promote her work points to a significant shift in attitudes. The reviewer of the published version of the play decided to extend the same dispensation, arguing that

It bears every mark of a female production. Without much strength of fable, force of character, novelty of sentiment, or humour of dialogue, a certain delicacy pervades the whole, which in some places interests and attaches us, and in all places induces us to overlook greater deficiencies.

(ibid.)

We can only wonder at the nature of the deficiencies that were withheld from the reader. The profound disapproval of such bias and condescension felt by some female authors is exemplified by Mary Wollstonecraft's candid response to Mary Hays, whom she criticized for special pleading:

I do not approve of your preface – and I will tell you why. If your work should deserve attention it is a blur on the very face of it. – Disadvantages of education etc. ought, in my opinion, never to be pleaded (with the public) in excuse for defects of any importance, because if the writer has not sufficient strength of mind to overcome the common difficulties which lie in his way, nature seems to command him, with a very audible voice, to leave the task of instructing others to those who can. This kind of vain humility has ever disgusted me – and I should say to an author, who humbly sued for forbearance, 'if you have not a tolerably good opinion of your own production, why intrude it on the public?'

(Letter 12 November 1792, in Wollstonecraft 1979: 219)

On the other hand, the reason for many such intrusions was clearly money, and if by marshalling the 'deficiencies' of her sex in her defence the hard-pressed professional could increase the performances or sales of her material, it is likely that she would take the opportunity to do so. We confront the paradox again; the emergence of women's professional writing was at least partly dependent upon the confirmation of more reductive notions of women's abilities. As I discuss in the following chapter, writing became one of the few occupations available to middle-class women and we may reasonably assume that the issue of remuneration was of major importance when alternatives were so scarce.

4

PROFESSIONAL AUTHORSHIP: THE ALTERNATIVES FOR WOMEN

But the matter is this – Mankind have taken it into their heads, that authors who are worth countenance are those only who write without hopes of reward, whose independent spirit soars above the paltry profits obtained by divinity, law, physic, or war. Authors should write by inspiration and live on air. I confess myself in this respect to have been always ill qualified for an author; my ambition from the first being to present the public with such fruits as Hope flattered me they would not grudge to pay a price for.

(Jean Marishall 1789: vol.2, 198)

THE SOCIAL AND ECONOMIC BACKGROUNDS OF PROFESSIONAL WOMEN WRITERS

The expansion of women's literary professionalism was an integral part of the development of women's fiction during the eighteenth century. In the context of this study the term 'professional' is used simply to distinguish between those who received payment for their work and those amateurs who did not. This definition, therefore, includes authors for whom payment was a concomitant but inessential accompaniment to publication, and those – occasionally identified in the text as 'dependent professionals' – who used writing as a means of earning a living.

A hundred years after Aphra Behn and Delarivière Manley chose authorship as their main occupation, many women had taken up the pen for money with varying degrees of success. As we have seen, it became increasingly acceptable for women to offer the need for 'Bread' as their reason for seeking publication. This remarkable development is a major theme of the remainder of this study, beginning with a closer examination of the social and economic backgrounds of the writers concerned.

The following discussion is based upon the lives of sixty-four prose-fiction writers for whom it has been possible to establish either that they received money for their publications, or that at some stage during their careers they wrote expressly in response to financial hardship.[1] These women are identified in Appendix A by the notation (P). It is important to stress that, by focusing upon a particular genre, I have excluded those professionals, like Laetitia Pilkington, who used a number of literary forms with the apparent exception of prose fiction, and those, including Hannah Cowley and Mary Barber, who concentrated on other genres.[2] None the less, it has been possible to find evidence of payment for over a third of the writers in Appendix A and it would be reasonable to assume that many more, and particularly the 'Minerva' authors, were remunerated for their work.

Most of the women in the sample were dependent upon their income from writing for at least part of their working lives, and for a few it was their principal occupation. Examples can be drawn from throughout the period, suggesting a fairly continuous presence of 'dependent professional' female writers in the literature market, and there is reason to think that this aspect of women's fiction continued into the early 1800s. We can trace it in the career of a highly successful writer like Maria Edgeworth, who attained market eminence during the first decade of the nineteenth century, and at a more prosaic level in the continued entry into the market of writers like Elizabeth Isabella Spence, a physician's daughter, who avoided destitution by publishing novels and travelogues.

On the eve of the industrial revolution English society was a complex and subtle hierarchy within which men were placed according to various criteria, including the source and amount of their income, and their occupation, religious convictions, and political affiliations. The status of women was derived largely from that of their presiding male, whether father or husband, and thus considerable changes in circumstances could occur upon the death of their parents, or upon marriage. As will become evident, many of the authors referred to in this chapter turned to writing after such an event, either as a means of preventing, or of surviving, a marked downturn in their fortunes. For example, the novelist Lady Dorothea Dubois was the eldest daughter of Richard Annesley (later the sixth Earl of Anglesey) but she spent her life in poverty after her father repudiated his marriage, declared his children illegitimate, and reclaimed Dorothea's £10,000 annuity.[3] Similarly, Ann Emelinda Skinn was expected to inherit an annuity estimated at £3,000 as the sole heir of her wealthy grandfather. This fortune eluded her when she was disinherited at the age of sixteen following a family dispute.

Other women were more successful in securing their inheritance only to lose their wealth after marriage. Elizabeth Villa-Real Gooch was left an heiress following her father's death but an unhappy arranged marriage resulted in her abandonment in France, where she attempted to survive on a dwindling annuity. Her subsequent imprisonment for debt was the spur to becoming a professional author. Delarivière Manley's incentive for writing was similar. On the death of her father, Sir Roger Manley, she received £200 and a share in the residue of his estate. This was soon dissipated after she was deceived into a bigamous marriage and then deserted by her husband on the birth of their first child. These women represent the higher levels of potential wealth amongst the sample. In contrast, Ann Yearsley was one of several working-class poets, including Mary Collier, Mary Leapor, and Elizabeth Hands, who attracted curiosity and acclaim after the publication (mainly through subscription and the helpful offices of a patron) of their verses. Ann's literary success was achieved against a background of little education and menial work undertaken to supplement her husband's income as a labourer. Her sobriquet, 'Lactilla', was derived from her first occupation of selling milk from door to door.

The majority of the sixty-four women in the sample, however, came from the middle social stratum. In the eighteenth century the term 'middle ranks' described a subtle organism which embraced a wide range of occupations, wealth, and status:

> Distinguished at the top from the gentry and nobility not so much by lower incomes as by the necessity of earning their living, and at the bottom from the labouring poor not so much by higher incomes as by the property, however small, represented by stock in trade, livestock, tools, or the educational investment of skill or expertise.
>
> (Perkin 1969: 23)

Between the extremes of merchant princes and those surviving through their crafts lay a multiplicity of occupations with their own minutely graded hierarchies. Thus, although the lives of the women authors in the sample had certain common features (which I shall examine later), there were considerable differences in their circumstances. A cursory glance reveals a husband who was a compiler, and another an actor, and fathers who worked as a captain on a Bristol whaler, a coal merchant, and a fashionable musician. Whilst recognizing this diversity, it is still possible to identify three sectors of the middle social stratum that were well represented: the confident and swelling ranks of those concerned with making and circulating wealth and capital; the professions; and the farming community.

Women authors came from various levels of wealth and influence within manufacturing and merchanting. Mary Wollstonecraft's grandfather was a rich Spitalfields manufacturer whose son dissipated the family fortune through abortive farming ventures and alcoholism. Charlotte Smith, who was born into the landed gentry, married the son of a wealthy West India merchant and director of the East India Company. Her husband reduced the family to destitution through his improvidence, resulting in their imprisonment in the Marshalsea for debt. Eliza Parsons fared little better. The daughter of a wine merchant, she made an unfortunate marriage to a man engaged unsuccessfully in the turpentine trade and, again, both were reduced to poverty. Eliza Haywood's origins as the daughter of a small London shopkeeper meant that she started life without an independent income. She married a clergyman with a living in Norfolk and when they separated it was necessary for her to support herself. She survived initially through a mixture of acting and writing before swiftly and successfully concentrating her efforts on publication. Priscilla Wakefield was forty when the misfortunes of her husband, a London merchant, required her to earn an income. Her resort to writing was the beginning of a highly successful literary career that lasted twenty years.

Not all the women from this broad category encountered such vicissitudes. Ann Radcliffe's father was a genteel tradesman and there were family connections with Cheseldon, the famous surgeon, and with Sir Richard Jebb, physician to George III. Most of her youth was spent in reasonable affluence and her marriage to a journalist and former Oxford student was financially comfortable, no doubt largely as a result of the considerable sums she earned through her writing.

Those authors who came from, or married into, the professional sector experienced a similar variety of economic and social circumstances. In this context, as distinct from its previous application in this chapter, the term refers to the professions of divinity, law, and medicine. This traditional usage is sometimes extended to include the army and navy, and that convention is followed here. There were considerable inequalities within each profession. To take an obvious example, in medicine the relatively few members of the Royal College of Physicians were the elite, above non-member physicians and surgeons, who were, in their turn, superior to the apothecaries who served the bulk of the population. As Perkin has suggested, the company of 'gentlemen' would include 'The nobility and gentry, the clergyman, physician and barrister, but not always the Dissenting minister, the apothecary, the attorney, or the school master' (1969: 24).

The lower levels of the professional hierarchies feature most frequently in the backgrounds of the authors in the sample. Mary Latter was the daughter of a country attorney and she earned her own income initially in trade, and eventually as an author. Despite becoming something of a local celebrity as a result of her writing, according to her own account, she was troubled constantly by financial insecurity and the fear of destitution. The erstwhile heiress Ann E. Skinn's first husband was a lawyer who divorced her after a few years on the grounds that she deserted him for another man. She went on to marry an army officer, who eventually abandoned her in poverty.

The families of poorer clergy were potential seedbeds of literary professionalism, combining the probability of education with the possibility of an insufficient income. Sarah Fielding's friend, Jane Collier, was the daughter of the rector of Langford Magna who, having sold his property in order to pay his debts, left his children with the need to earn their own living. Clara Reeve's father, who was the rector of Freston and Kerton,

Suffolk, and a perpetual curate in Ipswich, had an insufficient income to provide for his many offspring. As a result, Clara supported herself, first through domestic service and later through a highly successful career as a writer (Hecht 1956: 18).

A few women in the sample came from, or married into, military and naval families. Susannah Gunning married an army officer from a distinguished family; Charlotte Lennox's father was Captain James Ramsay, whose death left her unprovided for; Helen Maria Williams's father was an army officer; and Susanna Rowson, the daughter of Lieutenant Haswell of the British navy, married a hardware merchant and trumpeter in the Royal Horse Guards who later went bankrupt. Elizabeth Hervey's step-father was the wealthy MP William Beckford, making her a half-sister to William Beckford, author of the extraordinary Gothic novel *Vathek*. Unfortunately, the security she enjoyed in this affluent environment was eroded after her marriage to Colonel Thomas Hervey. He gambled away their fortune, forcing them to flee abroad. Elizabeth returned to England after his death and supported herself through her writing.

During the eighteenth century, the agricultural sector underwent fundamental changes in its structure and methods which had a mixed impact upon the farmers involved. Large landowners, able to afford enclosure and the implementation of progressive techniques, experienced a rise in their wealth and standard of living, as did substantial tenants in receipt of financial support from improving landlords. Inevitably, these groups sought to enhance their social status and their quest for gentility was reflected in a desire for better educated, more accomplished children. As Allan Macleod observed in response to disapproving comments from James Lackington:

> The farmers of England, who are qualified by fortune to have their daughters polished by the refinements of a liberal education, have as good a right as any set of men in this world to send their daughters to boarding schools, and run not half the risk the gentry do of losing, in their education, the affection of their children.
>
> (1804: 147)

Other contemporaries were less sanguine about the aspirations of this sector, and numerous squibs, songs, and cartoons satirized bucolic complacency. Hannah More made it the target of one of her moral tracts, describing in *The Two Wealthy Farmers* the dilemma of 'Mrs. Bragwell', who:

> Ventured to request her daughters to assist in making the pastry. They asked her scornfully, whether she had sent them to boarding-school to learn to cook; and added, that they supposed she would expect them next to make puddings for the hay-makers.
>
> (c.1810: 8)

Although these attacks were actuated often by social snobbery, they high-lighted the potential impact of important developments that were taking place within the farming household. These included the gradual withdrawal of some farmers' wives from their traditional tasks (for example, as mistress of the dairy), and the gentrification of their children who, it was suggested, were losing interest in agricultural employment.

However, not all farmers fared equally well and small freeholders with limited personal funds, possibly undermined by low grain prices in the first half of the century, found the viability of their businesses threatened by contemporary developments. This background was more likely to produce 'dependent professional' authors than those who wrote for pleasure or to be fashionable. For example, Jane West, who was self-educated, wrote in order to help support her family following her marriage to a yeoman farmer at Bowden. Remarkably, she continued to supervise the household and dairy, whilst publishing material in various genres, including poetry, plays, con-duct books, and prose fiction, during a literary career which lasted nearly fifty years.

Thus far, the evidence from this sample of known professionals suggests the emergence during the eighteenth century of two key features of their authorship: its function as a source of income for impecunious, literate women without apparently posing a threat to their respectability; and the ascendancy of the middle class amongst literary women. It is worth noting that a number of the other authors listed in Appendix A also came from backgrounds which included middle-rank occupations. Elizabeth Bonhote was the wife of a Bungay solicitor, Elizabeth Pinchard was married to a Taunton attorney, and Elizabeth Sophia Tomlins was the daughter of an eminent London solicitor; Susanna Keir married a man engaged in com-merce who eventually took over Boulton and Watt's enterprise at Soho, Birmingham; Elizabeth Rowe was the daughter of a Presbyterian preacher and prosperous clothier; Frances Sheridan, the only daughter of the Archdeacon of Glendalough, married the actor-manager Thomas Sheridan; Elizabeth Helme married a Brentford schoolmaster, and at a more elevated level, Sarah Trimmer's father, an architectural draughtsman, became a tutor to the Prince of Wales; Amelia Alderson (later Opie), was the daughter of a Norwich physician; Ellis Cornelia Knight was the daughter of a rear-admiral of the white who was knighted in 1773; and Jael-Henrietta Pye was the daughter of an affluent London merchant. Her first husband was a Mr Campbell (admitted to Lincoln's Inn in 1755), and she later married an ensign in the 1st Foot Guards.

The social and economic circumstances of writers such as Fanny Trollope, the Brontë sisters, and Elizabeth Gaskell attest to the continued predomi-nance of the middle ranks in the backgrounds of women novelists in the nineteenth century. This is, of course, entirely in accord with the literary historians' perception of the novel as a quintessentially middle-class development (however that term is defined),[4] entailing the market eminence of authors from that stratum.

PLAYERS, PAINTERS, AND PEDAGOGUES: THE OCCUPATION STRUCTURE

The rise of female literary professionalism, and particularly the number of authors who were dependent financially upon their writing, suggests that publication acquired a significantly different function in the lives of women during the eighteenth century. This can be understood more fully if we examine the position of writing within the range of occupations available to the 'unprotected female' from the middle ranks.

The majority of eighteenth-century women could anticipate a future that included marriage (whether through the church or through binding arrangements like verbal spousals and cohabitation) and motherhood. For women from the middle stratum upwards, these major undertakings acquired added significance due to the growing belief that the home was the rightful focus of their activity, unmixed with other areas of (remunerated) employment. Their steps along the path towards domestic fulfilment were guided by numerous commentators writing in magazines, pamphlets, and books. The entire proceedings were subjected to detailed and often humorous scrutiny, witness the 'young Lady's *Litany*' which pleaded: '*from the dangerous Delusions of young* Men *without Principles; from the artful Insinuations of Intriguing* Old Women, *and from the forward Presumption of* a Boarding School Breeding *may* Providence deliver us!' ([Anon] 1748: 33).

As contemporary readers would appreciate, this squib was satirizing a real predicament facing those caught up in the rigours of the market, and one that was raised frequently in the periodical press by those offering or seeking serious advice. Their plight is illustrated by the experience of one unfortunate correspondent to the *Lady's Monthly Museum* who signed herself 'Biddy Willing'. For three years Biddy's campaigning parents had transported her from their 'country seat to London, from London to Brighton, from Brighton to Bath, and from Bath to Cheltenham', thereby reducing her at twenty-three to a state of mind in which she was willing to accept any man 'who was neither ugly, nor ill-natured'. In response, the magazine was highly critical of parents who exerted 'all the grimace and cant of an auctioneer to engage purchasers' (1798: vol. 1, 289, 291). Clearly, dedication to the cause was not proof against failure and, furthermore, such expeditions were expensive. There were those who simply did not have sufficient resources 'to go to Market with . . . . to buy this haughty, saucy Thing, called a Husband' (Defoe 1720 [1869]: vol. 2, 187).

Spinsterhood, as depicted in the popular culture, was an unenviable condition. The 'Old Maid' was a favourite 'Aunt Sally' of contemporary satirists, who could wax highly abusive on the subject, as is demonstrated by Defoe's satirical proposition to establish 'An Office for Marriages':

Which I believe would be particularly useful to a set of despicable creatures, called Old Maids . . . those wretches who have languished out their insipid lives, perhaps without ever having an offer of a Husband; 'tis no wonder, if they, (lost to all sense of Modesty, and at their last Cast,) should (rather than sink with that heavy luggage of Virginity into their graves) depising the calumnies of a censorious World . . ., flock in Crowds to your office. . . .

(1719 [1869]: vol. 2, 115)

Execration was not, however, the most severe threat to the happiness of single women. As Jean Marishall explained:

What is the reason, it is alleged, there are so many fretful, ill-looking, discontented, old maids? Is it because they have not got husbands? No. If they have money enough to ensure their consequence, entertain their friends, dress in the mode of the times; take my word for it they will neither be particularly ill-looking, fretful, nor discontented: . . . Put as many of you mighty sovereigns of the creation under the same predicament, I am persuaded two-thirds of you would hang or drown yourselves in less than a twelvemonth.

(1789: vol. 2, 114–15)

The greatest problem was economic vulnerability. Marishall's own solution was the voluntary levying of a county tax to augment the income of the 'deserving', who would each be given the full responsibility of caring for two orphaned or neglected children. She intended that her annuitants should obtain not only financial security, but also a degree of respect that would 'wear out that illiberal practice of ridicule and neglect' (ibid.: 117). It was a forthright and ingenious proposal which touched upon one particular aspect of a larger problem that was gaining increasing attention: the plight of ill-trained, indigent women from the middle and upper ranks, married as well as single.

Under more favourable circumstances, the daughters of wealthy landed or commercial families had little need or, one assumes, desire to leave the parental home to earn a living. Although their chances of inheriting the family estate were negligible,[5] their financial future was normally secure, at least until marriage. Provision for younger children during the eighteenth century was more generous than had previously been the case, and it was fixed under strict settlement at their parents' marriage. A family gathering at this stage could ensure an equitable balance of interests between the parents and the expected issue, who would have a legal claim to portions which were secured customarily by a trustee. These enabled or induced the younger sons to enter a profession, and they provided the daughters with a stake in future marriage (and jointure) negotiations.

It was expected that after marriage the financial security of such women would depend upon their husbands' income and within this arrangement their own duties were quite clear. *The Lady's Museum*, addressing its literate, middle- and upper-class readership, argued that upon the wife

> Lies the education of her children; of the boys to a certain age, of the girls till they be married; the government of her domestics, their morals, their service; the disembursements of housekeeping, the method of living with oeconomy, and at the same time in figure; often even the letting of farms and the receiving of rents.
>
> (Fénelon, Archbishop of Cambray 1761: vol. 2, 847)

Later in the century, the *Lady's Monthly Museum*, basing its views upon Priscilla Wakefield's *Reflections on the Present Condition of the Female Sex* (1798), maintained that the 'Duties of Women in the Superior Classes of Society' should include some attention to the 'female poor of the neighbourhood':

> Not only for a liberal distribution of pecuniary assistance in cases of sickness or unavoidable distress, but also for part of their time, proportioned to their leisure. Without any impertinent interference with the exclusive departments of men, in the administration of parochial business, there are many important benefits which might be derived from the co-operation of women of enlarged understandings, in the superintendence of the poor of their own sex. . . . The patronage and management of useful institutions for the improvement of their morals, and the increase of their happiness, the inspection of work-houses, schools of industry and cottages, not merely once or twice in a twelve month, but so frequently as to become acquainted with the wants and condition of the inhabitants, would . . . correct many abuses, . . . particularly with respect to the rearing of children, and the preservation of the morals of female apprentices.
>
> (1798: vol. 1, 35)

This view of women's responsibilities was advanced and, indeed, enacted by the writers More, Trimmer, and Hamilton, but difficulties arose when women of such 'enlarged understandings' were confronted by drastically reduced incomes. Inherited wealth was not a guarantee against poverty, and disinheritance or an unpropitious marriage could lead to destitution. The options available to middle- and upper-class women in these circumstances were limited by an enduring opposition to the very idea of gentlewomen undertaking paid work. Although this attitude did not preclude the kind of active, protective interest in her family's wealth displayed by Mrs Montagu, who assumed a vital role in the management of her husband's northern collieries, it did censure severely any form of direct remuneration. The problem was outlined by Hestor Mulso in a letter to Richardson. She observed: 'Custom indeed allows not the daughters of people of fashion to leave their father's family to seek their own subsistence, and there is no way for them to gain a creditable livelihood, as gentlemen may' (3 January, 1750–1, in Chapone 1808: vol. 2, 117).

This proscription filtered through the social structure to those amongst the middle ranks who desired gentility. Thus the daughters and wives of merchants, manufacturers, farmers, and the professions could be affected also. Richard Brinsley Sheridan's response to his wife's work as an eminent singer illustrates well the impact of this view upon a promising and vital career. Despite being desperately in need of money, Sheridan refused to allow Elizabeth to continue, much to the approval of Dr Johnson. When questioned about Sheridan's behaviour and whether or not it was 'foolishly delicate, or foolishly proud', Johnson remarked that 'He resolved wisely and nobly to be sure. He is a brave man. Would not a gentleman be disgraced by having his wife singing publickly for hire? No, Sir, there can be no doubt here' (Boswell 1799 [1927]: vol. 1, 598). Like Swift and Richardson, Johnson was at times very supportive of individual professional women writers and therefore it is tempting to speculate that his opinion in Sheridan's case was strengthened by the very public nature of Elizabeth's occupation. Similar to the acting profession, it was impossible for a successful singer to preserve a diffident anonymity which, significantly, was possible for the writer.

Problems arising from condemnatory attitudes were compounded by those resulting from inadequate training. The daughters of the upper and aspiring middle classes often received a limited education which made them literate but did not train them in cheese making, spinning, dress or mantua making, bookbinding, or a host of other possible areas of paid employment. Furthermore, without a portion or another source of finance, they faced the difficulty of acquiring the initial capital necessary to buy an apprenticeship, or to purchase or rent suitable premises and equipment. Once established, they required sufficient working capital and business acumen to survive in the face of competition. The novelist Laurence Sterne, writing to his uncle, recounted how he and his wife had settled upon mantua making as a suitable occupation for his dependent sister, and that (once she had learned her craft) he offered '*That* we would give her 30. pounds to begin the World & Support her till Business fell in' (1751, in Sterne 1935: 37–8). Although this was a substantial sum, Pinchbeck tells us that for some crafts

> A five or seven year apprenticeship was required and a milliner in good business demanded a fee of at least £40–£50. The capital required to set up in business afterwards varied from £100 to £1,000 according to the scale of business, but at least £400 to £500 was considered necessary to 'set up genteelly'.
>
> (1930 [1981]: 287)

The difficulties facing such women were acknowledged by increasing numbers of their contemporaries. At an individual level, some parents (for example, those of Hannah More) tried to equip their daughters with skills that would enable them to make their way in the market for genteel trades. In the public domain, enlightened views on training for women were advanced throughout the century, usually as part of the wider issue of 'Female Learning'. The vexed questions of how much education it was desirable for girls and women to receive, and for what purposes, were themselves linked with concerns about social change and stability. On the one hand, there were those who perceived the potentially subversive impact of learning upon women and who advised caution. In the opinion of Lady Pennington,

> It has been objected against all female learning, beyond that of household oeconomy, that it tends only to fill the minds of the sex with a conceited vanity, which sets them above their proper business – occasions an indifference to, if not a total neglect of, their family-affairs – and serves only to render them useless wives and impertinent companions. – It must be confess'd that some reading ladies have given but too much cause for this objection; – and could it be prov'd to hold good throughout the sex, it would certainly be right to confine their improvements within the narrow limits of the nursery, of the kitchen, and the confectionary.
>
> (1784: 40–1)

On the other hand, the converse was argued by those who regarded an extension of the curriculum for female education as a prerequisite for contented family life and well-trained children. To Mary Wollstonecraft, writing towards the end of the century, it was morally imperative: 'So forcibly does this truth strike me that I would rest the whole tendency of my reasoning upon it, for whatever tends to incapacitate the maternal character, takes woman out of her sphere.' Her axiom that 'The weakness of the mother will be visited on the children' underpinned the conclusion: 'Make women rational creatures and free citizens, and they will quickly become good wives and mothers – that is, if men do not neglect the duties of husbands and fathers' (1975: 298, 299).

Wollstonecraft's equation between improved education for women and successful motherhood was clearly part of her explication of a larger challenge to existing relations between the sexes and between different social strata. However, she was not the first to enlist education in support of a desire to buttress the moral nature of women and to enlarge their sphere of influence and activity. In *An Essay Upon Projects* (1697), Defoe added his voice to those of Bathsua Makin and Mary Astell by proposing the founding of 'An Academy for Women', to counter the

> Most barbarous Customs . . . that . . . deny the advantages of Learning to women. We reproach the Sex every day with Folly and Impertinence, while I am confident, had they the advantages of Education equal to us, they wou'd be guilty of less than our selves.

One wou'd wonder indeed how it shou'd happen that Women are conversible at all, since they are only beholding to Natural Parts for all their Knowledge. . . . And I wou'd but ask any who slight the Sex for their Understanding, What is a Man (a Gentleman, I mean) good for, that is taught no more?

(1697 [1969]: 282–3)[6]

Defoe's stance in support of women's learning was adopted by a number of later writers, including Samuel Richardson, Wetenhall Wilkes, and the mysterious 'Sophia'.[7] The latter, in her first pamphlet, *Woman Not Inferior to Man: or, A short and modest Vindication of the natural Right of the FAIR-SEX to a perfect Equality of Power, Dignity and Esteem, with the Men* (1739), anticipated key elements of Wollstonecraft's exposition by suggesting that

It is a very great absurdity, to argue that learning is useless to *Women*, because forsooth they have not a share in public offices, which is the end for which *Men* apply themselves to it. *Virtue* and *Felicity* are equally requisite in a private, as well as in a public station, and *learning* is a necessary means to both. It is by that we acquire an exactness of thought, a propriety of speech, and a justness of actions: Without that we can never have a right knowledge of ourselves: It is that which enables us to distinguish between right and wrong, true and false. . . . But let truth speak for once: Why are they [men] so industrious to debar us that learning, we have an equal right to with themselves, but for fear of our sharing with, and outshining them in, those public offices they fill so miserably? The same sordid selfishness which urged them to engross all power and dignity to themselves, prompted them to shut up from us that knowledge which wou'd have made us their competitors.

(2nd edn 1740: 27–8)

The debate was not entirely theoretical. Significant changes were taking place in the provision of schooling for children from the middle ranks upwards which gave greater pertinence to questions of curriculum and purpose. During the eighteenth century, as in earlier periods, the daughters of enlightened parents could receive a good education at home. The work of the Anglo-Saxon scholar Elizabeth Elstob, who was encouraged in her studies by her mother and later by her brother, is eloquent testimony to the potential of this kind of tuition.[8] Indeed, home-based education was strengthened during this period by the arguments of moralists and educational theorists who stressed the importance of early training. The implementation of such ideas was facilitated by a complementary growth in children's literature, games, and toys, and the expansion in retailing and the library system which made these accoutrements of successful parenting increasingly accessible.

71

Despite these developments, this mode of education was still very haphazard, being so dependent upon the vagaries and skills of family and friends. Laetitia Pilkington's later career as a professional writer was nearly prevented by her mother's prohibition against her reading. She was forced to study surreptitiously and to risk harsh punishments until her father intervened and brought an end to the situation. Similarly, the author Frances Sheridan had to be taught in secret by her brothers because her father disapproved of her literacy. The employment of a governess, although increasingly fashionable, was not necessarily a solution to the problem. In 1753, Lady Mary Wortley Montagu recalled how her education at home

> Was one of the worst in the World, being exactly the same as Clarissa Harlowe's, her pious Mrs. Norton so perfectly ressembling my Governess (who had been Nurse to my Mother) I could almost fancy the Author was acquainted with her. She took so much pains from my Infancy to fill my Head with superstitious Tales and false notions, it was none of her Fault I am not at this day afraid of Witches and Hobgoblins, or turn'd Methodist.
>
> Almost all Girls are bred after this manner.
>
> (1967: vol. 3, 25–6)

In this context, the appearance after 1750 of numerous ladies' academies offered a substantial improvement in girls' access to at least an elementary education. As J.H. Plumb (1975: 75–8) has demonstrated, the quality of tuition at these schools varied greatly but the supply of places was plentiful. Furthermore, they came well within the purchasing power of the middle ranks, particularly after intense price competition in the 1780s and, according to Plumb, they 'almost certainly' attracted the children of 'small squires, farmers, tradesmen, merchants, shopkeepers, and clerks' (ibid.: 78). Many of these institutions offered vocational subjects as part of the curriculum. For boys, this could include handwriting for clerks, merchanting accounts, and surveying. For girls, the emphasis was upon enhancing their chances in the marriage market and improving their ability to uphold future familial responsibilities. On the whole, such instruction was not intended to equip them for paid work, nor to enable them to dispute the 'natural' order of accomplishments, 'for who would wish to see assemblies made up of doctors in petticoats, who will regale us with Greek and the systems of Leibnitz' (Fénelon, Archbishop of Cambray 1760: vol. 1, 10).[9]

We know from the experience of Hannah More, whose father gave her a good education at home but excluded mathematics when he discovered her disturbing aptitude for the subject, that restrictions to the curriculum applied equally to girls able to study at home. Nevertheless, through all these means – parents, governesses, schools, and even autodidacticism (facilitated by a growing body of educational literature) – girls from the middle ranks were receiving a greater measure of education than they had enjoyed before.

This enhanced the quality of their leisure and enabled them to embrace new areas of knowledge which, as I shall demonstrate later, became increasingly accessible to them. Most importantly for this study, it enabled them to write books as well as to read them, and to offer learning to others. In other words, education became a resource that middle-class women could turn to financial advantage.

In view of their background, education was clearly a potential area of work for such women; it was securely respectable, it drew upon their skills, and a few individuals had demonstrated already that it had the potential to offer satisfying and profitable careers. By 1700, women had broken new ground by running schools, tutoring in the highest circles, and by contributing to public debates on principles and curricula.[10] Employment opportunities in the field expanded after 1750 in tandem with the rapid growth in the number of institutions, and it was possible for women with pedagogic talent, business acumen, and the right social contacts to make a comfortable living. As Priscilla Wakefield noted in her *Reflections*:

> The presiding over seminaries for female education, is . . . a suitable employment for those, whose minds have been enlarged by liberal cultivation, whilst the under parts of that profession may be more suitably filled by persons whose early views have been contracted within narrower limits.
>
> (1798: 138)

Fortunately for such 'persons' a concomitant of the growth in seminaries was a rising demand for resident and peripatetic teachers. Although, here again, success was at least partly dependent upon contacts as well as talent. Mrs Thrale, in a letter to Dr Johnson, described the income and status of a well-employed practitioner:

> A taylor's daughter, who professes musick, and teaches so as to give six lessons a day to ladies, at five and threepence a lesson. Miss Burney says she is a great performer; and I respect the wench for getting her living so prettily; she is very modest and pretty-mannered, and not seventeen years old.
>
> (1780, as quoted in Boswell 1799 [1927]: vol. 2, 318–19)

Although the growth in schools was rapid, its geographical concentration left substantial opportunities for work within what Charlotte Brontë described later as 'governessing slavery' (1847 [1969]: vol. 2, 340). As an upper domestic servant, material benefits were determined largely by the beneficence of the employer, and for gentlewomen there was a degree of social degradation with even the most secure and well-paid position. The experiences of the hapless Mary Ann Radcliffe illustrate well the vulnerability of the profession. Her *Memoirs* reveal how her family was thrown into financial turmoil as a result of her husband's disastrous investments in the sugar business. After selling her silver and other possessions, she sought employment from 'the millinery line' (1810: 101), only to be rejected because of her lack of experience and apprenticeship. The response was the same when she applied to become a governess and then a housekeeper, and she was forced to take in 'a little sewing to supply [her] . . . own immediate wants, and [to] keep [her] . . . from selling any part of the remaining property' (ibid.: 104). Relief came when a friend helped her to obtain a position as a governess in Scotland. After sending her boys to school, placing her youngest daughter with a dressmaker, and her two eldest with her own servant to comfort her aged mother, she took up her post in the family of, as she discovered, an old school friend. Radcliffe did not complain directly about ill-treatment or exploitation, but the disadvantages of her dependent status were conveyed clearly enough:

> At length no cooking was approved of, if I had not a finger in the pie; and consequently, I had an appartment appropriated for my use in cookery also. So, my dear friend, you may figure to yourself the abundant share of business that fell to my lot; one time cooking, the next in state to receive the congratulatory visits, on the birth of the young nobleman; then carving, and assisting the good Lady in bed; in fact, I cannot ennumerate the variety of honourable posts I held . . . indeed I do not know what I was not . . . and I dare venture to say was *supposed* to have obtained an abundant reward for my trouble; an acknowledgement for which, I doubt not would have been considered, had not her Ladyship's finances at that time precluded it, (for she was naturally of a generous as well as friendly disposition).
>
> (ibid.: 121–2)

Despite such disadvantages, life as an upper servant was almost certainly preferable to some of the alternatives. Thomas Hood's 'Song of the Shirt' (1843), with its well-known evocation of the misery of 'sweated' needlework, was no less pertinent to the condition of the poorly paid 'sempstress' in the eighteenth century. On the other hand, since it required quite basic skills and little capital, this type of sewing had the advantage of being a relatively accessible option for women who failed to break into the market for teachers or servants, or to buy an apprenticeship; as Radcliffe discovered to her cost, there were families who would employ neither 'gentlewomen . . . nor gentlewomen's daughters' (ibid.: 254).

Service and sewing lay towards the poorer reaches of what Roy Porter has called the 'client economy servicing the Great' (1982: 86). At a higher level, working for the 'Quality Market' could include the potentially more lucrative options of either dress and mantua making, creating designs for needlework and other ornamental crafts, or even a position at Court. For women with the requisite talent, professional painting could be a viable alternative, offering 'a mode of subsistence, congenial to the delicacy of the most refined minds' (Wakefield 1798: 126). For example, Boswell reported how Joshua Reynolds's sister was 'much employed in miniatures', and that she had painted the portrait of 'the literary lady', Mrs Montagu (1799 [1927]: vol. 2, 186). On a more impressive scale, Catherine Read became one of the best known and most sought-after English portraitists of the early 1770s. We can glimpse the profitability of such success through the career of Mrs Grace, who, with no formal artistic training, earned £20,000 from her portraits (Greer 1979: 279).

The demand for this work was not confined to elite circles. As the middle ranks grew more affluent, their social aspirations were reflected in their commissions for paintings and these were obtainable by those who lacked social contacts above this stratum. However, success at all levels in this market was still dependent upon talent, fashion, and the ability to secure patrons, and therefore this option was restricted to relatively few women. In addition, there was some doubt as to its suitability for young ladies; Dr Johnson, for example, maintained that the 'Publick practice of any art, and staring in men's faces, is very indelicate in a female' (1775, as quoted in Boswell 1799 [1927]: vol. 1, 593).

There were, however, a number of other possible occupations within the arts that might be undertaken without challenging propriety. According to Wakefield, women could paint 'The drapery and landscape both of portraits and historical pieces', draw the frontispieces of books, and design and colour prints (1798: 131). They might also produce designs for needlework, do painting in enamel, draw the animals and plants for books on natural history, colour maps and globes, and create patterns for calico-printers and paper-stainers (ibid.: 132–3).

Wakefield was less sanguine about another area of the visual arts 'to which many women of refined manners, and a literary turn of mind have had recourse' (ibid.: 135). Although, as she acknowledged, women had demonstrated an ability to succeed in the theatre that was equal to that of their male contemporaries, celebrity had not altered the disapproving light in which actresses were viewed. This was due partly to the indelicacy of the 'courage requisite to face an audience', and partly to the 'situations incident to it, which expose moral virtue to the most severe trials' (ibid.: 136).

It is reasonable to assume that the fear of dishonour acted as a significant deterrent for many women, but for those who persisted, wealth, public acclaim, and social status were the possible rewards. Women from the middle stratum, like the famous Mrs Spranger Barry (daughter of an eminent apothecary), were still tempted. With talent, resilience, and tact it was possible for an actress to maintain a respectable reputation and to move in cultured and influential circles. Boswell recorded how Johnson 'seemed much pleased with having made one in so elegant a circle' after he had had supper at the home of the actress Mrs Abington (1799 [1927]: vol. 1, 584).

The artistic abilities and intentions of women like Mrs Woffington, Mrs Siddons, and Mrs Bellamy were taken seriously, and they could make a very good living through the theatre, particularly if they had built up a sufficient following to make their benefits worth while.[11] Anne Oldfield, who was one of the leading players at Drury Lane, became sufficiently wealthy to bequeath a house in Grosvenor Street and £5,000 to her son, a lifelong annuity of £60 to her mother, and one of £10 to a Mrs Margaret Saunders.[12]

Such affluence was the reward for success on the London stage or in the major provincial centres like York, Norwich, and Bath. This required talent and also the favour of influential men of the theatre, for example, Cibber, Garrick, Harris, Colman, Reddish, and King. Difficult as this might be to cultivate, it could take years to acquire a following amongst the public. Mrs Barry spent nine years in Dublin gaining recognition before moving to London to face an indifferent initial response. Many women who tried the stage never accomplished this transition, remaining in the provinces where opportunities were improving as the number of theatres grew. As an anonymous contributor to *The Annual Register* for 1761 complained:

> The effects of this easy communication have almost daily grown more and more visible. The several great cities, and we might add many poor country towns, seem to be universally inspired with an ambition of becoming the little *Londons* of the part of the kingdom wherein they are situated; . . . they [the aspiring country ladies] too, have their balls and concerts by subscription: their theatres, their mall, and sometimes their rural *Ranelagh*, or *Vauxhall*.
>
> (4th edn 1779: vol.2, 207)

Those who fell through this expanding net could still land within the profession by joining a company of itinerant players but, according to Charlotte Charke, daughter of the actor-manager Colley Cibber, such people were subjected to all kinds of indignity and inconvenience. In the *Narrative* of her life, Charke described how circumstances prevented her from carrying forward her intention of writing for money and how she was forced to 'trust to Providence from Time to Time for what I could get by occasionally Acting' (1755: 176). After the failure of several other possible avenues of employment, she 'went into the Country', where she remained for nearly nine years working as a strolling actress (ibid.: 184).[13] Her experiences made her scathing about the 'impudent and ignorant Behaviour' of the generality of such players, and she concluded that 'it wou'd be more reputable to earn a Groat a Day in Cinder-sifting at *Tottenham-Court*, than to be concerned with them' (ibid.: 187).

In common with other poorly paid women engaged in uncertain employment (for example, needlework or the lower levels of domestic service), it is probable that actresses had recourse to prostitution. The potential of the latter to supplement an income and to advance a career attracted women from throughout the social structure. Mary 'Perdita' Robinson, who came from a prosperous and genteel background, was forced by financial difficulties, both before and after her marriage, to find a profession. She chose acting, and having studied with Garrick, she went on the stage at Drury Lane to great popular acclaim. Her performance in the role of Perdita was, apparently, the initial cause of a very public affair with the Prince of Wales which lasted approximately a year. Her reign as a royal mistress ended when, 'like an April flower, Florizel's love withered and died, 'ere it bore any of the golden fruit, which a settlement was to contain; and Perdita, after blazoning in all the *gew-gaw* of splendid royalty, now . . . [reverted] to her former situation' (1784: 179). She demanded payment of £20,000 which, she claimed, had been promised to her, and after various acrimonious exchanges she obtained a lifetime annuity of £500. Her *Memoirs* record how, after her disappointment with the Prince, she went to the benefit of the actress Mrs Cuyler where, with typical bravado, she 'insinuated, that her house in B——y square is new painting, . . . and that she intends to write over the door QUICONQUE VOLT!' (ibid.: 180).

Although Robinson encountered persistent financial difficulties during the remainder of her career, the substantial income she acquired through her brief affair demonstrates that, at the higher levels of the occupation, prostitution could be very profitable. A successful courtesan could enjoy a luxurious existence and, with good fortune and judicious management, acquire sufficient funds to establish herself later in another business. Alternatively, she could follow in the footsteps of Phebe Phillips, Anne Sheldon, Lady Vane, and the notorious Teresia Constantia Phillips, and exploit the contemporary vogue for salacious autobiographies.[14] It would seem likely that this was the market anticipated for the *Memoirs* of 'Perdita,' and for the *Faithful Memoirs of the Life, Amours* and *Performances, of That justly Celebrated, and most Eminent Actress of her Time, Mrs. Anne Oldfield* (1731). Such works tended to strengthen the assumption, which was probably more prevalent in the early eighteenth century, that the three female professions of acting, prostitution, and writing were linked.

For most women life ran a more prosaic course and prostitution was the unglamorous and hazardous result of their inability to earn their living in any other way. The kind of crisis which might lead a middle-class woman into this life was described by Mary Ann Radcliffe in *The Female Advocate* (1799). By following the decline into poverty of a genteely educated mother and daughter who had both been 'Abandoned by friends, and left . . . without a provision, or any probable means of gaining a subsistence' (1810: 412), Radcliffe confronted her readers with 'the great and shocking alternative between vice and death' (ibid.: 415). As her 'poor victims of wretchedness' exclaimed, ' "extreme oppression maketh us desperate!" ' (ibid.: 416). The dramatic tone of the polemic was actuated by her own experience of poverty and of the limited options available to gentlewomen. In her *Memoirs* she referred frequently to the plight of 'unprotected females' and to the misery behind that '*Magna Charta* of female wretchedness' (ibid.: 261), the advertisements for work in the *Daily Advertiser*.

Radcliffe's proposed solutions to this problem included a heightened public awareness of its existence, an institution to save 'unfortunate' gentle-women, and enhanced employment opportunities. In *The Female Advocate* she linked the latter with improved education for women and to an ending of the 'vile practice of men filling such situations as seem calculated, not only to give bread to poor females, but thereby to enable them to tread the paths of virtue, and render them useful members, in some lawful employment' (1810: 409). Although she disclaimed the 'Amazonian spirit of a Wolstonecraft [*sic*]', their arguments against 'unremitted oppression' (ibid.: 399) were predicated upon the same belief: that inadequate education, and insufficient opportunities for employment and rational activity, led to idleness for some women and to poverty for others; and that both results were corrupting for the individual and for society in general.

Their contemporary, Priscilla Wakefield, presented the same reforming verities in her influential *Reflections on the Present Condition of the Female Sex; with Suggestions for its Improvement*. Her suggestions included a 'Female College', better schools, and a general acceptance of the need for women from all social strata to be educated for paid employment. These were advanced in the context of an attempt to provide a comprehensive review of the occupations that were, or should be, available to women. The analysis was ordered according to a class structure and for women from the 'first and second classes' her options lay within the familiar areas of education and the arts (including landscape gardening). Significantly, however, her enumeration began with literature, which, she argued, could afford:

> A respectable and pleasing employment, for those who possess talents, and an adequate degree of mental cultivation. For although the emolu-ment is precarious, and seldom equal to a maintenance, yet if the attempt be tolerably successful, it may yield a comfortable assistance in narrow circumstances, and beguile many hours, which might other-wise be passed in solitude or unavailing regret.
>
> (1798: 125–6)

THE ROLE OF AUTHORSHIP

Wakefield's proposal confirms that by the end of the eighteenth century literary professionalism was clearly an established employment option for women from the middle and upper classes. Various reasons for this have been examined already in chapter 3 and we can now add to those the simple fact that, by comparison with the cost of apprenticeships in acting or mantua making, or the initial capital requirements of a seminary or a dressmaking business, the entry fee for authorship was low. Thus, it is possible that many women were tempted or impelled to try their luck. The resulting competition was probably intense and it is likely that the failure rate was high. In view of this it is reasonable to conclude that authorship was more significant statistically than this study reveals as by definition it has been restricted to women who actually published and who were, therefore, at least partly successful.

In the sample of professional female writers presented at the beginning of this chapter, there were a few, including Hannah More, Ann Radcliffe, and Fanny Burney, who acquired national status and a very comfortable standard of living through their publications. There were also women who relied primarily upon their income from authorship to support themselves and their families, for example Charlotte Smith. Without underestimating the significance of these developments, it should be stressed that writing was still a very precarious option for women. Market preferences for particular writers or genres were hard to predict, and publishers with a plentiful supply of manuscripts could be selective and parsimonious towards the material on offer. Attempts to bypass 'the Trade' through subscription could be outstandingly successful but, as I shall demonstrate later, this alternative had its own attendant difficulties.

Therefore, it is not surprising to find that the careers of the 'dependent professionals' in the sample reveal a mixture of occupations within which writing was only one element, albeit an important one at times. The range of work undertaken by these women corresponds closely with the occupation structure outlined above. Education emerges as a particularly important field, not least for those, like Charlotte Palmer, who used their experience of many years in teaching to inform their books for children. Reversing this process, the Lee sisters were able to invest the profits from Sophia's comedy, *The Chapter of Accidents* (1780), in a school at Bath which ran successfully for over twenty years, and probably counted amongst its pupils the celebrated novelist Ann Radcliffe (Rogers, in Todd 1987: 262). The potential for profitability in such ventures is demonstrated by the success of the More sisters in Bristol. Hannah More, who had been trained by her father to become a teacher, established a girls' boarding school with her sisters in 1757, and after five years they had earned enough to build themselves larger premises.

Although this market was relatively easy to enter, requiring some capital but no formal qualifications, it was becoming increasingly competitive as new seminaries mushroomed into existence. Having endured 'toad eating' as a lady's companion and taken in sewing, Mary Wollstonecraft, with her sisters Eliza and Everina, and their friend Fanny Blood, set up a small academy in Islington, and waited in vain for pupils to enrol. They moved premises to the rural suburb of Newington Green, and by taking in lodgers as well as pupils, the sisters' establishment survived for over a year. After its failure, Mary went to Ireland to work as a governess before returning to concentrate on her literary career.

Teaching was far more accessible than aspiring to set up an academy and a number of women in the sample were engaged as schoolmistresses at various points in their working lives. For ten years the northern heiress Ann E. Skinn combined teaching with sewing and writing, whilst after the death of her insolvent husband, Anna Maria Mackenzie maintained herself and four children by working as an assistant at a ladies' boarding school. Similarly, Jane Gosling helped to support her family by teaching at a dame school near Sheffield, and the poet and novelist Eliza Mathews was also a teacher by profession.

A few women from the sample were engaged in commerce outside the field of education. For example, Mary Latter probably became the proprietor of a linen draper's and millinery business upon her mother's death and, like Mary Ann Radcliffe (1810: 177, 216) and the Wollstonecraft sisters, she took in boarders. Unfortunately, her business interests foundered and she was reduced to a debtors' prison. Rather more unusually, the didactic author Lucy Peacock worked as a bookseller in London, and there is also evidence to suggest that Eliza Haywood ventured briefly into publishing during the 1740s.[15] In fact, although Haywood's principal occupation was writing, she began her working life as an actress, and she returned to the stage in the 1730s when her writing career was apparently experiencing difficulties. Reversing this balance of interests, Maria Hunter's novels appeared after her highly successful career as an actress was on the wane.

There are women in the sample for whom acting and writing seem to have been of similar significance, or who pursued both professions concurrently. Elizabeth Inchbald sustained a moderately successful career as an actress for well over a decade whilst attempting to supplement her income by writing comedies. Upon her retirement from the stage in 1789, she concentrated upon authorship and her plays and novels were the source of her considerable wealth. However, she did not abandon her earlier occupation entirely as she continued to appear occasionally in her own pieces. Similarly, Frances Brooke's activities were inextricably linked to her connections within the theatre. Her acquaintance in these circles included the actresses Peg Woffington and her sister Mary Cholmondeley, the manager Tate Wilkinson (who had employed Inchbald in her early days as an actress), and the tragedian Mary Ann Yates with whom she became co-manager of the Haymarket Opera House in 1773. In the meantime, she had written poetry and plays since the 1750s, and had succeeded in publishing a weekly periodical, two novels, and several prose translations. She later secured productions of her tragedy (with Mrs Yates in the leading role) and of both her comic operas. Susanna Rowson, after working briefly as a governess, began writing, singing, and acting. She continued to combine these activities successfully in England, and then in America, until her retirement from the stage in 1797. However, this did not herald the onset of idleness. Rowson persisted with her busy literary career whilst undertaking new duties as a teacher in her own ladies' academy.

If Susanna Rowson's exemplary diligence would fit comfortably into a conduct book of the period, so the careers of some of the other women in the sample would translate well onto the pages of a picaresque novel. 'Perdita' Robinson's progress had a solid beginning at the More sisters' school in Bristol which equipped her for her first brief employment as a teacher in her mother's school. She later supplemented her royal annuity by setting up an academy in France. The responsibility to provide for her daughter and mother meant that she eventually concentrated her efforts on authorship, which was facilitated by the notoriety that helped to boost the sales of her publications. Her work was admired by contemporaries, although her Jacobinical tendencies did little to erase the controversy attached to her reputation.

Charlotte Charke's alleged route to professional writing is best described in her own words. Having entered into an early and unsuccessful marriage, she turned grocer and then puppeteer, went 'into men's cloaths [*sic*]' (for reasons she preferred not to give), was widowed twice, and then:

> My being Gentleman to a certain Peer; after my Dismission, becoming *only an Occasional Player*, while I was playing at *Bo-peep with the World*. My turning Pork-Merchant; broke, through the inhuman Appetite of a hungry Dog. Went a Strolling. . . . My Return, and setting up an Eating-House in *Drury-Lane*; undone again, by pilfering Lodgers. Turning Drawer, at St. *Mary-la-Bonne*. . . . Going a Strolling a second Time, and staying near nine Years . . . my being sent to G——— Jail, for being an Actor; . . . My settling in *Wales*, and turning Pastry-Cook and Farmer. Made a small Mistake, in turning Hog-Merchant. Went to the Seat of Destruction, called *Pill*. Broke, and came away. Hired myself to a Printer at *Bristol*, to write and correct the Press. Made a short Stay there. Vagabondized again, and last *Christmas* returned to *London*, where I hope to remain as long as I live.
>
> (1755: 273–4)

Her intention, once at rest, was to apply herself to her pen and to open an 'oratorical Academy, for the Instruction of those who have any Hopes, from Genius and Figure' (ibid.: 268) of acting in London or the major provincial theatres.

In some cases, successful publication facilitated an author's move into other types of employment, witness the career of Ann Yearsley, who used the profits from her poetry to establish herself as the proprietor of a circulating library at Hotwells, Bristol. This aspect of authorship is particularly striking in relation to Fanny Burney, whose social and literary success as the writer of *Evelina* (1778), and then *Cecilia* (1782), helped to secure her employment in the Royal service. She found her role as Second Keeper of the Robes to Queen Charlotte constraining but it brought her an income of £200 a year, followed by an annuity of £100.

The deliberate use of writing to engineer a move into another area of work was the stated motivation behind Elizabeth Boyd's venture into print. She deflected charges of ambition for the 'Name of Author' in an 'Advertisement' in her novel *The Happy-Unfortunate* (1732) by claiming:

> I have printed this Manuscript, (which otherwise I never had done) with a View of settling my self in a Way of Trade; that may enable me to master those Exigencies of Fortune, which my long Illness hath for some Time past reduc'd me to suffer: That I may be capable of providing for my now ancient, indulgent Mother; whom Age, and the Charge of many Children hath render'd incapable of providing for herself: And as I shall directly sell Paper, Pens, Ink, Wax, Wafers, Black Lead Pencils, Pocket Books, Almanacks, Plays, Pamphlets, and all Manner of Stationary [*sic*] Goods.
>
> (1732 [1972]: 'Advertisement')

It was also possible, as we have seen in relation to those teachers who wrote children's books, for another occupation to facilitate an attempt at literary professionalism. This applies, more unusually, in the case of the novelist Mary Davys. After the death of her husband, who had been a master of a free school in Dublin, Mary was confronted with the need to earn her own living. This she achieved successfully for twenty-seven years by running a coffee shop in Cambridge and by writing. Her student customers were amongst the subscribers to her novels.

From these brief sketches a picture of 'dependent' female literary professionalism begins to emerge. It includes outstanding successes, the creation of fortunes, and the acquisition of national reputations. It also encompasses women who responded to exigent circumstances by attempting the occupation most easily to hand, moving from one type of work to another, or undertaking several concurrently: 'like a bubble upon the surface of the water, ready to be tossed aside by every breeze . . . without protection – and almost without money' (M.A. Radcliffe 1810: 236). Amongst these writers we can observe a flexible, at times desperate, at times highly successful accommodation of pressing need and inadequate resources. In this context, the value of authorship as a new occupation was immense, and the persistence with which these women pursued it is not at all surprising.

5

WOMEN NOVELISTS AND
THEIR PUBLISHERS

Your Booksellers are but Pedlars. – Though really there is a good deal
of melancholy Truth in what they say, after all. – A two Guinea, and a
two hundred Guinea Novel, must be pretty much the same to them. A
new Thing is a new Thing; and though the Reader may send one down
Stairs to the Scullion, to singe his Fowl, and send the other to be
bound, for his Library, yet the Books must be first bought.-And then
what avails the Preference to the Bookseller?

(Richard Griffith 1786)

THE IMPACT OF EXPANSION IN 'THE TRADE'

The development of women's prose fiction and the emergence of their
literary professionalism brought increasing numbers of female authors into
contact with the book trades. Desirous not only of seeing their work
published, but of securing the maximum payment for it, these writers were
compelled to negotiate with publishers and booksellers and to become
sensitive to the market they sought to exploit. That they succeeded in doing
so is evident from both the growing numbers who achieved publication, and
the women throughout the century who sustained literary careers that lasted
years and even decades. The process, so essential to women's literary
production, of identifying and eventually dealing with prospective purchasers was clarified and made easier for female writers as the eighteenth
century progressed. This was due largely to major changes in the book
business itself which were rooted in the substantial expansion that occurred
from the late 1600s.

Henry Plomer, in his three dictionaries of booksellers, printers, and
publishers working in England, Scotland, and Ireland between 1641 and
1775, has effectively recorded that growth.[1] Although a simple head count of
the number of bookselling and printing firms at various moments in time is
not a clear index of market expansion, concealing as it does the size of
businesses and the number of short-lived enterprises and bankruptcies, none
the less a rapid rise in the total (aggregate) can be taken as an indicator of a

climate of growth and buoyancy. According to his information, there were approximately 1,700 firms working between 1668 and 1725, which was almost double the total of 940 for the previous twenty-six years. In addition, the later period included a marked spread of businesses outside London. For the period 1725 to 1775 the figure increased to approximately 2,500 firms with provincial growth much in evidence. The cumulative total for 1725 of 142 locations rose to 217 in the following fifty years, incorporating a spread into parts of Scotland and Ireland.[2] This growth reflects a rising tide of demand for the printed word which meant that 'By the 1790s, the publication of new book titles was running at four times the level of the beginning of the century' (Vincent 1989: 11). This development was stimulated, particularly outside London, by improved educational opportunities for the middle ranks, the growth of the periodical press and number publication, and (as I shall discuss in chapter 7) the reading and lending facilities offered by circulating libraries, book and pamphlet clubs, and private subscription libraries.

How did this marked expansion in the supply and demand for literature influence the development of women's fiction? Most obviously, it resulted in an increase in potential publishing outlets which was of particular importance to those who were dependent upon an income from their writing. Moreover, greater competition amongst booksellers for manuscripts could help to sustain their market value. As the historian and writer Catherine Macaulay suggested later in the century, 'there are at present too many in the trade, for an author to be reduced to the necessity of disposing of a saleable copy for less than it is worth' (1774: 30).

However, it is important to stress that opportunities for remunerative publication did not necessarily increase *pari passu* with the number of traders. The determining factor was the publishers' willingness to accept material and to pay for copyright. It is reasonable to assume that most firms were reluctant to take risks or to make unnecessary payments and it was often possible for publishers, wishing to swell their lists for minimal cost, to reissue old novels under new titles in cheap and pirated editions. According to one disheartened critic reviewing Harriet Thomson's *The Labyrinths of Life* (1791):

> To a publisher, there are many advantages attending this mode of proceeding; and the saving of copy-money is to be reckoned as the chief. A novel of two or three volumes, . . . may be thus new vamped from an old one, by a compositer who dabbles a little with his pen, for perhaps half a guinea; . . . so that, neither author nor bookseller knowing his own book again, a prosecution for copy-right need not be apprehended.
>
> (*The Monthly Review* 1791: vol. 5, 338)

These practices must have appealed to the many small firms that appeared during these years and, indeed, Blakey (1939: 30–1) has suggested that William Lane made use of them when he was struggling to establish himself. Such behaviour would inhibit publishing opportunities for writers irrespective of their sex. However, women faced an additional problem in the resistance to 'She-Authors' which seems to have been more prevalent in the early 1700s, and which probably contributed to any reluctance to accept their fiction until a market for it was clearly established. With this in mind, it is not surprising to discover that most of the known publishers of women's fiction were well-established members of the occupation.

The provincial development of printing and bookselling facilitated the growth of local newspapers and the production of a host of parochial publications including sale and auction catalogues, guides to nearby places of interest, copies of the psalms and recent sermons, sheet almanacs, and broadsides reporting local crimes and scandals in lurid detail. Such productions should be considered in conjunction with serial publications and the stocking and distribution of circulating libraries, as prime agents in the promotion of the secular demand which underpinned both the rise of prose fiction and the emergence of a profession of women authors. Furthermore, although their output was highly localized, these firms occasionally issued novels and titles that were strongly suggestive of contemporary fiction, such as *Dialogues Between Two Young Ladies* (1728), which was published at Gainsborough in Lincolnshire.

Apart from their role in the spread of the reading habit during the eighteenth century, provincial presses made a specific contribution to the distribution of work by women. They published a wide range of their writing, consisting mainly of volumes of occasional poetry, musical scores, songs, and domestic manuals like the enormously successful *Experienced English Housekeeper* (1769) by Elizabeth Raffald.[3] They were also responsible for the publication of novels by Jane Barker (Cambridge), Eliza Clarke (Liverpool), and Ann Thomas (Plymouth), amongst others. Given the existing population distribution, these firms were inevitably, in the aggregate, less significant to the growth of women's writing than those based in London. None the less, they were instrumental in promoting women's publications on a national scale, thereby familiarizing those living in areas remote from London with that contentious phenomenon, the 'Petticoat Author'.

Earlier expansion within the printed book industry had been accompanied by trade specialization, and during the eighteenth century the publishers emerged as the most influential occupation, superseding the printers' traditional supremacy. According to James Boswell: 'As Physicians are called *the Faculty*, and Counsellors at Law *the Profession*; the Booksellers of London are denominated *the Trade*' (1799 [1927]: vol. 2, 216, n. 1). Within the world of letters, substantial booksellers like Dodsley, Strahan, and the Dilly brothers were often as well known as the famous authors with whom they frequently had close and convivial dealings. The integration of bookselling and publishing was largely unaffected by this development, and the terms 'bookseller' and 'publisher' remained broadly interchangeable throughout the eighteenth century. Indeed, the prosecution of the bookseller J. Almon for seditious libel in 1770 suggests that in legal terms the two categories were indistinguishable.[4]

Publishers, therefore, working either as individuals or in combination, had a crucial influence over the literary and financial success of authors. Their interpretation of demand was a key determinant of publication, and, if they chose, they could promote or suppress a writer's material. As the bookseller James Lackington acknowledged, 'it is inconceivable what mischief booksellers *can* and often *will* do to authors, as thousands of books yearly are written for to London that are never sent; and . . . many plausible reasons are assigned by them for such omissions . . . '(1792: 359–60). The formation of the Society for the Encouragement of Learning in 1736, and John Trusler's Literary Society in 1765, were attempts to challenge the dependent status of authors by securing to them the entire profits from publication. Indeed Trusler's intention was to abolish 'the Trade' altogether.

Conversely, publishers could, and did, exert themselves to beneficial effect. They were in a position to nurture a literary career by advising upon the content of material, thus guiding the author towards a larger readership and a higher income. The professional novelist Mrs Meeke was probably reflecting the foundation of her own success as one of Lane's 'Minerva' novelists when she advised the aspiring writer that

> She must (which, as being a more competent judge than herself of the prevalent taste, she ought to do) consult with her publisher. Indeed to secure their approbation is rather the general aim; for should you fail of meeting with a purchaser, that labour you hope will immortalize you is absolutely lost; a most mortifying circumstance in every sense of the word; and the gentlemen or ladies who sit in judgement upon the fine spun webs from the prolific brains of female authors, are very competent to decide upon the taste of the public.
>
> (1802: vol. 1, 4)

Furthermore, publishers invested their money at source by acting as patrons to particular authors. For example, as she often told him, Mary Wollstonecraft was heavily indebted in this way to the publisher Joseph Johnson. He set her up in a house of her own, supplied her with work, and introduced her to other authors, artists, and like-minded intellectuals. She was sufficiently confident of Johnson's enduring good will to address him with considerable frankness on professional matters. For example, in one of her many letters to him she declared, 'If you do not like the manner in which I reviewed Dr. J———'s S——— on his wife, be it known unto you – I *will* not do it any other way' (*Posthumous Works* 1798: vol. 4, 89).

Previously, the aristocracy were the primary source of this type of support but their relative significance within the patronage system decreased around the turn of the century. The political and cultural supremacy of court circles was eroded by fundamental changes in the distribution of power within the body politic which, J.W. Saunders (1964: 113–14) has suggested, gave rise to an increasing expectation that writers should earn their keep by serving partisan interests. This transition was disadvantageous for some authors but others were still able to obtain an income from more overtly political patronage. Delarivière Manley, for example, was a notably success-ful propagandist; witness the £50 she received in 1714 from John Harvey for her services to the Tory faction.

On the whole, however, the emergence of easily accessible, additional forms of financial support was a prerequisite for any significant expansion of professional writing by women. The growth of a reading public which was delimited only by its literacy and propensity to consume, supported the development of genres, like the novel, which were open to the less educated writer, or certainly to the writer (including most female authors) who had not experienced a classical education. The availability of alternatives to patronage removed the necessity of acquiring personal contacts and recom-mendations which could be problematic for any writer living beyond the fringes of affluent circles or outside court life. This alone would have inhibited the emergence, during the eighteenth century, of substantial num-bers of women authors from the middle social stratum. By comparison with more impersonal relations based on market forces, patronage was exception-ally susceptible to the investor's opinions and prejudices. An opprobrious contemporary reaction to the 'She-Author' could discourage potential patrons from giving, and the authors from seeking, such support. Furthermore, the customary familiarity between writer and patron was incompatible with the anonymity that some women preferred. The level of commitment to authorship and the degree of public exposure involved in obtaining patronage could preclude the tentative anonymous first offering which was a feature of eighteenth-century women's fiction. Such anonymity was not always a matter of preference and for some professional women, as we have seen, it was an absolute necessity.

IDENTIFYING THE PUBLISHERS

Although a number of eighteenth-century women authors continued to receive significant levels of support through various forms of patronage, like their 'unpatronized' contemporaries, these women also found it necessary at some stage in their careers to deal with 'the Trade'. This presented the inexperienced author with at least two key problems: whom to approach, and how to accomplish the transaction successfully. As far as the former is concerned, it is clear that during the century, there were certain booksellers who might be identified relatively easily on the basis of their interest in fiction, and more particularly, their evident willingness to promote work by women writers.

Of the novels for which the relevant details are known, approximately a half were produced by only one publisher, whilst the rest were either 'Printed for the Author' or produced by various types of association between two or, in a few cases, more publishers. Such combinations were quite usual in the eighteenth-century literature market as a device for spreading the risk or the cost of publication (particularly if the work was a large or lavish edition), and for protecting copyright by controlling distribution. The corollary of this type of arrangement was the formation of permanent, larger organizations for joint copyright ownership and the protection of investment by the control of wholesaleing: for example, *The Printing Conger* (1719), *The New Conger* (1736), and the powerful 'Chapter', which extended the old custom of co-operative publishing onto a systematic share basis.[5] Becoming a part proprietor of more than one book was a means of spreading investment, minimizing risk, and of increasing opportunities for speculation, particularly as shares could be traded within the business community. Temporary liaisons for this purpose, involving from two publishers to 'all the principal booksellers of London and Westminster', were more common than permanent partnerships.

However, even those involved in associations behind prestigious works by well-established writers could not guarantee a substantial or even commensurate return on their investment. Boswell maintained that:

> Indeed, although they ['the Trade'] have eventually been considerable gainers by his [Johnson's] *Dictionary* it is to them that we owe its having been undertaken and carried through at the risk of great expence, for they were not absolutely sure of being indemnified.
>
> (1799 [1927]: vol. 1, 203–4)

The market for women's fiction, particularly in the early eighteenth century, was highly speculative. Indigenous prose fiction was a relatively young genre and women writers were regarded with uncertainty and disapproval by many. Under these circumstances, until a writer had clearly established a demand for her work, associations would be sound business practice. As might be expected, therefore, combinations of booksellers behind women's fiction were more frequent in the first half of the century, and the earliest of these involved the greatest numbers of publishers.

However, if we look more closely at the authors who were involved in these transactions, uncertainty about the profitability of their work does not seem to be an entirely adequate explanation. At least thirty of the novels in Appendix A were published by three or more booksellers and a high proportion of these were written by Penelope Aubin and Eliza Haywood. Aubin's material was almost invariably produced by the same large consortium of up to ten publishers. Haywood, on the other hand, attracted a considerable range of booksellers during her long career (at least thirty-one), although some were frequently associated with her work. These were popular authors whose marketability was well established. Therefore, it is possible that, with some of this material, associations were the result of the traders' desire to remain or to become involved with a good investment. In this context it is interesting to note that, although female booksellers were not usually involved in the production of women's fiction, Mrs Billingsly and the controversial Anne Dodd both joined a consortium of publishers behind Haywood's *The Dumb Projector* (1725).[6]

Taking the century as a whole, most of the partnerships behind women's fiction consisted of either two or three publishers; for example, Curll and Francklin (1718), Parker, Jackson, and Joliffe (1733), Becket and De Hondt (1769), Payne and Cadell (1782) and Carpenter and Hookham (1796).[7] However, the majority of the novels listed in Appendix A were the responsibility of publishers operating on their own. Amongst those most frequently involved were members of the bookselling elite, including Robert Dodsley, Andrew Millar, the Dilly brothers, and Thomas Cadell, all of whom were part of Johnson's circle and acquainted with the *literati* of their day. Boswell's picture of their world evokes the fraternal atmosphere of a gentleman's club in which the booksellers and their authors were social companions as well as business partners. The participation of these men in the production of women's fiction therefore seems surprising, particularly when we take into account the generally low contemporary cultural status of the genre and of women writers.

A closer look at the authors concerned may help to explain the involvement of such publishers. Some of these women, like Susannah Gunning, Ellis Cornelia Knight, and Fanny Burney, had considerable social status and moved in the fashionable and literary circles of their day, including those of Johnson and the Bluestockings. Other writers, for example Fielding, Sheridan, and Lennox, although less elevated socially, had contacts with major literary figures and, like Scott, Reeve, and Smith, they were amongst the most talented female novelists of the period. A few female authors had personal connections with their publishers. For example, Andrew Millar had already worked for Sarah Fielding's brother Henry when he published her books, whilst T. Payne was selected for Fanny Burney's novels by her father, on the basis that his nephew was courting the publisher's daughter. Such factors distinguished these writers from the many other women entering the market and gave them easier access to particular producers.

In their history of the publishing industry, Mumby and Norrie (1974) have emphasized a distinction between these men and other reputedly less honourable publishers like Edmund Curll. This generally held view should not mislead us into thinking that the women who dealt with these putative gentlemen of 'the Trade' were thus removed from the pressures of the cash nexus. Profit was presumably the motivation behind the actions of 'that thing Dodsley' when he printed some previously circulated, anonymous verses in his *Collection of Poems* (1758) under a title that implied that they were written by Lady Mary Wortley Montagu 'to a very contemptible puppy [Sir William Yonge]'. Alongside these, Dodsley included (without permission) some stanzas that were in fact by Montagu but which had been written extempore as a private piece of fun between friends after she had read the unattributed 'passionate addresses'. Dodsley printed these under a title that suggested that they were Yonge's response to Montagu's entreaty (1758, in Montagu 1986: 283). Even Cadell – regarded by Mumby and Norrie as inheriting the chief honours of 'the Trade' after Johnson's death and as the centre of a remarkable group including Hume, Robertson, Gibbon, and Smith (1974: 176) – was criticized by the *Gentleman's Magazine* in a review of Mrs Brooke's *Excursion*, for stretching slight works into several volumes by using wide margins, many divisions, and short paragraphs (1777: vol. 47, 88).

A substantial number of the authors in Appendix A dealt with either Curll or Lane, publishers who were notorious for their commercial orientation. Indeed, they have been held responsible by many for the reduction of literature to a mere commodity and the denigration of the writer to a factor of production in a labour-intensive industry. Without wishing to underestimate the ruthlessness of Curll's methods (which, as I shall show later, were applied equally to women writers), or his promotion of scurrility, it should be noted that the range of material listed in the *Catalogue of Poems, Plays, and Novels, Printed for, and Sold by E. Curll next the Temple Coffee-House in Fleet-Street* (1720) shows that he spread his investment quite widely across the market. Included amongst his publications were several plays by Susanna Centlivre and a number of novels by women. Having begun with Barker's *Love's Intrigues* (1713), Curll went on to issue her later material and also works by most of the early women novelists, including Sarah Butler, Delarivière Manley, and Mary Hearne.[8] As an important force behind the early growth of women's fiction, he was, by implication, an important contributor to the 'rise' of the novel.

William Lane, as was noted in chapter 3, played a critical role in the development of the fiction market at the end of the century and was exceptionally active in cultivating the production and sale of women's material. He published at least fifty-six of the books in Appendix A and a further twenty-two are known to have been printed at his famous Minerva Press; it is probable that he published most of these. As a specialist in the market for novels, Lane was not merely responding to an existing demand for women's fiction, he actively promoted it. He sought out new authors and developed the market for their material by consistently recording the names of female writers (mostly, but not exclusively, novelists) in his *Catalogues*. Furthermore, he publicized specific women novelists as the 'particular and favourite Authors' at the Minerva Press.[9] This successful publisher was demonstrating those qualities regarded by Charles Wilson as quintessential to the entrepreneur of the period, 'a sense of market opportunity combined with the capacity needed to exploit it' (1957: 103). It is indicative of the popularity of women's fiction by the late eighteenth century that their novels were his chosen commodity.

It has been argued that, until the appearance of the Noble brothers (in the mid-eighteenth century), there is 'very little evidence that the booksellers played a direct part in stimulating the writing of novels' (Watt 1957 [1972]: 61). This impression is mistaken. Plomer has recorded several late seventeenth- and early eighteenth-century publishers who dealt primarily in this material, for example, Jeremiah Batley, Richard Bentley – referred to as 'Novel Bentley' by Dunton in his *Life and Errors* – and C. Hitch in partnership with L. Hawes.[10] Furthermore, once we acknowledge the contribution of early women's fiction to the rise of the novel, it becomes clear that certain publishers played a direct part in the evolution of the genre, not simply by issuing material but also by evincing a continued interest in particular authors. Curll was conspicuous amongst them, but he was by no means alone in his early involvement in women's fiction. A. Bettesworth was a member of the consortium behind Aubin's publications and he also worked with Jane Barker. John Morphew published virtually all Manley's fiction, and James Roberts, as part of his involvement in at least sixty-five works of fiction between 1710 and 1736, worked in partnership with Curll on material by Barker and Hearne. Roberts was largely responsible also for eleven of Haywood's novels and was involved in a further five as part of various combinations including W. Chetwood, R. Francklin, J. Millan, and T. Green, amongst others. Haywood's later fiction (after 1761) was placed, apparently exclusively, with T. Gardner. Most of the subsequent editions of material by these writers were issued by various combinations of the same men.

NEGOTIATIONS WITH THE PUBLISHERS

On this evidence we may reasonably conclude that an inexperienced writer could identify, with relative ease, a suitable publisher to approach, but she then faced the greater problem of how to carry her project forward. Inevitably, some women preferred to protect their identity completely by using intermediaries to present their material. Frances Sheridan placed the manuscript of *Memoirs of Miss Sidney Bidulph* (1761) in Samuel Richardson's hands after they had become acquainted through her husband Thomas Sheridan, the theatre manager. Richardson was sufficiently impressed with the novel to arrange for its publication. Other authors took even greater pains to remain unknown to their publishers. Fanny Burney's biographer tells us that the novelist

Never forgot the warning she had been given by her step-mother . . .
that a young woman's reputation could not easily survive her being
known as a writer. Consequently she was desperate to preserve her
anonymity if and when she published her book. . . . Dodsley refused
to consider an anonymous work, and so a lengthy and evasive missive
was sent to Mr Lowndes in December asking him to reply to a Mr
King at the Orange Coffee House in the Haymarket.

(Kilpatrick 1980: 59)

Not all contacts between female authors and their publishers were characterized by such discretion. Dr Johnson's advice to those who had 'written in
order to get money . . . to go to the booksellers, and make the best bargain
they can' (quoted in Boswell 1799 [1927]: vol. 1, 469) applied equally to
writers of both sexes. We know, for example, that Sterne, unable to obtain a
fee from Dodsley for *Tristram Shandy*, borrowed sufficient funds to pay for
a small and highly successful print run which eventually secured him a
copyright payment of £650 from the publisher. Similarly, Charlotte Smith
resorted to this solution when she met with the same response from
Dodsley. Her biographer (Hilbish 1941: 102) has revealed that, although
Smith felt disgraced by writing for money, she was none the less careful of
the products of her labour. She rejected Dodsley's proposal to print her
poems without cost (he claimed that there was no demand for such things),
and after persuasion from her brother, she took them to Dilly, who rejected
them outright. Undefeated, she decided to test the quality of her material by
writing to William Hayley, whom she then knew by name only, requesting
his opinion of her work. He read and approved her poems, and with her
confidence in their merit (and perhaps saleability) substantially restored, she
again approached Dodsley, who remained sceptical. She eventually financed
the publication herself and the exceptional success of this gamble formed the
basis of her literary career. The poems passed through eleven editions,
including a lucrative fifth issue financed by a subscription which attracted
the support of Walpole, Cowper, Fox, and the Archbishop of Canterbury.
The publication established her literary reputation and enabled her to obtain
publishers (notably Thomas Cadell) for all her later works.

To judge by the comments of other women writers, Charlotte Smith's
battle for remunerative publication was not unusual. Elizabeth Griffith, in
her correspondence with her future husband, reported that

I have gone on with my Novel briskly since we parted. The
Encomiums of my Friends spirited me up, and I have finished the First
Volume – At least all that ever I shall write more of it.

For, after all, I find it is good for nothing. – . . . And I find the
Booksellers will give nothing worth taking for it. –
Mr. J——— has tried them. They say that they do not dispute the
Merit of it, but that while the Public continue equally to buy a bad

Thing as a good one, they do not think an Author can reasonably expect that they will make a Difference in the Price.

(1786: vol. 5, 15)

Without the weight of a previous publication to add substance to her negotiations, a prospective author could soon find her expectations of profit frustrated. Partly to alert other female writers to this danger, Jean Marishall wrote a detailed account of her own difficult progress into print (*A Series of Letters* 1789). Encouraged into the belief that she could write for publication by a 'more than commonly stupid' (1789: vol. 2, 148) novel borrowed from a circulating library, she began her first work, *Clarinda Cathcart*. At her friend's suggestion, a sample of the novel was sent to Noble's circulating library using an intermediary because Marishall had 'often heard female wits and authors spoke of with a degree of contempt' (ibid.: 152). This elicited a promise from the publisher of a 'very genteel price' (ibid.: 151) for the completed piece, which was interpreted by Marishall and her friends as meaning at least a hundred guineas. Her hopes were shattered when, after submitting the manuscript, her intermediary returned with a final offer of five guineas. According to her messenger:

He [Noble] has a great many volumes by him which he got sent him from ladies in a present; a number of which he would not be at the expence of printing. He likewise, continued she, told me, that Mrs C———r is a very pretty writer of novels, and she has sold him several manuscripts at two guineas a volume: so that his offering five guineas for a first performance is a very great price. He says he often loses by his purchases; but desired me to tell the lady, that if her novel should have a more than ordinary quick sale, he would afterwards make her a present. A present indeed!

(ibid.: 158–9)

An attempt to secure a better offer from more 'capital' and 'eminent' booksellers failed when not one of them 'would so much as look at the title-page; they never purchased the productions of ladies, and advised her to carry it to Mr N———le, or to some other circulating library' (ibid.: 160). Recovering from this second disappointment, Marishall eventually struck a slightly more advantageous deal with Noble in which she stipulated 'that the errors should, under my inspection, be corrected by Mr A———n', and that she was to have 'as many copies of it as I choosed at the under price at which they are sold to brothers in trade' (ibid.: 168–9). This added a few more guineas to her profit.

The significance of her retention of some control over the quality of the publication was greater than might at first appear. To Marishall, her book was a source of some pride, her 'fair offspring', but to a publisher like Noble, anxious to keep his lists full of new titles, it was probably an unremarkable two-volume library novel that could be rushed through the press with little attention paid to the details of production. Indeed, Noble's reputation was characterized by his emphasis upon quantity not quality, even to the extent of (reputedly) paying his writers by weight. The potentially disastrous consequences of such carelessness were described in a review of an epistolary novel *The Maiden Aunt* 'Written by a Lady':

> We should have thought ourselves under the necessity of censuring this female Writer for the incorrect manner in which her work appears before the Public, had we not received *information* . . . that since the copy passed out of the Author's hands, the beginning of every letter in the first volume was altered, many of them in the most absurd and vulgar manner; – that the carelessness of the publisher has suffered the grossest blunders in sense, grammar, and spelling to pass into print, for which the copy was not answerable, and that he has added fifteen letters just before the conclusion, beginning with the 42nd, and ending with the 56th, which the Author entirely disclaims, and considers as a compound of inconsistency, added merely to spin out the work.
>
> (*Monthly Review* 1776: vol. 54, 161-2)

At about the time that Marishall was producing her account of her earlier disappointments, William Lane was attempting to facilitate the process of initial contact between author and publisher by advertising his desire for new material. He used magazines and his own publications for this purpose. Apart from the kind of explicit exhortation that Mrs Meeke incorporated into the start of her *Midnight Weddings*, allusions to Lane's approachability were even woven into the narrative of the novel. Blakey (1939: 69–71) has recorded how a description of a young female author, who was relieved to find Lane courteous and prepared to examine her work after two previous failures with different publishers, was incorporated into the Minerva novel *The Follies of St. James's Street* (1789). Furthermore, Blakey reveals that Lane was even prepared to communicate basic details of business through the columns of a newspaper, witness his notice to 'Matilda', author of *Ill Effects of a Rash Vow*, informing her when the copies of her novel would be ready for collection (1939: 49). Clearly, it is always possible that 'Matilda' was neither new to authorship nor particularly diffident about her writing, or even, for that matter, a woman. The significance of such a notice was that it gave a clear signal to any 'timid adventurers for fame' that Lane was willing to accommodate their interests.

During the eighteenth century, many of the novels that appeared in the market had apparently been written by 'Young Ladies'. Some of this fiction was certainly written by women who preferred to hide their identity and a number of the novelists in Appendix A, such as Elizabeth Bonhote, Sarah Harriet Burney, and Mrs Woodfin, published at least their first novels in this way. A few women, like Sarah Scott, issued all their material either anonymously or pseudonymously. The general reasons why female authors preferred to remain unknown are not difficult to identify: the detrimental impact that their sex might have upon the earning power of their writing, particularly early in the century; the fact that it could undermine a proper evaluation of literary merit, either through premature rejection and ridicule, or through over-indulgence and condescension; and because the stigma of 'unfeminine' behaviour remained attached to authorship throughout the period. On the other hand, a niche had appeared within the literature market for these particular products of the female pen which was easily identifiable and potentially lucrative. A clear understanding of the demand encouraged many women to create their novels of domestic sensibility, and it is tempting to speculate that some male hacks were induced to don petticoats to earn a few guineas. The accepted mechanism of an intermediary would protect the fraud, and certainly it would seem that female impersonation was not unknown in other genres.[11] In a review of *Sermons Written by a Lady* (1770) the *Gentleman's Magazine* commented:

> As among other literary frauds it has long been common for Authors to affect the stile and character of ladies, it is necessary to apprize our readers that these sermons are the genuine productions of a female pen, to which the public was some time ago indebted for an excellent translation of Four select Tales from Marmontel.
>
> (1770: vol. 40, 273)

The use of literary disguises by female authors did not necessarily reflect a requirement to remain unknown, nor did it always entail anonymity with publishers. Pseudonyms were sometimes employed by authors solely to add an appropriate quality to their publication. This is demonstrated by the number that were used by well-established women writers (see Appendix A) and which had stylistic associations with their texts. For example, Jane West's educational books acquired an aura of sensible respectability when she became 'Prudentia Homespun'; Lady Eleanor Fenn became an eminently suitable writer of children's books as 'Mrs. Teachwell' and 'Mrs. Lovechild'; whilst 'Mrs. Penelope Prattle' (possibly Eliza Haywood (Adburgham 1972: 77–8)) promised a comfortable garrulity to the readers of the periodical *The Parrot* (1746).[12] In this context the use of pseudonyms would seem to demonstrate an understanding of market manipulation, rather than a need for protection. Once authors like Haywood, Smith, Reeve, Radcliffe, Bennett, Roche, Meeke, Charlton, Parsons, Bonhote, and More had established a reputation with the reading public, they could approach 'the Trade' with the confidence of popular, even best-selling writers. Good, direct relations with their publishers brought not only useful advice on market preferences, but also, as I shall demonstrate in chapter 6, the additional benefit of supplementary payments, the 'present' so derided by the (then) inexperienced Marishall.

If we contrast Wollstonecraft's friendship with Johnson, with Marishall's dealings with Noble, it is clear that female authors' relations with their publishers were very diverse, ranging from enlightened patronage to a basic exchange of words for money. Negotiations were clearly affected by the character of the writer, of her material, and of the publisher. We know from Fanny Burney's letters that this highly successful, celebrated author was sufficiently involved in the development of her career to exchange 'many messages of business' with Andrew Strachan, 'who was the friend of Johnson and the principal printer of "Camilla" ' (Burney 1842–6: vol. 6, 203). Later on, she disapproved heartily of the booksellers' behaviour over *The Wanderer* (1814) on the grounds that they

> Erroneously and injudiciously concluding the sale would so go on, fixed the rapacious price of two guineas, which again damped the sale. But why say *damped*, when it is only their unreasonable expectations that are disappointed? for they acknowledge that 3,600 copies are positively sold and paid for in the first half year.
>
> (1842–6: vol. 7, 21)

Burney's concern about the booksellers' effect upon the sale of her material was natural enough for a writer who had a considerable market status to protect, but this unusual position did not make her uniquely vulnerable to the rapacity of self-interested publishers.[13] All writers, however pedestrian and obscure, could be exposed to such difficulties although the extent to which careers and reputations were threatened was linked to the individuals concerned. Not surprisingly, Edmund Curll provides us with a glimpse of the more ruthless extreme in his dealings with Delarivière Manley. After she became aware of a proposal by Gildon to write *The History of Rivella, Author of Atlantis* (1714) which she suspected would be 'A severe Invective upon some Part of her Conduct', she 'generously' (according to Curll) resolved to write her own account under the same title (1725: iv, v). During this process she wrote to Curll a number of times concerning the publication, approving his 'Design of continuing the same Name and Title' (ibid.: vi), and apparently pleading for his indulgence over the deadline:

> Judge that I have not been idle, when I have sent you so much Copy. How can I deserve all this Friendship from you? I must ask you to pity me; for I am plagued to Death for want of Time, and forced to write by Stealth. I beg the Printer may not have any other to interfere with him, especially because I shall want Time to finish it with that *Eclat* I intend.
>
> (ibid.: vii)

Notwithstanding the flattering tone in which Manley addressed him, Curll had effectively coerced this well-known writer into producing what was almost certain to be a best-selling work; far better for his purposes to have the account written by Manley than by Gildon. Shortly before the fourth edition of *Rivella* was published (in which he offered 'proof' that the work was autobiographical), Curll attempted to use Manley once again to advance his interests. He reported to Walpole that:

> Yesterday Mr Henley [initiator of the pro-Walpole *Hyp Doctor*] and myself were eye-witnesses of a letter, under Mrs. Manley's own hand, intimating that a fifth volume of *The Atlantis* had been for some time printed off, and lies ready for publication; the design of which, in her own words, is, 'to give an account of a sovereign and his ministers who are endeavouring to overturn that Constitution which their pretence is to protect; to examine the defects and vices of some men who take a delight to impose upon the world by the pretence of public good; whilst their true design is only to gratify and advance themselves'.
>
> (2 March 1723–4, in [Anon] *Curll Papers* 1879: 61)

This disclosure was made in the hopes of securing government patronage in the form of 'something in the Post Office', or 'some provision in the Civil List' (ibid.: 61).

Curll's contemporary reputation for mistreating his writers was strengthened by the accusation that he had starved one of his authors, William Pattison, to death. This charge was repeated in *An Author to Let* (attributed to Richard Savage) in which the writer claimed that Curll

> Arrested me for several months board, brought me back to my garret, and made me drudge on in my old dirty work. 'Twas in his service that I wrote Obscenity and Profaneness, under the names of Pope and Swift . . . I abridged histories and travels, translated from the French what they never wrote, and was expert at finding out new titles for old books.
>
> (Savage 1777: 266)

Whatever the truth of such claims, it is clear that Curll was a difficult and potentially even dangerous publisher to associate with. His dealings with Manley show that he could be equally unscrupulous with his female authors and this is confirmed by the recollections of Laetitia Pilkington. In her *Memoirs* she recorded how Curll attempted to defraud her out of some 'valuable manuscripts', including some of Swift's letters, at a time when she was desperately in need of money. Although subsequently imprisoned in the Marshalsea, she reflected, 'I comforted myself that Mr. Curl had not made a Fool of me, as he has done of many a better Writer, and secured me a Prisoner in his poetical Garret' (1749: 192, 193). Such evidence is hardly impartial, but there is no reason to assume that women were exempted from 'hard-headed' or deceitful business practices.

As the market for fiction expanded, the essence of a successful business in novels was the rapid issue of new titles, but this did not necessarily involve new material. Magazine stories were published together as novels, unsuccessful books were reissued under new covers, and unaltered novels were sometimes offered as 'new and improved' editions by booksellers who were secure in the knowledge that a review might not expose the fraud until the main sales were achieved. Publishers like Curll, the Noble brothers, and Lane reputedly required their writers to translate old continental romances and to 'ornament' and 'puff' out short, used stories for resale. Such pressures upon authors were compounded by the urgency of production schedules and the necessity of meeting deadlines. Charlotte Smith, an accomplished writer who produced an average of four volumes a year, struggled constantly to deliver her manuscripts on time and was forced to complete novels that were already partly in print. A correspondent of Bishop Percy wrote in 1801 that 'Charlotte Smith . . . is writing more volumes of the "Solitary Wanderer" for immediate subsistence. . . . She is a woman full of sorrows. . . . One of her daughters . . . has come to her mother, not worth a shilling, and with . . . three young children' (Andrew Caldwell, 8 June 1801, as quoted in Nichols 1858: 35). Smith's difficulties, like those of other married female authors, were exacerbated by her other time-consuming responsibilities towards her family. For example, Frances Sheridan's most famous novel, *The Memoirs of Miss Sidney Bidulph* (1761), was written in secret between her domestic duties. This conflict of interests for women writers was highlighted wryly by the 'dependent professional' poet, Mary Leapor:

> *Parthenia cries*, 'Why, *Mira* [Leapor], you are dull,
> And ever musing, till you crack your Skull;
> Still poking o'er your What-d'ye-call – your Muse:
> But pr'ythee, *Mira*, when dost clean thy Shoes?
> ('An Epistle to Artemisia. On Fame' 1751: vol. 2, 52)

COPYRIGHT: A BASIS FOR NEGOTIATION

Earlier in this chapter, I argued that a movement away from dependence upon the patronage system was essential to the emergence of female professionals, yet the resulting emphasis upon commercial priorities in author–publisher relations raised other difficulties for those seeking remunerative publication. As we have seen, an author's success in negotiation varied according to the circumstances of her case, such as the type of publisher and material involved, and whether it was the first unsolicited offering of a diffident unknown, or the eagerly awaited product of a respected best-selling author. However, a fundamental requirement of all such transactions was a clarification of the author's entitlement to literary property.

The concept of authors' copyright was stated for the first time in the 1709 Act of Queen Anne. Before its passing, ownership of a manuscript was not determined by authorship, but rather *de facto*, by possession. With the exception of royal patents granted for particular works, the copyright for printed books was secured largely by the laws of the Stationers' Company. Once a printer had obtained a manuscript, by whatever means, the usual method of formally securing copyright was by entry into the Stationers' register and the payment of a minimum fee. Only members of the Company were permitted to register books and this gave them perpetual copyright over the material, which was transferable only to another member of the Company through a further entry in the register.

The situation altered when the Licensing Act of 1694 lapsed and the Stationers' Company lost its monopolistic position. Subsequent petitioning for the restitution of the old system of control resulted, paradoxically, in an Act which, in theory at least, placed authors in an unprecedentedly favourable bargaining position. Their work was now defined as their property, along with measures to defend their rights of ownership, and this ostensibly gave them greater security and power in the market. Until the late seventeenth century, it was customary to regard any sale of copyright as total, but under the new Act it was possible for authors to publish and to retain final control. If they preferred, they might offer their work for a single issue and then negotiate a better price for subsequent editions on the basis of sales and reputation. Thus writers were able, in principle at least, to enhance the financial value of their material beyond the fee from the original copyright sale. Greater confidence and flexibility would help writers working without the support of patronage, and during the eighteenth century this included most female 'dependent professionals'. Futhermore, an unequivocal statement of their right of ownership was perhaps particularly necessary as a basis for the negotiatons of those female authors whose genteel upbringing and education within the aspiring middle social stratum had not prepared them for the world of business. It was at least an identifiable place to start.

Although the Act introduced substantial changes in principle, in practice its measures could be undermined. It remained more practicable for authors to continue selling their work outright because 'where authors keep their own copy-right they do not succeed, and many books have been consigned to oblivion, through the inattention and mismanagement of publishers' (Lackington 1792: 358). Furthermore, retaining copyright could restrict an author's redress against piracy as the penalties under the Act were applicable only if the book had been entered in the Stationers' records. Although injunctions restraining the printing, publishing, and selling of pirated editions could be granted regardless of registration, such lawsuits were expensive and there was no guarantee against the sale of the entire pirated edition before an injunction was granted. Additionally, the 1709 Act gave no protection against editions imported from abroad. This applied particularly to Ireland, where booksellers managed to issue pirated novels shortly after their publication in England. This was a common practice, and novels by Anna Maria Cox, Susannah Gunning, Frances Sheridan, and Phebe Gibbes, amongst others, were all published in Dublin. Usually the copyright holder had no legal redress against these 'Trespassers'.

Such behaviour influenced the actual status of literary property for all writers, but one factor affected married women in particular. Under the common law concept of *femme covert*, once a woman married she became totally dependent upon her husband and vested all legal rights in him. This position remained substantially unaltered until the late nineteenth century and therefore it pertained to all married eighteenth-century women writers. The essence of their situation was expressed by William Enfield in *Observations on Literary Property* (1774) in which he argued:

> The right of property in literary works rests on the solid grounds of primary possession and labour. . . . This point being established, it follows, that whatever can be asserted with truth concerning property in general, may fairly be applied to this particular kind of property.
>
> (1774: 19,22)

Thus, novels by married women were legally the literary property of their husbands, as were any profits from publication. This was demonstrated with cruel irony in the nineteenth century when Caroline Norton wrote a pamphlet in 1839 condemning the absence of a mother's custodial rights and then discovered that, like her children, the profits from her publication were the property of her husband and subject to his disposal.

It is important to note that the number of women possibly affected by this situation was less than might appear as the appellation 'Mrs' was also a customary, courtesy title given to or adopted by single women to denote their dignity and maturity.[14] None the less, a wife's legal position could present her with a number of difficulties. In principle, it entitled her husband to alter or even to destroy her work, and to arrogate to himself the authorship of a successful or potentially successful publication. I have no evidence to support this pessimistic interpretation and, whilst not precluding this possibility, it would appear that, on the whole, the work of female authors was treated by publishers, the public, and by the authors as their own, to dispose of as profitably as they could and to acknowledge if they chose.

Of greater concern to married 'dependent professionals' was their lack of legal control over the profits from publication. In many instances women turned to writing in order to contribute to the domestic finances, and in some cases their work was the sole means of their families' economic survival. Husbands had a legal claim to this income which they could use for entirely different purposes, thus exacerbating the authors' already difficult task of protecting their families' welfare. Desertion or divorce were not solutions to this problem, and separation was fraught with difficulties. Upon deserting her husband a woman forfeited her children and her property, and no matter what the provocation, she could take nothing with her. Divorce was very expensive, it required an Act of Parliament and therefore it was not a feasible option for the vast majority of people. Lawrence Stone has commented that between 1670 and 1799 'there were only 131 such Acts, virtually all instituted by husbands, and only seventeen passed before 1750' (1979: 34).

The alternative of a formal separation was apparently becoming more common amongst the upper classes during the eighteenth century and Stone has argued that there is a 'distinct impression' that more of these were being sought by women during this period (ibid.: 222). Even in these circumstances, the husband was in the position to dictate terms. If he chose to do so, he could seize her earnings and any other funds. He could compel her to return or insist she stay away, and he automatically had the right to custody of the children. According to Hilbish (1941: 125), Charlotte Smith's close friends at the time of her estrangement from her husband were less concerned at any possible scandal arising from her separation than with the fact that there were no legal arrangements to secure her fortune, including the profits from her publications. Her correspondence reveals that after the separation she paid out of her 'book money many debts that distressed him, & supplied him from time to time with small sums', and she referred to him and the legal inadequacies of her marriage articles as offering her 'no other prospect than being the slave of the Booksellers' (as quoted in McKillop 1951–2: 239).

The growth of the book trades and the rise of powerful publishers were part of a significant trend within the contemporary market that slowly removed literature from the primary influence of patronage into the commercial arena and under the control of profit-based economics. This was itself part of a far wider, more profound process of change which was apparent in other sectors, for example in agriculture, which reflected the development of industrialization and the social and economic structures and attitudes of modern capitalism.

This process necessarily had a profound effect upon the social, economic, and cultural status of authors in general, and particularly of 'dependent professionals'. The employment of writers by entrepreneurs with seemingly little or no interest in literary merit was attacked by the reviewers, who referred to 'workmen' engaged in a 'manufacture', and by writers as diverse as Alexander Pope (*The Dunciad*) and Catherine Macaulay. According to the latter, 'great pecuniary encouragement to literary publications creates a number of needy writers, who . . . obtrude their works upon the public, and rather retard than assist the progress of science and literature' (1774: 44). This fear of a threat to the dignity of letters was a driving force behind contemporary hostility towards the emergent literary professionals for whom writing, quite blatantly, need be little more than an appropriate means of earning a living. A significant number of eighteenth-century female 'dependent professionals' belonged to that category and their association with a commercial ethos was an important and enduring component of any adverse contemporary reaction to their fiction.

101

6

PROFESSIONAL WOMEN NOVELISTS: EARNING AN INCOME

Well, but the joy to see my works in print!
My self too pictur'd in a Mezzo-Tint!
The Preface done, the Dedication fram'd,
With lies enough to make a Lord asham'd!
Thus I step forth; an Auth'ress in some sort.
My Patron's name? 'O choose some Lord at Court.
'One that has money which he does not use,
One you may flatter much, that is, abuse.
For if you're nice, and cannot change your note,
Regardless of the trimm'd, or untrimm'd coat;
Believe me, friend, you'll ne'er be worth a groat.'
(Mary Jones, 'An Epistle to Lady Bowyer' 1750: 3)

THE ROLE OF PATRONAGE

Securing the maximum payment for their work was perhaps the major concern for all 'dependent professional' writers and, significantly for women, the methods for achieving this became more accessible during the eighteenth century. With more than one possible source of income available to them, writers could aspire to earn a reasonable, even comfortable standard of living through the pen, but this required more than literary skill alone. Adroit management, luck, persistence, and flexibility were all important ingredients of a successful literary career. As Samuel Johnson depicted in a satirical letter to 'Mr. Idler', an author who expected to be 'repaid by profit' could not sustain a fine resolution 'to maintain the dignity of letters, by a haughty contempt of pecuniary solicitations' (1759 [1816]: 221, 222). All too soon, approaches to potential patrons, subscribers, and booksellers had to be made, and their rejections endured.

Although aristocratic patronage was declining in significance within the world of letters, the system of preferment itself was endemic in most areas of social, economic, and political activity. As might be expected, therefore, throughout the century benevolent individuals were prompted to offer occasional and regular support of this kind to female authors. Early in the period Elizabeth Rowe obtained the patronage of Lord Weymouth and his family as a result of her *Poems on Several Occasions* (1696), and later, in 1775, Mary 'Perdita' Robinson received support from the Duchess of Devonshire on the basis of a manuscript of poetry written whilst she and her husband were imprisoned for debt. As we have seen in relation to Wollstonecraft and Johnson, some patrons acted more in the renaissance tradition by providing accommodation for their protégés. At the beginning of the century, Catharine Trotter was housed temporarily by Lady Piers after a judicious dedication in the dramatist's only comedy, *Love at a Loss; or, Most Votes Carry It* (1701). Similarly, Mary Latter's tragedy, *The Siege of Jerusalem by Titus Vespasian* (1763), secured money, accommodation, and tuition from John Rich, the patentee of the Covent Garden theatre, who also organized a subscription edition of her *A Miscellaneous Poetical Essay in three Parts* (1761). His death a short while later was a considerable blow to her prospects.

The relationship between an author and her patron included (apart from disinterested benevolence) varying degrees of mutual self-interest. Money or other forms of support were given in return for flattery, entertainment, the projection of favoured opinions and beliefs, and social éclat. The requirement to please meant that nurturing the favour of a patron could be as delicate a task as obtaining it in the first place. We can see this reflected in the exchanges between Laetitia Pilkington and her patron Lord Kingsborough. Her poems, drawings, and letters elicited substantial sums of between £20 and £100, an offer of support 'without limit' on application to his agent (Kingsborough 20 May 1748, in Laetitia Pilkington 1760: 249), and a promise of 500 subscribers for a requested 'panegyrick on the world' (ibid.: 268). It is clear from their correspondence that in return, Kingsborough expected to be pleased and uplifted; he did not want to be burdened with her anxieties:

Madam,
Your letter found me alone, I expected a fund of humour and entertainment on the receipt of it; but, good God! how much was I affected at your alteration of stile. Surely, Madam, you are troubled with vapours, and this must be the effect of them. When I last had the honour to see you, you were full of health and spirits; neither did I ever see more vivacity in any person living. For heaven's sake, Mrs. Pilkington, be yourself, and think no more of quitting the world, wherein the longer you live the more you will be admired. . . .
You were so obliging to promise, in one of your former letters, to entertain me with a transcipt of your humerous epistle from C———
D———m, I shall take it extremely kind, Madam, if you will, at a leisure hour, send it to me; . . .

P.S. I beg, dear Madam, you'll send something to raise my spirits, which your last has much depressed.

(Kingsborough 13 April 1748, in ibid.: 230–1)

Her response was a frank acknowledgement of her obligation: 'As you desire me to be merry, whether I will or not, my duty obliges me to comply with your injunction, and rattle out every thing I think entertaining, without once considering who I am prating to' (Pilkington 18 April 1748, in ibid.: 231).

Poetic tributes were a customary means of eliciting money from their recipients, although the outcome could be unpredictable. Halsband (1976: 57–8) has described Pilkington's less successful approach to Lord Hardwicke, who gave her a 'dish of Chocolate' in return for her celebration of his appointment to Lord Chancellor. On the other hand, Delarivière Manley obtained a welcome twenty guineas from John Harvey for a poem written in praise of his sister. Dedications were another source of additional income and a useful means of making advantageous contacts with influential people. Susanna Rowson's dedication of her novel *Victoria* (1786) to the Duchess of Devonshire led to an introduction to the Prince of Wales, who subsequently granted her father a pension; whilst Sophia Lee's dedication of her blank verse tragedy *Almeyda, Queen of Granada* (1796) to Mrs Siddons ensured that the famous actress took the leading role when the play was produced at Drury Lane.

Again, the outcome of such petitions for favour could be less than expected. Johnson's definition of a patron as 'one who looks with unconcern on a man struggling for life in the water, and, when he has reached ground, encumbers him with help' (Letter to the Earl of Chesterfield 1755, in Boswell 1799 [1927]: vol. 1, 174), was prompted by the derisory £10 he received from the dedicatee of the great *Dictionary*. In addition, for those entering the profession for the first time, or moving in more modest circles, there was the question of how to negotiate the etiquette involved in obtaining the dedicatee's permission. After her frustrating encounter with Noble, Jean Marishall decided to supplement her modest profit from *Clarinda Cathcart* by dedicating it to the Queen. She settled upon 'General G———' as the most eligible person to present her novel (partly because her brother was serving in his Regiment), and she used yet another intermediary (a relative, 'Colonel M———') to approach the General on her behalf (1789: vol. 2, 170–1). Having read the novel, the Colonel agreed and within a week she had heard that the General was equally compliant. Unfortunately, the latter decided to withdraw from the project after consideration because 'a novel was not a work of consequence enough for him to present to her Majesty, and that it would be much better to have it presented by a lady' (ibid.: 174). Undaunted, Marishall wrote to the Duchess of Northumberland explaining her predicament and she obtained the help of the eloquent 'Miss E———' to deliver her petition. To her surprise, the Duchess readily undertook to present the novel which was received favourably. Apart from her pleasure 'beyond expression' at this successful resolution, Marishall received (via 'General G———' and 'Colonel

M———') a reward of ten guineas from the Queen (ibid.: 183–4). Although she used intermediaries throughout her negotiations, Marishall's approach to authorship was hardly diffident. Her persistence in the face of rejection had more than doubled the initial profit from her novel, and the subsequent newspaper coverage of the Royal presentation was useful publicity (ibid.: 183).

A number of women incorporated dedications 'with permission' in their novels and a few, like Eliza Parsons, announced this distinction on their title pages.[1] The tone of these pieces varied from dignified appeals to the most precious and obsequious declarations. The latter species is represented well by Eliza Haywood's offering to Lady Abergavenny at the beginning of *Philadore and Placentia* (1727):

> The greatest happiness as well as glory of an author being the privilege we have of imploring the protection of the great and good, the eminence of your Ladyship's character in both these capacities, while it justifies my choice to the world, will also induce you to excuse my presumption for laying at your feet an offering not otherwise worthy of acceptance than by the motives which prompted me to present it.
>
> To go about to make any just description of those excellencies which render your Ladyship the pride and emulation of our sex and the admiration of the other is a task which, as conscious of my inability, I dare not undertake. . . . 'Tis the pretenders to merit who delight to hear their imaginary virtues the theme of flattering panegyric, but true perfection stands in need of no light but its own luster to make itself conspicuous.
>
> (1727 [1964]: 155)

The convention invited ridicule and Charlotte Charke responded with an ironic dedication from, and to, herself in *A Narrative of the Life* (1755), on the grounds that she was '*The properest Patroness I could have chosen*, as I am most likely to be tenderly partial *to my poetical Errors, and will be as bounteous in the Reward as we may reasonably imagine my Merit may claim*' (1755: 270). Similarly, in the Dedication to her *The Accomplished Rake*, Mary Davys satirized the customary effusions by concluding her address 'To the Beaux of Great Britain' with her 'unfeigned' wish that their 'fine faces . . . [would] receive no freckles, . . . [their] embroideries no tarnish, nor . . . [their] fortunes any shock' (1727 [1964]: 240).

Integral to the rich pattern of eighteenth-century middle- and upper-class culture were the various groups of writers, artists, and intellectuals who gathered around notable authors, influential publishers, and members of the social elite. These cultural and social matrices had an economic aspect in that they helped to establish the links between talent and wealth which were essential to the functioning of patronage. Historians have described the intricacies of these contacts in relation to major male authors, noting, for example, the importance of Robert Dodsley as both publisher and patron to Samuel Johnson, but there were a number of similar networks which offered opportunities to contemporary women. For example, Swift, Johnson, Thrale, Richardson, and the Bluestockings played notable roles in the creation of supportive links with and between female writers. These not only increased the authors' awareness of the work of other women, they also facilitated their efforts to secure financial help from patrons and subscribers.

Swift's friendships with women attracted unflattering contemporary attention. Lady Mary Wortley Montagu reported that 'D[ean] S[wift] . . . was so intoxicated with the Love of Flattery, he sought it amongst the lowest of people and the silliest of Women' (Letter to Lady Bute 1754, in Montagu 1967: 56); whilst Lord Orrery noted Swift's 'constant seraglio of very virtuous women' (*Remarks on the Life and Writings of Swift* 1752, in ibid.: 56, n. 2). Neither epithet seems particularly applicable to Delarivière Manley, with whom Swift shared an interest in political journalism. They were involved in joint ventures and he supported her application to Lord Peterborough for some reward for her services to the Tory cause, particularly through her *Atlantis*.

Swift's 'circle' also included the erudite Mrs Grierson and the 'dependent professionals' Laetitia Pilkington and Mary Barber, who 'as it becomes the chief Poetess is but poor' (Letter to Pope 1729, in Swift 1963: 369).[2] He applauded the work of these writers (although he fell out dramatically with Pilkington after 1738), and he used his influence to assist them in practical ways. Pilkington's *Memoirs* reveal that Swift went to some lengths to establish her husband comfortably in England when he took up his post as chaplain to the Lord Mayor of London, giving Pilkington letters of recommendation to various influential people. Additionally, it was the Dean's persistent approaches to his friends that eventually secured enough subscribers for a proposed volume of Barber's poetry. Furthermore, when she was in financial difficulty a few years later, he allowed her to publish his *Treatise on Polite Conversation* (1738) by subscription for her own benefit.

Johnson's acquaintance included many major cultural figures. Burke, Gibbon, Goldsmith, Reynolds, and Garrick were all attracted to the luminary, as were important women writers of the day, such as Sheridan, Seward, More, Elstob, Carter, Burney, and Lennox. Despite his clearly stated disapproval of certain activities for women (preaching, public singing, and portrait painting), he adopted a generally encouraging approach to female writers. He openly admired the literatae in his own circle, declaring in 'fine spirits' that 'Three such women [as Carter, More, and Burney] are not to be found: I know not where I could find a fourth, except Mrs. Lennox, who is superiour to them all'. It is interesting to note that later in the same exchange, Johnson implicitly acknowledged the professionalism of these writers by distinguishing between them and Mrs Montagu on the grounds that 'Mrs Montagu does not make a trade of her wit' (Boswell 1799 [1927]:

vol. 2, 537). As a professional writer he understood the difficulties of other 'labourers in literature', and when his assistance was requested, amongst other acts of kindness, he 'found time to translate for Mrs. Lennox's English version of Brumoy, "A Dissertation on the Greek Comedy", and "The General Conclusion of the book" ' (Boswell 1799 [1927]: vol. 1, 230). Johnson's base for many years, and the location of many of the distinguished literary and social occasions over which he presided, was the Thrales' house at Streatham. It was through an invitation from Hester Thrale (who had nurtured an impressive circle of aquaintances) that Burney, recently acclaimed as the author of *Evelina*, first met Johnson and members of the Bluestockings.

Through his novels, Samuel Richardson became particularly associated in the public mind with women: as their champion or corrupter (interpretations of *Pamela* varied considerably); as a writer who presented life from a 'feminine' perspective, appealing to a large female readership; and as the progenitor of a mass of epistolary novels by 'Young Ladies'. He cultivated a substantial correspondence with a number of women, engaging in discourses on topics like filial obedience and women's education, and it is characteristic of his approach that the coterie at North End consisted mainly of women. John Duncombe, the husband of one of that circle, praised Richardson in *The Feminiad* (1754) for his patronage of the sex, and Richardson was himself openly proud of his predominantly female acquaintance. This included Charlotte Lennox, Sarah Fielding, Jane and Margaret Collier, Frances Sheridan, Laetitia Pilkington, Susanna Highmore, and her daughter, the poet and illustrator Susanna Duncombe. He appears to have enjoyed nurturing literary talent – as his young correspondent Hester Mulso Chapone observed, 'I never was a writing lady till you made me one' (Chapone 1808: 132) – and he consulted with these friends about his own novels and gave advice to those women writers who sought it. He wrote collaboratively with Jane Collier and it is possible that he provided lodgings for at least one of the Collier sisters (Jarvis in Todd 1987: 89). Pilkington recorded that Richardson was charitable towards her, and he helped to promote Fielding's *Lives of Cleopatra and Octavia* (1757) by procuring subscribers and by buying several copies himself. He had a very high opinion of the latter's talents and printed three of her works.

The Bluestockings provided perhaps the most influential social, intellectual and literary network to include a cluster of women writers. These groupings evolved around salons hosted by Mrs Montagu, Mrs Boscawen, and Mrs Vesey, and they included poets, critics, and scholars. There was a degree of overlap with Johnson's circle as Chapone, More, Burney, and Catherine Talbot frequented both. Burney was perhaps the only true novelist amongst the 'Blues', and, although this female network acted as an important source of patronage for women writers (including some amongst themselves), they were inter ested primarily in poetry and scholarly material. For example, Elizabeth Montagu patronized Hannah More, the poet Anna Williams, and her good friend, the poet, translator, and essayist, Elizabeth Carter. She settled an annuity upon the latter and also on Sarah Fielding, whose scholarly as well as novelistic abilities were acknowledged widely. These preferences reflected the Bluestockings' desire to foster serious and intellectual interests amongst their members, but in fact they also mirrored those of patrons generally, who favoured women's poetry, translations, erudite texts, and plays. With the exception of dedications, therefore, the importance of patronage in the careers of women novelists was attached primarily to their work in other genres.

A paradigm example of such patronage amongst women writers was Hannah More's discovery and presentation of Ann Yearsley. More's cook, who was aware of Yearsley's impoverished domestic life and large family, brought Ann's poetry to the notice of her employer. More was impressed by her work, particularly in the light of the poet's background and lack of formal education, and she undertook to help her. She gave her protégée a dictionary and a grammar, and wrote to Mrs Montagu (the 'Queen of the Blues') amongst others, seeking support for the aspiring author. In a 'Prefatory Letter' to Yearsley's *Poems* she assured Montagu that

> It is not intended to place her in such a state of independence as might reduce her to devote her time to the idleness of Poetry. I hope that she is convinced that the making of verses is not the great business of human life; and that, as a wife and a mother, she has duties to fill, the smallest of which is of more value than the finest verses she can write: but as it has pleased God to give her these talents, may they not be made an instrument to mend her situation, if we publish a small volume of her Poems by subscription? . . . it is not fame, but bread, which I am anxious to secure for her.
>
> (More 1785: xi–xii)

The cautious tone of More's appeal was entirely characteristic of her efforts in other areas to improve the education of the poor whilst retaining a conservative interpretation of its function within their lives.[3] She was extremely successful, securing over a thousand subscribers, including Reynolds, Walpole, Blake, at least 115 members of the aristocracy, the Lord Primate of Ireland, and the Bluestockings; over half the subscribers were women. More and Montagu became trustees of a fund for Yearsley which contained over £600. The poet later entered into a dispute with her patron over her exclusion from control of the money and the affair became public through various prefaces in Yearsley's subsequent publications. More withdrew her support and, without her mediation, Yearsley's two later attempts at publishing her poetry by subscription (in 1787 and 1796) were comparatively disappointing.

THE ROLE OF SUBSCRIPTION PUBLICATION

The scale of More's intervention was exceptional and, on the whole, such patronage would not have been available to the many little-known, middle-class female novelists who appeared towards the end of the century and who worked outside the sphere of More and the Bluestockings *et alia*. Of necessity these authors looked elsewhere. At least thirty-two of the books in Appendix A were 'Printed for the Author', implying either that the writer provided the capital herself, or that other people were persuaded to subscribe to the work. The latter method of publication was used widely during the eighteenth century and involved the procuring of sufficient advance sales of copies to fund a projected work. The investors paid their contributions partly before, and partly on receipt of the book. Various devices were employed to attract support, including advertisements in newspapers, selling subscription tickets in parks and other public places, or inserting a proposal into a current publication, a method used (unsuccessfully) by Mrs Brooke for a projected translation of 'Il Pastor Fido'.

It is difficult to determine exactly how many women's novels were published by subscription. Not all novels published in this way have been recorded by bibliographers as 'Published for the author', and clearly not all novels so recorded were published by subscription. However, it has been possible through a search of secondary sources, primarily Robinson and Wallis's (1975) study of extant subscription lists, to establish that at least twenty-one of the novels in Appendix A were subscription publications.[4] The most famous of these, Fanny Burney's *Camilla* (1796), was exceptional due to both the £2,000–£3,000 the author allegedly cleared from its sale, and the circumstances surrounding its publication. As the third novel of a fêted and successful author it was awaited eagerly and sold well. Burney had influential friends in the royal court where she had earlier lived and worked, and the lists of subscribers were kept in these circles by the dowager duchess of Leinster, Mrs Boscawen, Mrs Crewe, and Mrs Locke, and not, as was usual, by the publishers.

The spectacular success of *Camilla* has attracted the attention of literary historians and, when this is conflated with the increased use of this method in other genres, the tendency has been to assume (by implication) that subscription was a very significant force behind the growth of women's novels during the eighteenth century. Undoubtedly it made a major contribution to the careers of a number of writers in Appendix A: Susannah and Margaret Minifie accumulated nearly 800 subscribers for their first novel; and Sarah Fielding obtained a welcome 500 investors for her *Familiar Letters* (a collection of miscellaneous essays and fictive correspondence). On a more modest scale, the possibility of earning far more than could be secured through a direct sale of copyright was probably a strong inducement for an impoverished provincial writer like Sarah Emma Spencer, who gathered about a hundred investors for her only known novel. That subscription was a resource for such 'dependent professionals' was acknowledged by the reviewer of *The Traditions, a Legendary Tale* 'Written by a Young Lady' [Mary Martha Sherwood] (1795) who deduced:

From an advertisment prefixed to this novel, and from an uncommonly numerous list of subscribers, under whose patronage it makes its appearance, we are led to consider it as an offering of benevolence to distress. It appears to have been written by a young lady, probably of some distinction, certainly of some talents, to serve one of those unhappy foreigners whom the convulsion of the times has thrown into this country.

(*Monthly Review* 1795: vol. 18, 229)

However, despite its potential for profitability, there were significant disadvantages attached to this method. Although Robinson and Wallis have argued that the growth of subscription during this period was an aspect of the gradual transition from individual patronage by an elite to the more general support of commercial enterprise, it was still heavily dependent upon personal contact and the favour of individuals.[5] We have already seen this in relation to Ann Yearsley but it applied equally to Eliza Parson's excellent start to her career. Her first novel attracted subscriptions from the Prince of Wales, Mrs Fitzherbert, Elizabeth Montagu, and Horace Walpole, who were no doubt encouraged to invest by the Marchioness of Salisbury, Eliza's patron and the novel's dedicatee.

Unfortunately, having a distinguished friend to present the proposals, and even the advantage of literary status, were not guarantees against painful rebuff. In 1775 Johnson wrote a proposal for publishing the works of Charlotte Lennox (which had already received royal approval) in which he expressed her hope that she would 'Not be considered as too indulgent to vanity, or too studious of interest, if, from that labour which has hitherto been chiefly gainful to others, she endeavours to obtain at last some profit for herself and her children' (Boswell 1799 [1927]: vol. 1, 542). Despite his support, the project was a failure.

In the absence of a well-placed intermediary, the author either paid for the services of an agent, relied upon the help of friends, or upon the generosity of an immediate circle of potential subscribers, like Mary Davys's coffee-house supporters. Securing investments could be an uncomfortable experience. Marishall recalled that she 'cleared about a hundred guineas' from a subscription publication of her second novel, *The History of Alicia Montague*. This was considerably more profitable than her earlier venture and therefore it

Would have been sufficient to have made me go on, had it not been the great difficulty which I understood there had been in procuring subscriptions. My zealous friends were confined to a few; and they, I had reason to believe, were exceedingly disappointed to find that not one in twenty were disposed to throw away a crown on what they could get a reading of when published for a few pence.

(1789: vol. 2, 193)

Marishall's unease about the process was shared by others who felt that subscription was tainted with commercialism, involving an undignified touting of work or reputation for profit. In an 'Advertisement' in Pope's *Works*, Warburton claimed proudly that 'The Editor hath not, for the sake of profit, suffered the Author's Name to be made cheap by a *Subscription*' (Warburton 1757: ii). This attitude may help to explain Fanny Burney's reluctance to undertake what was almost certain to be a highly rewarding venture. In a letter written shortly before the publication of *Camilla*, she stated:

> Should it succeed, like 'Evelina' and 'Cecilia', it may be a little portion to our Bambino. We wish, therefore, to print it for ourselves in this hope; but the expenses of the press are so enormous, so raised by these late Acts, that it is out of all question for us to afford it. We have, therefore, been led by degrees to listen to counsel of some friends, and to print it by subscription. This is in many-many ways unpleasant and unpalatable to us both; but the real chance of real use and benefit to our little darling overcomes all scruples, and, therefore, to work we go!
>
> (15 June [17]95, in Burney 1842–6: vol. 6, 45)

Apart from an understandable reluctance amongst the public to invest in something about which they knew relatively little, by someone possibly completely unknown, and which might not materialize at all,[6] the novelists' difficulties were compounded by prevailing attitudes towards the genre. As Burney complained: 'In the republic of letters, there is no member of such inferior rank, or who is so much disdained by his brethren of the quill, as the humble Novelist' (*Evelina* 1778 [1909]: Preface). Unlike such prestigious projects as Pope's translation of Homer's *Iliad* (which attracted an exceptionally high number of subscribers), there was little kudos attached to the proposals for a novel, thus removing an important motivation for investors. According to Blakey, the method was unpopular amongst Minerva novelists, and she cites the *Critical* (1794), which claimed that a respectable list of subscribers was 'a circumstance rarely attendant on Novels' (1939: 75–6). Thus, it seems probable that the average female novelist could not expect sufficient profit from this method to justify the exertion involved.

Furthermore, despite the increasing public acceptance of female authors in the second half of the century, a residual uncertainty about the suitability of novel writing for women persisted throughout the period. In the range of female literature, poetry and didactic material were probably more likely to attract subscribers than fiction, since these genres were perceived as unequivocally appropriate for the female pen.[7] This approval underlies the tone of the *Monthly's* review of *Miscellanies, on moral and religious subjects. In prose and verse*, by Elizabeth Harrison:

> As this publication is the work of benevolence, and a sacrifice, not to

111

vanity, but to PIOUS OLD AGE, and INDUSTRIOUS POVERTY;[*]
it has a natural claim upon us, to an entire exemption from any
criticism that might tend, in the least, to obstruct the progress of so
worthy an intention.

[*] Vid. Mrs. Harrison's Preface, containing her grateful acknowledge-
ments to her friends, whose generous subscriptions enabled her to
provide for an aged parent.

(1755: vol. 15, 537)

The extant subscription lists from this period also hint at some compatibi-
lity between poetry and this method of publication. Robinson and Wallis
record at least seventy-one works by female writers and about half of these
were volumes of poetry, occasionally including letters and dramatic entertainments. The remainder were typical of contemporary women's publications, including musical lessons and scores, sermons, songs, discourses on
religious, moral, and philosophical subjects, books on cookery and household affairs, erudite texts, and only twelve (original) novels.

Whatever direct contribution subscription may have made to the rise of
the professional female prose-fiction writer, it is clear that it played an
important role in the wider growth of women's involvement in the literature market. Women from the social elite continued to act as benefactors of
the literary profession, including its female members, but the broader social
base of subscription compared with that of patronage meant that the support of the middle ranks was becoming increasingly influential. Within
this, women subscribers emerged as a significant source of funding.
Through this means they were involved in financing work by women from
the earliest years of the century, and the lists, such as those for Elstob's *An
English-Saxon Homily* (1709), Haywood's *Letters from a Lady of Quality
to a Chevalier* (1721), and Boyd's *The Happy-Unfortunate* (1732), reveal
that particular works attracted substantial numbers of female subscribers.
This development reflects women's growing participation in print culture –
as readers, as writers, and as patrons – and their increasing familiarity with
and support of writers of their own sex. As we shall see in chapter 7, this
was itself nurtured by a number of other major developments within the
literature market, such as the growth of both the periodical press and of
circulating libraries.

Some authors, perhaps despairing of ever procuring either sufficient
subscribers or an adequate copyright fee, financed their own publications.
This strategy was adopted by Manley in 1707 as a result of financial
difficulties. Her biographer, Paul Anderson, tells us that having accepted
two commissions for funeral elegies in May of that year, Manley became
'tired of waiting for another performance of *Almyna*, . . . [and] printed the
play and dispatched it to her patroness the Countess of Sandwich, asking her

for pecuniary aid' (1935–6: 272). Self-financed publication could result also from a combination of a strong desire to get into print coupled with the money to finance it, or it might be an attempt to avoid sharing the profits with 'the Trade', a practice which was discouraged by the booksellers.

Whatever the motivation, this action required a substantial investment on the part of the author, reflecting either desperation, or the author's considerable faith in the value or saleability of her work. Hannah More claimed that she spent £5,000 publishing *Coelebs in Search of a Wife* (1809). This passed through eleven editions in nine months and by 1810 she had recovered £2,000. The book (her only novel) later achieved thirty editions in America and she retained the copyright of this and other publications until the end of her life. More was unusual in her actions, which demonstrated a degree of flexibility that was possible only for a well-known author who was confident of both her entitlement to literary property, and the demand for her material.

DIRECT SALE OF COPYRIGHT

For the overwhelming majority of the increasing number of novelists who entered the market at the end of the century, a direct sale of their copyright was the easiest means of obtaining some income from their labours. As the contemporary historian Catherine Macaulay argued:

> If authors had no better dependence than private patronage or public generosity; if they had not a more certain resource in their right to sell their works to booksellers, they would probably sometimes be obliged to feed on the insubstantial breath of fame.
>
> (1774: 37)

Aspiring female novelists could identify relatively easily those publishers who were most likely to be interested in their fiction, and recourse to men like Curll, the Noble brothers, Bell, Hookham, and Lane reduced the risk of rebuff and, if anonymity was sought, of exposure. A sale was not necessarily dependent upon social status, personal contacts or funds, or even literary talent. 'Certainly there was a time', recalled a critic writing for the *Lady's Monthly Museum* in 1798, 'when the rage for novel-writing was so indiscriminately managed that every wretched author who could produce his five, nay *two* guinea MS. was sure to meet with a ready sale for it in Holborn or Fleet-Street' (1798: vol. 1, 435).

Although there were distinct advantages to direct sale of copyright for women authors, the prices paid for novel manuscripts were generally low. Overall, there seems to have been a slight upward trend in payments for unexceptional material concurrent with the rise in retail prices, from a span of between two and five guineas in the earlier eighteenth century, to between five and ten guineas towards the end of the period. For example, Mary Davys recalled how her first literary attempt, written in 1700 and later published in 1704 as *The Amours of Alcippus and Lucippe. A Novel. Written by a Lady*,

> Was sent about the world as naked as it came into it, having not so much as one page of preface to keep it in countenance. What success it met with I never knew, for, . . . I took three guineas for the brat of my brain and then went a hundred and fifty miles northward.
>
> (1725 [1964]: 236)

The bulk of popular novels, including those by women, were probably sold to their publishers for around the five guineas received by Phebe Gibbes from T. Lowndes on 14 April 1763 'for the novel called "The Life of Mr. Francis Clive" ' (*Gentleman's Magazine* 1824: vol. 94, 136). There were, of course, a number of authors who managed to secure substantially more for their material. Booksellers were occasionally induced to pay over twice the normal price for a better-quality manuscript, or for one by a well-known author. Lowndes paid £20 for Burney's *Evelina* (1778), which in the event was well under its market value, and he paid a similar but more appropriate sum of twenty guineas for Sophia Briscoe's *Fine Lady* (1772); Anne Dawe obtained the same price for her *Younger Sister* (1770) (*Gentleman's Magazine* 1824: vol. 94, 136). A few authors received considerably higher sums. Charlotte Smith usually secured £50 a volume (Spencer in Todd 1987: 288), and after the success of *Evelina*, Fanny Burney was able to extract £250 from Payne and Cadell for her second novel. Ann Yearsley, famous as Hannah More's 'Milkmaid', received £200 for *The Royal Captives* (1795). Such prices were paid only rarely for copyright, particularly for novel manuscripts, but they were exceeded by the remarkable £500 and £800 reputedly paid for Ann Radcliffe's *The Mysteries of Udolpho* (1794) and *The Italian* (1797), respectively.

The prices secured by contemporary male novelists covered a similarly broad spectrum, ranging from the few guineas netted by the hack's two- or three-volume library novel, through Lowndes's generous (or far-sighted) fee of thirty guineas for Robert Bage's first novel *Mount Henneth*, to the exceptional sums of £183. 10s., £700, and £1,000 received by Fielding for *Joseph Andrews*, *Tom Jones*, and *Amelia*, respectively. Comparison of these fees with the sums paid to women novelists suggests that there was not a significant differential between the sexes as far as copyright payments were concerned. Indeed, if one views such fees as an indicator of saleability, women novelists were amongst the most commercially successful authors of their day.

The sale of the copyright of a novel was not always the end of the transaction between author and publisher as the latter sometimes augmented the original payment with a further sum in recognition of a success. For example, Cadell supplemented the original fee for Smith's first novel *Emmeline, The Orphan of the Castle* (1788), and gave Sophia Lee £50 more than they had agreed for the copyright of her novel *The Recess* (1783–5). Lowndes added a further £10 to his bargain payment for Burney's *Evelina* (1778) and, if we are to believe the squib *A Full and True Account of a Horrid and Barbarous Revenge by Poison, On the Body of Mr. Edmund Curll, Bookseller* (1716), even Curll was moved during his illness to recommend to his wife that she give a 'Week's Wages Advance to each of his [Curll's] Gentlemen Authors, with some small Gratuity in particular to Mrs. *Centlivre*' ([Anon] 1716: 6).[8] Such satire aside, although extra payments may well have been shrewd investments on the part of publishers to ensure that they had first call on subsequent manuscripts, they were, none the less, financially beneficial (at least in the short term) for the author.[9]

As we have seen, a judicious dedication could have a similarly advantageous effect, whilst the careful marketing of copyright could increase the author's profits substantially. Elizabeth Inchbald received initial payments of £200 and £150, respectively, for her novels *A Simple Story* (1791) and *Nature and Art* (1796). These were high fees, but not unprecedented for a celebrated writer. The novels were a major success, and a second edition of *A Simple Story* was ordered less than three months after the first. On the basis of this, Robinson was prepared to pay £600 for their extended copyright before they were sold again in 1810 to Longman. In total, Inchbald earned over £1,000 from the two novels.

A few 'dependent professional' women novelists became unusually wealthy. After her death in 1833, Hannah More left a fortune of approximately £30,000 (mostly in the form of legacies to charitable institutions), representing the accumulated profit from years of literary activity in various genres.[10] By the early nineteenth century, Fanny Burney was in a position to anticipate £3,000 from one novel, *The Wanderer* (1814). Shortly before its publication she wrote to her father:

> I am indescribably occupied, and have been so ever since my return from Ramsgate, in giving more and more last touches to my work, about which I begin to grow very anxious. I am to receive merely £500 upon delivery of the M.S.; the two following £500 by installments from nine months to nine months, that is, in a year and a half from the day of *publication*.
> If all goes well, the whole will be £3,000, but only at the end of the sale of eight thousand copies.
>
> (12 October 1813, in Burney 1842–6: vol. 7, 14–15)

Burney's concern at the prospect of receiving a *mere* £500 as an initial payment is a measure of her contemporary popularity as a novelist who enjoyed 'the astonishing *éclat* of a work in five volumes being all bespoken before it was published' (3 April 1814, in ibid.: 20). By contrast, most professional writers, including many of the female novelists mentioned in this study, expected to make their living by selling a lot of material cheaply. The chequered careers of women like Manley, Haywood, Robinson,

Lennox, Latter, Skinn, Griffith, Brooke, and Fielding were a continual struggle against the prospect of poverty, and they required opportunism, assiduity, luck, and talent in order to survive.

PROFESSIONAL WOMEN NOVELISTS' WORK IN OTHER GENRES

In both literary and financial terms, the novel was a major resource for the eighteenth-century female professonal writer; at the very least, the genre offered the chance to earn a few essential guineas. None the less, like the famous quintumvirate of Defoe, Richardson, Fielding, Sterne, and Smollett, it is doubtful whether such authors as Manley, Haywood, Brooke, Lennox, Inchbald, and Wollstonecraft conceived of themselves solely as novelists, and, as will become apparent, the term is an inadequate description of the scope of their work. Apart from the literary, political, moral, and educational motives for writing in other genres, the financial reasons were compelling. The average copright fee from one novel was roughly equivalent to the annual wages of a laundry, scullery, or dairy maid, and therefore entirely inadequate for anyone attempting to maintain middle-class status. To obtain a respectable income of at least £50 per annum, a novelist would have to write and publish as many as ten novels a year (even the prolific Eliza Haywood only achieved this in 1725), or, like most professionals, she had to venture into as many other types of literature as possible. The information in the *Dictionary of National Biography* provides a rough-and-ready guide to the extent of this diversification. Forty-seven of the fifty eighteenth-century female novelists in the *Dictionary* wrote in at least one genre other than the novel. Thirteen of those used at least five different types of literature, including novels, plays, poetry, didactic non-fiction, translations, and journalism, and of these, at least ten were professional.

The periodical press

The emergence of women's written contribution to the periodical press was coincident with the development of a female readership for this ephemera. Dunton, through his *Athenian Mercury* (1691–7), and Motteux, through his *Gentleman's Journal* (1692–4), are credited with recognizing first the vast potential of this market, although their accommodation of overtly feminine interests did not meet with universal approval. For example, included in Dunton's autobiography is a letter written by a 'friend in earnest' who pleaded with him to leave out all his 'female trumpery', adding that he was of 'too public a rank not to know that taste of the age; and I can assure you the mentioning of female correspondents and she-wits would ruin the sale of the best Authors we have' (J.W., 5 November 1718, in Dunton 1818: xxix). Prominent amongst his women contributors was Elizabeth Rowe, who made regular submissions of her poetry under the name of 'Philomela'; her success encouraged Dunton to devote two issues to her material. These publications were followed by John Tipper's *Ladies Diary* (1704), which was designed specifically for women readers. It had a large circulation and encouraged and received contributions of enigmas, stories, and poems from its readers. Before the *Ladies Diary* disappeared, *Records of Love* (1710) came onto the market, also targeted at women and offering the attraction of at least one novel in each number. This was additional to the usual fare of biographies, poems, and advice on marriage, etcetera. Virtually from its inception, the pattern of most later popular miscellanies for women was established.

Professionalism amongst female authors developed concurrently with the emergence of women's periodicals and naturally such writers took advantage of the opportunities offered by the medium. Early in the eighteenth century, Delariviere Manley began her thrice-weekly *Female Tatler* (1709–10) with the apparent intention of capitalizing on the popularity of Steele's *Tatler*, particularly amongst women readers. As with so much of Manley's other material, the periodical was largely a vehicle for Tory ideas and propaganda until her resignation from its editorship after issue fifty-one.[11] She later succeeded Swift as editor of the *Examiner* (in 1711), and produced a number of pamphlets on behalf of the cause.[12] It is interesting to note that Manley was not the only female insurgent into this particular minefield. Sarah Popping was a Whig propagandist and political opponent of Manley. As joint proprietor with Benjamin Harris of the *Protestant Post Boy* (1711), she was responsible for frequent attacks upon Swift.[13] Later in the century, Ann Jebb wrote political articles for the *London Chronicle* under the name of 'Priscilla' as part of her campaigning activities; and intriguingly, the *Dictionary of National Biography* suggests that Elizabeth Ryves 'wrote political articles for newspapers' when she came to London to earn her living by writing (1922: vol. 17, 560).

Manley's *Female Tatler* bears witness to a belief that the emergent interest in women's periodicals could be turned to good effect. Expansion in demand did not, however, make this an easy market to exploit, and, as Robert Mayo (1962) has demonstrated, numerous titles were printed during the eighteenth century only to disappear almost immediately. The aspiring author Jean Marishall was advised 'that these publications seldom answered at first', and Lord Lyttleton's view of her projected periodical was: 'If you write for fame, go on; if for money, desist, unless the Dutchess [*sic*] of Northumberland or Lord Chesterfield will enable you to bear the expense' (1789: vol. 2, 229–30). None the less, Haywood had at least two attempts with her *Female Spectator* (1744–6) and the *Parrot* (1746), and she was followed by another professional, Frances Brooke. The latter's *Old Maid* (1755–6) ran for thirty-seven weeks, presenting the novelist's work under the pseudonym of 'Mary Singleton, Spinster'. Brooke's editorship of the periodical was her first conspicuous literary activity. In contrast, Charlotte Lennox (like Haywood) turned her talents to the genre when she was already established as a novelist. Her *Lady's Monthly Museum* (1760–1) was an innovative attempt to break into the market through a type of essay-miscellany. It included a long series of articles on women's education and, following in the footsteps of Addison and Steele, she sought to improve her readers' understanding through informative pieces. This was in addition to a substantial amount of original and translated prose fiction.

Haywood, Brooke, and Lennox catered largely to the interests of the daughters of the middle and upper ranks, but, towards the end of the century, another writer entered this market who steered women's journalism onto a significantly new course. Like Manley's political journalism, Sarah Trimmer's *Family Magazine* (1788–9) had strong thematic links with the fiction she published in book form. Her magazine was written with the same high moral intention to counteract the contagion of atheism threatened in the circulation of irreligious books amongst children and the poor. It was not an immediate publishing success but the venture initiated a major new trend in British magazines which was to become hugely popular during the nineteenth century. Indeed, Trimmer continued to pursue the objective herself in her later periodical *The Guardian of Education* (1802).[14]

These women were largely responsible for the entire issue of their respective publications. On a less ambitious scale, numerous other female writers contributed material to periodical miscellanies, and not solely to those designed for female readers. After 1731, Edward Cave's *Gentleman's Magazine* gave many women the opportunity to publish their poetry and short prose items: Jane Hughes contributed verses regularly under the pseudonym 'Mellisa' in an effort to support herself and her two children after her husband's death; Elizabeth Carter's earliest compositions appeared in the magazine; and late in their careers, the playwright Catharine Trotter and the novelist Jane West published in the periodical; indeed, the latter contributed material for many years.

Elizabeth Griffith had a number of stories published in the *Westminster Magazine* (thirteen of which were published in 1780 in a collection of novelettes edited by Griffith), whilst the *Rambler* (1750–2) attracted material by Hannah More, Mrs Chapone, and Mrs Talbot. Elizabeth Hamilton published essays and poetry in the *Lounger*, Elizabeth Sophia Tomlins had material issued in various periodicals, and, appropriately, the children's author Lucy Peacock contributed stories to the *Juvenile Magazine*. The dramatist Hannah Cowley and the novelist Mary 'Perdita' Robinson frequently appeared in Bell's enormously successful *World, or Fashionable Gazette* (1787–94), both authors allegedly participating in the Della Cruscan literature with Cowley as 'Anna Matilda', and Robinson writing under various signatures.[15] Mary Wollstonecraft wrote frequently for Johnson's *Analytical Review* and, like Mary Hays and Fanny Burney, she contributed pieces to the *Monthly Review*.[16] According to Tompkins, the reviewers' pay 'was not high; two to two and a half guineas a sheet was the usual rate, and on this scale it would take a goodly batch of novels to fetch a crown' (1932 [1962]: 17). The fee for material was, to some extent, linked to the status of the writer, and well-known literary figures might elicit higher sums. For example, Inchbald received £50 for her first article for the *Edinburgh Review*, which was probably seen as an investment by the proprietor.

Whilst the growth of periodicals was undoubtedly a boon for professional writers, it is important to note that they did not have the field to themselves. As the century advanced, the desire to see their words in print inspired a growing band of enthusiastic amateurs. Their offerings of verses, biographical sketches, articles, reviews, recipes, and prose fiction were encouraged by fictitious editors (such as 'Sylvanus Urban' in the *Gentleman's Magazine*, or 'Mira' in the *Female Spectator*) who replied to correspondents and contributors. Towards the end of the century, this 'new-type amateurism' (Mayo 1962: 320) undermined the standards of some miscellanies and encouraged the proprietors' belief that they could fill their pages successfully with gratuitous contributions. The potential of this competition to undermine the earning power of the professional is illustrated by the attitude of the *Lady's Magazine* ('the very seat of the new amateurism' (ibid.: 317)) towards Clara Reeve. Mayo has described how, through its pages, the magazine invited Reeve to submit for publication any piece she chose but it failed to elicit a response despite persistent public reminders. He suggests that Reeve intended to engage in a professional transaction with the periodical until she realized that she, 'an author of reputation', was being asked 'to write *gratis* for a very lucrative publishing enterprise that had only recently been boasting of its "uncommon, rapid, and increasing sale" ' (ibid.: 316).

Didactic material and the children's market

As was discussed in chapter 3, the evolution of women's perception of their responsibility to guide society on moral and social issues was facilitated by the development of prose fiction, which offered a new outlet and an imaginative dimension to that undertaking. A number of the writers listed in Appendix A were well known amongst their contemporaries for the didactic nature of their fiction, and for a substantial amount of instructional and religious non-fictive prose which, in some cases, constituted the major part of their literary canon.

Early in the eighteenth century, Elizabeth Singer Rowe's exemplary reputation was based largely upon her highly successful *Friendship in Death*, but she also wrote various sacred and meditative pieces including *Devout Exercises* (1738), which was reprinted until the mid-nineteenth century. The prolific writer Hannah More utilized almost all the available genres. She wrote successful plays and poetry prior to the death of her friend and mentor Garrick, and thereafter sermons, anti-slavery pamphlets, *Cheap*

Repository Tracts (1795–8) (similar in intention to Trimmer's *Family Magazine*), annotated paraphrases of the Scriptures, *Sacred Dramas* (1782), and pamphlets on the manners and religion appropriate to 'polite society', 'the Middle Ranks', and 'The Common People'. Similarly, Sarah Trimmer's *Exemplary Tales* were part of a range of material that included *The Oeconomy of Charity* (eventually a standard guide to the management of Sunday Schools), and abridgements of the Old and New Testaments. After 1793, the latter were placed on the lists of the Society for Promoting Christian Knowledge, which continued to issue them for over seventy years, reputedly selling 250,000 copies.

Trimmer was first inspired to venture into print by Anna Laetitia Barbauld's *Early Lessons for Children* (1778), which had encouraged her to publish the first of several works of children's literature. Barbauld herself issued a wide range of material including a popular Gothic prose fragment, poetry, sermons, polemical pamphlets (against slavery and the oppression of Dissenters), and she was well known to her contemporaries as the author of books of lessons and hymns for children. The market for this material expanded significantly during the eighteenth century under the entrepreneurial influence of such publishers as J. Marshall and J. Newbery, both of whom specialized in the field. Women writers were outstanding contributors to the range of publications that became available, from educational theory (such as Maria Edgeworth's *Practical Education* (1798), written with her father), through numerous collections of instructive and entertaining stories, to school texts like Isabella Kelly's *The Child's French Grammar* (1805).

A number of writers developed their literary careers within this market. Dorothy Kilner (an acquaintance of Trimmer) and her sister-in-law Mary Ann Kilner wrote at least eighteen and six such works respectively, and it has been suggested that their publisher, Marshall, may have 'sought them out' as potential authors (MacDonald in Todd 1987: 185). A number of other women, including Elizabeth Pinchard, Mary Collyer, Elizabeth Helme, Mrs Ives Hurry, and Mary Wollstonecraft, wrote didactic juvenile fiction ranging from instructive fables and anecdotes, to Sarah Fielding's full-length novel *The Governess: or Little Female Academy* with its pioneering concentration upon a female readership. Fielding's design 'to cultivate an early Inclination to Benevolence, and a Love of Virtue, in the Minds of young Women' (1749 [1987]: xi), was customary amongst writers in this field, although there were a few who extended the boundaries of instruction into less orthodox regions. Priscilla Wakefield, for example, published several juvenile travelogues and introductory texts on natural history.[17]

Didacticism was clearly a motive behind these publications, but it is worth noting that most of the novelists (listed in Appendix A) who wrote this type of material were 'dependent professionals' at some stage during their careers. If these writers had profit in mind, their experience of teaching (Palmer and

Mathews) and of rearing children in their own families (Edgeworth, Trimmer, and Bonhote) gave them the advantage of a first-hand understanding of the consumers' requirements. The potential of didacticism to offer opportunities for money making is illuminated by the career of Hannah Robertson. During a lifetime fraught with disaster and financial difficulty, Robertson published two extremely successful instructive domestic works for 'young ladies' which drew upon and complemented the skills she had developed as a teacher of such subjects in Edinburgh.[18]

Women's poetry

By comparison with didacticism and journalism, which were both nascent areas of women's writing, poetry was well established in the repertoire of literary women by the dawning of the Augustan Age. Earlier female poets had come primarily from amongst the aristocracy and this social elite continued to nurture such skilful writers as Lady Winchilsea and Lady Mary Wortley Montagu. However, the growth of educational opportunities for middle-class children, and the contemporaneous expansion of the book trades, encouraged a major broadening of the base of authorship during the 1700s. Not only could more women write poetry, they could also publish their verses more easily.

In his introduction to *Eighteenth-Century Women Poets*, Roger Lonsdale has charted the considerable development of women's poetry during this period, pointing out that 'In the first decade of the eighteenth century two women published collections of their verse. In the 1790s more than thirty did so' (1989: xxi). The richness of his anthology is a welcome revelation of the better-quality material hidden in the titles recorded in the magazines, circulating library catalogues, and publishers' lists of the period. He is right, therefore, to argue that 'Condescension to "magazine" verse in the eighteenth century is unjustified' (ibid.: xxvi). Equally, however, the willingness of these periodicals to accept amateur material, the advent of subscription, and the growth of provincial presses, encouraged many far less skilful versifiers into print. The quality of such effusions is not of interest to this study but the fact that they reflect an ease of access to print most certainly is. A slim volume of *Original Poems on various subjects by a young lady eighteen years of age* (1772) published by subscription, or verses printed in the *Lady's Monthly Museum*, could constitute the initial tentative steps towards a longer career in authorship. It is worth noting in this context that Charlotte Smith first ventured into print when she was only fourteen by sending her poetry to the *Lady's Magazine*.

As we have seen in relation to Yearsley, writing poetry could also be lucrative. Hannah More, for example, received forty guineas from Cadell for her poem *Sir Eldred of the Bower and The Bleeding Rock* (1776). The unfortunate Elizabeth Thomas, who became notorious as Curll's 'Corinna' after Pope's reprisal in *The Dunciad*, first published her *Poems* in 1722 in an effort to avoid destitution; and Anna Williams, a close friend of Dr Johnson, supported herself after the death of her father through a precarious mixture of needlework and translation, until a subscription edition of her *Miscellanies in Prose and Verse* (1766) generated sufficient funds for her to survive with supplements from benevolent friends.[19] Occasionally a 'natural' poet like Yearsley was discovered and their work taken up by 'persons of quality' through subscription. Mary Leapor, a gardener's daughter from Brackley, achieved a similar level of national fame when her *Poems upon Several Occasions* (1748) was published posthumously for the benefit of her father. The work attracted approximately 600 subscribers, largely as a result of the efforts of Bridget Freemantle, daughter of the former Rector of Hinton. Leapor was later praised in *The Feminiad* (1754), and her work attracted the active interest of Richardson, who printed a second volume in 1751.

Approximately half the fifty authors in the *DNB* sample published verse, either in anthologies including material by others or in their own collections, and many of the 'dependent professionals' identified in this study used the genre. Some women novelists, including Mary Heron, Charlotte Lennox (under her maiden name of Ramsay), Harriet Chilcot, and Charlotte Smith, entered the market as poets rather than as novelists, and for a few, like Ann Yearsley, this medium was more important to their careers than prose fiction.

Translations

The inclusion of foreign languages, particularly French and Italian, in the education offered to children from the middle stratum upwards, contributed to the continuing popularity of translations amongst the reading public. As Elizabeth Griffith complained to her future husband, this was becoming a very congested market for the professional to negotiate:

> I am no Translator, by Profession. – It was by mere Accident I happened to fall into an Essay of this Kind. . . .
>
> The Success of that Work, notwithstanding a *Folio* or *Press Errata* to a *Duodecimo*, did, I own, encourage me to undertake some other Work of the same Kind, but before I could get the French Books from England, I read Advertisements of them in the London Papers, notifying their being then *under Translation, by an able Hand*, for P. Vaillant, or T. Becket, and P.A. de Hondt, or some other *Traducer* of the French Language, . . .
>
> A Gentleman told me, that in some of the blind Alleys of the City of London, he has seen such Labels as this stuck up. – *Here lives A.B. Scrivener, and Translator from the foreign Languages*. These Hackneys are paid so much *per Sheet* for translating Poems, Plays, or *Modeles des Conversations*, as they are for copying out *Bills* or *Actions* in

Chancery. – What horrid Stuff must they give us! And yet there is no helping one's self; for should any Person be every Way capable of executing such a Work to Advantage, he would never be able to sell off the smallest Impression of it. – The Book has been in every one's Hand's already, and there are but few People nice enough to go to the Expence of a good Edition, after having paid for a bad one.

(1786: vol. 4, 28–30)

Despite the competition, Griffith eventually produced eight translations, Eliza Haywood is credited with seven, and Elizabeth Gunning with four. In fact, twenty of the novelists in the *DNB* published translations, mostly of French prose. Less typical were those by Ellis Cornelia Knight, Mary Collyer, and Mary Wollstonecraft, who worked from German originals; Sarah Fielding, who accomplished a highly regarded translation of *Xenophon's Memoirs of Socrates* (1762);[20] and Griffith, Anna Plumptre (from German originals), and Elizabeth Inchbald, who translated and adapted material for the stage. There is evidence that, in some cases, payments could be high, witness the £200 reputedly received by Mary Berry (1763–1852) in the early nineteenth century for her four-volume annotated translation of Madame Deffand's correspondence with Walpole and Voltaire.

Women and the theatre

Although early women professionals wrote in a number of genres, drama played a dominant role in their output. Aphra Behn and Susanna Centlivre can best be described as dramatists, whilst Manley and Haywood, who concentrated successfully on prose, wrote at least four and three plays, respectively, and had their material produced on the London stage. The development of prose fiction through the 1700s affected the role played by the theatre in the careers of women writers and with notable swiftness novels assumed the prominent position held previously by drama. Thus, Fidelis Morgan, in her analysis of Restoration women playwrights, is broadly correct in her suggestion that Centlivre's death 'may be seen to close a chapter' (1981: xi). But this conclusion does not complete the story. Women continued to write for the theatre throughout the eighteenth century, and, as Hannah Cowley's career demonstrates, it was still possible for a female professional to work almost exclusively in this medium.

Twenty-four of the eighteenth-century women novelists in the *DNB* wrote plays that were both produced and published, and in some cases these were perhaps their most important literary achievements. Sophia Lee's *The Chapter of Accidents* was performed many times during the eighteenth century at the Haymarket, Covent Garden, and Drury Lane theatres, and after publication it reached a second edition in a year, and was translated into French and German. Similarly, Frances Brooke's musical entertainment

123

Rosina (1783) reached an eleventh edition in three years (passing through a number of versions in the nineteenth century), whilst *Marian*, produced at Covent Garden in 1788, was still being performed into the early 1800s. Elizabeth Griffith was equally alert to the potential for profit and after a successful run of twelve consecutive nights at Covent Garden for her comedy *A Double Mistake* (1766), she wrote to Garrick introducing herself and requesting employment. She persisted in these approaches for several years and her efforts were eventually rewarded by the occasional commission; for example, Garrick paid her to translate Beaumarchais's *Eugénie*, which he produced successfully at Drury Lane as *The School for Rakes* (1769) and which later went through several printed editions.[21]

Griffith's difficulties in obtaining Garrick's approval were shared by Marishall, who sent him her comedy 'Sir Harry Gaylove', hoping to secure a performance. He returned it unread, saying that 'he had more new ones in his hand than he could possibly bring on the stage for a number of years' (1789: vol. 2, 237). Approaches to Mr Dagg (patentee for the Covent Garden Theatre), Mr Colman (recently moved to Covent Garden Theatre), Mr Foote (Edinburgh Theatre), and again to Garrick, were ineffectual, despite the recommendations she had obtained from two peers. When her persistence continued unrewarded, she decided to publish the play by subscription on the advice of a friend, who immediately secured 100 subscribers. Another acquaintance found her a further 300 and so the project was salvaged.

Marishall's experience conveys something of the difficulties involved in moving between genres, and particularly in trying to enter a highly competitive world like the theatre, where the good opinion of influential individuals like Garrick was still critical. Even those who were known already in these circles could encounter problems in transferring their efforts from one medium to another. Elizabeth Inchbald had a long career in the theatre as an actress. She became a close friend of Mrs Siddons and whilst touring the northern theatres she met Tate Wilkinson, whose company she joined after many applications. Following the death of her husband and the completion of the novel *A Simple Story* (finished in 1779 but not published until 1791), she obtained an engagement at Covent Garden and left the York Company in 1780. Eventually her salary as an actress rose above £3 per week. Early in her impecunious married life Elizabeth settled on the idea of writing comedies to augment the family income, and whilst employed at Covent Garden she sent several of her manuscripts to the theatre's manager, and to Colman, then at the Haymarket. Neither was interested initially but in 1782 Harris gave her £20 on account for one offering. Thereafter, he accepted eleven of her plays and was persuaded to pay as much as £600 for a single work. In time, Colman responded favourably, producing six of her plays and paying a hundred guineas for *The Mogul Tale, or the Descent of the Balloon*, which was produced successfully at the Haymarket in 1784. During her career, Inchbald wrote twenty plays as well as editing three substantial theatrical series (including the twenty-five volume *The British Theatre* (1808)). Her accumulated earnings from these and other works produced an annual income of over £260.

Inchbald was not a typical professional since her considerable social and literary prestige allowed her to command consistently high sums for her work, as is evidenced by the £1,000 offered for her memoirs. Nevertheless, her earnings confirm that the theatre remained a potentially profitable forum for the talented woman writer.[22] Of equal importance is the fact that, as was demonstrated by Haywood, Griffith, and Inchbald, it offered a route into the market for those making their first steps towards a literary career.

The novel has been perceived as giving the 'vast body' of eighteenth-century women writers the 'confidence to make the plunge' (Tompkins 1932 [1962]: 119), and in terms of the number who published such material, this view would appear to be correct. Yet, there were significant numbers of women who entered the market through other media – most notably poetry. Approximately a third of the women who published novels during the second 'phase' identified in chapter 3 are recorded in the *DNB*. According to this source, the first publication of twenty-one of these forty-six writers was a novel, for thirteen it was poetry, for three a play, for two journalism, and for seven a miscellaneous or didactic piece. Twenty of the forty-six are known to have written professionally and of these only seven began their literary careers by publishing a novel.

The sample from the *DNB* is a crude measure, not least because this source does not aim to provide comprehensive bibliographical information. None the less, the results are noteworthy because they do not concur entirely with the prevailing assumption. Additionally, as we have seen, once professionals were involved in the market they did not rely solely on the novel. Instead, they often ranged through several genres in order to sustain their careers. A number attempted the gamut of forms available to them and several achieved their greatest literary and commercial successes in these other fields. Indeed, we know of a number of women writers, like Elizabeth Raffald and Hannah Cowley, who attained, or partly attained, financial security without apparently ever publishing a novel.

A varied output from professional novelists is only to be expected since writing was a difficult, unpredictable, and, for the majority, not especially lucrative occupation. Competition between novelists intensified towards the end of the century and, according to the reviewers, publishers had a plethora of cheap manuscripts to choose from. Those female authors – amateur and professional – who looked to other material found their alternatives were improving. Although the eighteenth century was an early phase in the growth of women's participation in the literature market, the range of their publications was extensive. To appreciate the scope of their work we have only to think of the provincial poets whose material was issued through subscription; of women who submitted their correspondence, biographical portraits, reviews, social commentaries, and verses to magazines; the writers of polemical and reflective religious pieces and of controversial items on social issues; translators; and authors of travelogues, treatises on education, histories, and of books offering mixtures of prose and verse, recipes, and advice on childrearing, housewifery, and midwifery. Viewed in this context, the growth of prose fiction by female authors can be seen as a major part of both a broader expansion in women's publications and a concomitant spread of their literary professionalism. The critical role played by fiction in stimulating the greater involvement of women in our print culture will be examined further in the final chapter, when we consider more closely the composition of the readership.

7

ACCESS TO WOMEN'S FICTION

Never, surely, was there an age in which novels were more generally read than the present. New ones of every description, good, bad, or indifferent, are daily presented to the public; therefore, certainly, there must be some likely to please even the most fastidious readers; and I own, as I think no author ought to lose sight of the moral such works are required to inculcate, I consider the lecture of them as a very innocent, if not a very profitable recreation. The best of people have their moments of *ennui*, and if they can beguile a leisure hour by sympathising in the sorrows or pleasures of some imaginary hero or heroine, who can blame them for having recourse to a Circulating Library, from whence they may now select either the marvellous romance, teeming with ghosts and spectres, or the satyrical adventures of a political Quixote, replete with wit and judgment, or else the more simple narrations founded upon events within the bounds of probability, romantic love tales being very generally discountenanced.

(Meeke 1802)

The reception given to women's fiction changed during the eighteenth century as the public persona of female writers altered, and as their literary status was influenced by both the highly regarded work of writers like Fielding, Lennox, Burney, Reeve, Smith, and Radcliffe, and by the success of popular 'Minerva' authors. Women were amongst the most respected of contemporary novelists, and engaged in the new commercially driven 'manufacture' of words.

A critical factor underpinning the character of the response was a growing awareness amongst the reading public of the prevalence of the 'Fair Authoress'. This was signalled by Samuel Johnson, whose own contact with female professionals must have strengthened his conviction that the woman writer was no longer an isolated, 'eccentric being . . . rather to be gazed at with wonder, than countenanced by imitation'. On the contrary, 'the revolution of the years has now produced a generation of Amazons of the pen, who . . . have set masculine tyranny at defiance' (*Adventurer* 11 December

1753, in Johnson 1907: 252). Ballard's *Memoirs of Several Ladies of Great Britain who have been Celebrated for their Writings* (1752), Duncombe's *The Feminiad* (1754), *Poems by Eminent Ladies* (1755), and Mary Scott's *The Female Advocate; a Poem Occasioned by reading Mr. Duncombe's Feminead* (1774), did much to confirm a growing sense of a female literary lineage stretching from Katherine Philips and Aphra Behn in the seventeenth century through to the late 1700s and Hannah More and Elizabeth Inchbald.[1] These women were upheld 'not only [as] an honour to their sex, but to their native country' (*Poems by Eminent Ladies* 1755: vol. 1, i), and as being highly regarded by their male literary contemporaries.

The roll of honour consisted mainly of poets, and therefore it is interesting to note that a reviewer of Scott's *Female Advocate* argued that her throng of female geniuses (which embraced More, Barber, Fielding, Lennox, Brooke, and Aikin) might be extended to include 'a namesake of her own, and the sister of Mrs Montagu (Mrs Scott), the author of Millenium Hall, the History of Sir George Ellison, and the Life of Theodore Agrippa d'Aubigné' (*Gentleman's Magazine* 1774: vol. 44, 376). Novelists, it seems, were eligible for inclusion, despite the comparatively low cultural status of the genre.

Public awareness of the emergence of women writers was heightened by the booksellers themselves, who, for less disinterested reasons, took care to familiarize the reading public with the names of certain authors. From the early years of the century, when Curll was promoting works by Barker, Hearne, Butler, and Manley, to Lane's exceptional interest in the late 1700s, publishers issued catalogues and prospectuses in which certain female writers were cited regularly, along with the titles of their novels. Proprietors of ciculating libraries, including a number of publishers, produced catalogues in which these names occurred frequently. It was common practice for newspapers to be used to advertise newly published material by such authors, and for booksellers to list earlier works on the title pages of their latest novels.

Furthermore, Robert Mayo (1962) has noted that by the late eighteenth century, miscellanies carried hundreds of biographical sketches of novelists, including women writers, some of which were reprinted 'many times'. These occurred throughout the magazine market as these authors became figures of popular interest, but 'women's magazines in particular liked to dwell upon the lives of the female novelists from Aphra Behn to Mrs. Robinson' (ibid.: 268–9). These appreciative portraits were supplemented by reviews, bibliographical information, and even guidance for future reading. Under the *Lady's Monthly Museum*'s 'Review of Female Literature', for example, readers were recommended to select from a range of material that would 'instruct, improve, or amuse . . . female readers' (1798: vol. 1, 62); the periodical included women's fiction and children's books in its lists. In total, this type of promotion was intended (and could hardly fail) to draw consistent attention to the successful involvement of women writers in the fiction market.

That women were inspired by the work of other female writers is suggested by the cross-referencing that occurred throughout the period. For example, like Astell nearly forty years before her, Trotter invoked the achievements of Dacier in her poetical plea for the better treatment of women writers (*Gentleman's Magazine* 1737: vol. 7, 308), whilst Elizabeth Thomas wrote panegyric verses to both Chudleigh and Astell (1722: 145–50, 150–1, 218–19), celebrating their demonstration of female excellence. Women authors were also aware of the commercial appeal of some of their contemporaries, witness Hearne's dedication of *The Lover's Week* (1718) to her friend Manley, and the inclusion of an extract from the fashionable *Atlantis* on the title-page of Boyd's *The Happy-Unfortunate*.[2] This awareness was aided by the contacts that were established amongst them, and without having to delve too deeply, we can uncover many intersecting acquaintances and friendships. For example, Fielding knew Scott, Carter, Jane and Margaret Collier, and Sheridan; the latter was also acquainted with Catherine Macaulay. Amelia Opie knew Inchbald and had great admiration for Wollstonecraft, with whom she corresponded. Wollstonecraft's extensive contacts included Helen Maria Williams and Mary Hays and, initially, Sarah Trimmer and Anna Laetitia Barbauld (née Aikin). The latter had many literary friends including Elizabeth Montagu, Hester Chapone, Hannah More, and later Joanna Baillie, and, as we have seen, her work inspired Trimmer, who was herself a correspondent of More and Elizabeth Carter. Helen Maria Williams was surrounded at first by an extensive London acquaintance that included Fanny Burney and Elizabeth Montagu, and she corresponded regularly with Anna Seward. Williams's later Jacobinical sympathies alienated her early admirers (who did not include Burney) and led to her contact with like-minded writers such as Wollstonecraft and Anna Plumptre.

Although female authors throughout this period applauded the achievements of individual women and of their sex in general, as we have seen in chapter 3, awareness of the work of others did not necessarily create a sense of common cause, or approval. Indeed, at times during the century, literary women were harshly critical of work by other writers of their sex.[3] Wollstonecraft's description, noted earlier, of the corrupting effects of the popular novel (citing, as an example, the work of Mrs H. Cartwright)[4] was matched in its sincerity by More's condemnation of the current generation of female writers whose revival of the centuries-old challenge to the status of women had brought forward 'political as well as intellectual pretensions', rekindling a 'presumptious vanity' and 'impious discontent' amongst their sex (1799: vol. 2, 20).

THE READERSHIP FOR WOMEN'S FICTION

The gender base

The criticisms from both Wollstonecraft and More were actuated by strongly held moral beliefs rather than discomfort with the notion of women authors *per se*. This was not always the case and the occurrence of less high-minded hostility amongst women readers was satirized in Esther Lewis's poem 'A Mirror *for* Detractors. Addres'd to a Friend', in which her 'tattling' women accused a 'witty rhiming creature' of, amongst other things, dull-ness, plagiarism, vanity and immodesty (in Bowden 1754: 327, 329). Such unsympathetic responses were noted with regret; as Centlivre observed, 'even my own Sex, which should assist our Prerogative against such Detractors, are often backward to encourage a Female Pen' (1707: 3).

The conversion of both sexes to an acceptance, even approval, of female authors, which was a prerequisite for women's greater participation in the literature market, was indeed carried forward during the eighteenth century. This was achieved through the promotional activities of the book trades, by the advocacy of the writers themselves, and by a number of important changes in the literature market which extended women's access to litera-ture, increasing their familiarity with the work of past and current female writers. The effectiveness of these various factors is suggested by the number of women who subscribed to publications written by members of their own sex, and by the fact that during the eighteenth century women's novels were associated in the minds of their contemporaries with a primarily female readership. This predilection has been viewed by literary historians as part of a general rise in women's demand for fiction which eventually dominated the market by the end of the century.

Contemporary comment tends to support this view. There are many criticisms of the supposedly corrupting and enervating effects of the novel upon young women, who were depicted, often satirically, but at times with great concern, as voracious and susceptible consumers. According to Fénelon (Archbishop of Cambray), in his *Treatise on the Education of Daughters*, 'There is scarcely a young girl who has not read with eagerness a great number of idle romances, and puerile tales, sufficient to corrupt her imagination and cloud her understanding' (1760: vol. 1, 13). In addition, the preoccupation of many female novelists with the responsibilities, aspira-tions, and mistakes of their sex in courtship and marriage indicates that they had women readers in mind, and occasionally an author referred explicitly to this audience. In the Preface to *Evelina*, Fanny Burney criticized those novels that spread a 'distemper' amongst 'our young ladies in general, and boarding-school damsels in particular', and she aligned her work with 'attempts to contribute to the number of those which may be read, if not with advantage, at least without injury' (1778 [1909]: 7–8).

Whilst this interpretation of the demand for women's novels is probably correct, as a generalization it obscures interesting detail about the readership, including the possible extent of male interest in this material. The strong association, particularly of the later novel, with women authors and readers (which must have encouraged greater female participation), coupled with a critical response to their work that was at times either derogatory or excessively tolerant, probably dissuaded men from admitting that they read these books, but not necessarily from actually doing so. Jane Austen humorously suggested as much in *Northanger Abbey*, her satire upon the conventions of 'horrid' Gothic fiction. In response to Catherine Morland's conviction that 'young men despised novels amazingly', her hero, Henry Tilney, replied:

> It is *amazingly*; it may well suggest *amazement* if they do – for they read nearly as many as women. I myself have read hundreds and hundreds. Do not imagine that you can cope with me in a knowledge of Julias and Louisas.
>
> (1818 [1906]: 86)

Although the impact of the conversation is clearly enhanced by hyperbole, Austen's basic proposition is supported by other evidence. James Boswell recorded in his *London Journal* how Noble sent him 'from time to time a fresh supply of novels from his circulating library, so that [he was] . . . very well provided with entertainment' (1950: 187). In the nineteenth century, Leigh Hunt (editor of the *Examiner*) described in his autobiography how in his youth he had subscribed to Lane's library and had

> Continued to be such a glutton of novels ever since, that, . . . I can read their three-volume enormities to this day without skipping a syllable; . . . I think the authors wonderfully clever people, particularly those who write most; and I should like the most contemptuous of their critics to try their hands at doing something half as engaging.
>
> (1891: 127)

However, not all contemporaries were as sanguine about novel reading amongst young people. According to one correpondent of 'Sylvanus Urban': 'It must be a matter of real concern to all considerate minds, to see the youth of both sexes passing so large a part of their time in reading that deluge of familiar romances' (*Gentleman's Magazine* 1767: vol. 37, 580).

It is worth stressing in this context that only some novels by women were consigned to join 'the many trifling, the many wretched productions' that allegedly came before the disappointed reviewers.[5] Writing for profit or under difficult circumstances did not necessarily lead to poor material, and authors as hard-pressed as Fielding, Sheridan, and Smith produced novels that were upheld as fine examples of the craft. For example, in the opinion of *The Critical Review*:

If a copy drawn with the most exquisite skill, and heightened with the nicest touches of art, can be allowed merit equal to a justly admired original, the Memoirs of Miss Bidulph may deservedly claim a place in our esteem with the histories of Clarissa and Sir Charles Grandison.

(1761: vol. 11, 186)

In a review of *The Old Manor House*, the *Analytical Review* allowed Charlotte Smith, 'the ingenious author . . . to whom the public has been indebted for some other similar productions, great credit for her talents as a novelist' (1793: vol. 16, 61), and the *Monthly Review*, in its coverage of *The Mysteries of Udolpho*, ranked Mrs Radcliffe's romances 'highly in the scale of literary excellence' (1794: vol. 15, 278). The eulogistic response of London's literary circles to Burney's *Evelina* is well known, as is Richardson's highly favourable opinion of Sarah Fielding's *David Simple*.[6] Her brother Henry was similarly impressed by 'the inimitable author [Lennox] of the *Female Quixote*' (1755, in H. Fielding 1907: 23), which had earned a laudatory review from Johnson (author of the novel's dedication) in the *Gentleman's Magazine*:

Mr. Fielding, however emulous of Cervantes, and jealous of a rival, acknowledges, . . . that in many instances this copy excels the original; . . . he concludes his encomium on the work, by earnestly recommending it as a most extraordinary, and most excellent performance.

(1752: vol. 22, 146)

Clearly, there need be no uncomfortable connotations associated with novels by these writers and we may reasonably assume that they were read widely by both sexes. The same may be argued for the 'philosopher' novelists of the late eighteenth century – Mary Wollstonecraft, Mary Hays, and Elizabeth Inchbald – who had an accessible market for their work amongst individuals and organizations sympathetic to English Jacobinism and the French Revolution. These connections extended beyond London through Inchbald's strong links amongst the Dissenting intelligentsia centred in Norwich. Delarivière Manley may be added to the list of writers whose appeal was not especially 'feminine' in character. Her politically partisan scandal chronicles gave her a wide potential readership amongst delighted Tories and disgruntled Whigs of both sexes. Furthermore, juxtaposing two profoundy different authors separated by almost a century and a spectrum of moral opinion, we can assume that Eliza Haywood's eroticism and Hannah More's didacticism appealed strongly to both sexes, as indeed they were intended to.

The role of circulating libraries

Contemporaries linked the expansion of the novel market with the development of circulating libraries. These were criticized for supplying fiction to unprecedented numbers of women and people from the poorer classes, particularly domestic servants. Traditionally, historians have endorsed this view, regarding women as important library users and arguing that novels, if not the bulk of the stock, were certainly the main attraction to these establishments. Therefore, these libraries are a key element in the existing historical schema which embraces, implicitly, the growing demand for women's fiction.

Between c.1740 and 1800 there were at least 112 circulating libraries in London and 268 in the provinces, distributed over thirty-seven counties.[7] Despite these numbers there is a paucity of reliable information about their stock and readership. The main sources are a relatively few catalogues which, fortunately, cover a wide geograpical area and various points in time throughout most of the eighteenth century. An examination of twelve of these catalogues was undertaken for this study. These cover every decade between 1740 and 1820, and various towns including Bath, Bristol, Oxford, Darlington, Stamford, Edinburgh, and London.[8] Admittedly, the sample is small and all the information relates to quite substantial enterprises whose stock does not necessarily reflect that of numerous smaller concerns which probably consisted of 'about an hundred volumes' on a shelf at the back of a shop (*Annual Register . . . for the year 1761* 1779: vol. 2, 207). Nevertheless, the catalogues are a fruitful source containing details of hundreds, and in some cases thousands, of books listed in broad subject categories, often with their retail prices. Thus, they offer a glimpse of the breadth and diversity of the eighteenth-century literature market, including obscure and ephemeral works, and they can provide price series for folio, duodecimo, quarto, and octavo publications, pamphlets, and periodicals.

Novels were the largest single category of books in most of the catalogues examined although the majority of the libraries offered their subscribers works on history, music, antiquities, gardening, philosophy, religion, science, 'Livres François', plays, and poetry, as well as pamphlets, periodicals, and newspapers.[9] Therefore, although it would appear that fiction was important to the success of these establishments, the catalogues do not support the contemporary contention that the libraries were merely purveyors of 'agreeable Nothings' (*Monthly Review* 1787: vol. 77, 162). Certainly, as commercial enterprises they had to gauge demand accurately in order to survive in a difficult market. The anonymous author of *The Use of Circulating Libraries Considered: with Instructions for Opening and Conducting A Library Either upon a large or small plan* was 'perfectly satisfied that not one Circulating Library in twenty' was, 'by its profits, enabled to give support to a family, or even pay for the trouble and expense of attending it'. Therefore, in cities 'Bookselling and stationery business[es] should always be annexed, and in country towns, . . . Haberdashery, Hosiery, Hats, Tea, Tobacco and Snuffs; or Perfumery and the sale of Patent Medicines' ([Anon] 1797: 35). In this context, the stocking of varied and at times recondite material suggests the existence of subscribers with eclectic literary tastes.

Unfortunately, it is impossible to verify the thrust of the contemporary complaint that the 'ever-green tree, of diabolical knowledge' (Sheridan 1775 [1975]: 21) circulated only fiction, since the evidence of withdrawals which might illuminate the question is entirely lacking. The manuscript listings of the borrowings from various library societies and book clubs provide the only related quantitative information and the reading vogues discernible from these records are of limited value in this context.[10] Therefore, without the requisite factual information we can refer only to the notable weight of the contemporary emphasis upon novels as the major attraction of these libraries. However, the presence of so much other material raises questions for those interested in the eighteenth-century literature market, some of which I shall touch upon later in relation to the demand for women's fiction.

The twelve catalogues consulted for this study list the titles and, in some cases, the retail prices and publication dates of their stock of novels. Occasionally, they include the names of well-known authors and a large number of female novelists are recorded in this way, including: Behn, Manley, Haywood, Fielding, Collier, Scott, Sheridan, Lennox, Rowe, the Minifies, Brooke, Griffith, Burney, Smith, Radcliffe, Bonhote, Inchbald, and Reeve. This has implications for our perception of the anonymity that surrounded women's publications, suggesting that not only were these women known to be writers, but that they had suffcent public status to make it advantageous for the proprietors to name them.

Catalogues by Bathoe (1757), Noble (1767), Frederick (1774), Bell (1778), and Palmer and Merrick (1789) include novels by all the better-known women authors and some by obscure novelists who have virtually disappeared from our literary histories, such as Jane Timbury, Anna Meades, and Dorothy Kilner. In particular, Lane's catalogue (1796–1802) (which naturally lists material by the numerous women who worked for his Minerva Press) itemizes over 250 women's novels. In total these few sources record works by virtually all the authors in Appendix A.

Circulating libraries were undoubtedly an important force behind the growing demand for women's fiction. They offered easily identifiable and well-distributed outlets for publishers and, according to the novelist Elizabeth Griffith, they accounted for 400 copies from a print run of 1,000 (1786: vol. 5, 15). For the reader, the libraries provided not only the stock available at their premises but also mail order services for rural subscribers: for example, Bell advertised that customers who were 'residing in the Country may be supplied with a larger Quantity of Books, on paying double Subscription, and defraying the Expense of Conveyance' (1778: A1). According to the publisher Lackington:

> I am informed that when circulating libraries were first opened, the
> booksellers were much alarmed, and their rapid increase added to their

fears, and led them to think that the sale of books would be much diminished by such libraries. But experience has proved that the sale of books, so far from being diminished by them, has been greatly promoted, as from those repositories, many thousand families have been cheaply supplied with books, by which the taste for reading has become much more general, and thousands of books are purchased every year, by such as have first borrowed them at those libraries, and after reading, approving of them become purchasers.

(1792: 388–9)

Lackington's suggestion of a high level of transference from the renting of literature to its purchase may well be optimistic, but his basic argument, that these libraries introduced new and poorer sections of the public to a taste for reading, is supported by the differential fee structures that were available. Amongst the twelve catalogues in the sample, the lowest annual subscription charge was 12s., and the highest was Lane's fee of three guineas. With the exception of Fancourt, who offered a flat rate of one guinea a year plus 1s. extra a quarter, the proprietors presented a tiered structure of quarterly (at about three shillings) and sometimes half-yearly and monthly rates which, in total, were usually slightly more expensive than the straight annual fee. It is typical of Lane that his system was the most complex. He offered various fees linked to the number of books the subscribers were entitled to borrow and dependent upon whether they lived in the town or the country. His lowest charges of 16s. per annum, 9s. per half-year, or 5s. per quarter, permitted the borrowing of two books at a time, and subscribers were allowed to change these once a day, 'and not oftener' (1796–1802: iii).[11]

Non-subscribers were catered for in these fee structures: Gray charged 1d. a night; Palmer and Merrick 3d. per duodecimo or octavo volume (per week) and 4d. for folio and quarto; and at Lane's library they were required to make a deposit and pay 'per Week for each Volume as under: for Folios 1s. – Quartos 6d. – Octavos 4d. – Duodecimos 3d. – Single Plays 2d. per day – New Quartos, and Books of the Value of One Guinea and upwards, One Shilling per Week' (ibid.: iii). On this basis (and bearing in mind that the rates of these more substantial enterprises may have been higher than those charged by smaller libraries), it seems probable that potential readers in the lower-middle and upper working classes could afford to use these facilities, albeit on an occasional nightly, monthly, or quarterly basis.

Extending access to literature was not the full extent of the libraries' contribution to the growth of women's reading and writing. In addition to large numbers of novels (including many by female authors), these establishments stocked substantial quantities of other types of women's material and, again, many of these works were recorded in the catalogues under the authors' names. Bathoe's (1757) comprehensive mixture of seventeenth- and eighteenth-century material is typical. It included: poetry and plays by the

Duchess of Newcastle, Aphra Behn, Susanna Centlivre, Mrs Leapor, Katherine Philips, Laetitia Pilkington, Charlotte Ramsay (later Mrs Lennox), Mrs Tollet, the Countess of Winchilsea, Elizabeth Rowe, and 'Eminent Ladies' (listing the poets in each volume); letters by several women; an autobiographical account by the Quakers Katharine Evans and Sarah Cheevers; Mary Astell's *Serious Proposal*, Mrs Jones's *Miscellanies in Prose and Verse*, and memoirs by eleven women. This list is not exhaustive and a similar range, with different authors and supplemented by works of literary criticism, scholarly translation, and topical essays, may be found in the catalogues of Gray, Bell, Palmer and Merrick, and Yearsley.[12] It is interesting to note that, although William Lane is normally associated solely with the novel, he actually stocked the largest selection of other material by women in this sample of libraries.

Taken as a whole, this evidence suggests that the rise of women's fiction was a key element within, and a main stimulus to, a wider cultural development involving a broader-based incursion of women's material into the literature market. Circulating libraries contributed to that development and to the gradual identification of a canon of female authors through their holdings and listings of women's novels, and through their presentation of a wide range of other material to their subscribers.

Our received impression of the clientele at these establishments is that it consisted mainly of women. Again, we are not able to substantiate the conventional wisdom because of the lack of objective evidence. We have only one known record of subscribers, the manuscript ledger of James Marshall, a leading bookseller of Bath, which details every subscriber to his circulating library from 1793 to 1799. Kaufman (1967b [1969]), in his study of the document, has calculated that in 1793 women comprised 35 per cent of the membership, and in subsequent years they constituted 30 per cent, 29 per cent, 30 per cent, 32 per cent, 22 per cent and 29 per cent.[13] Although this information is hardly conclusive, it shows that men were the main subscribers at an establishment in a fashionable spa town where one might expect to find an unusually high proportion of women with the leisure and education to read. Indeed, noting the association made by contemporaries between such resorts, the 'heedless fair, who trifle life away' (*Poems by Eminent Ladies* 1755: vol. 1, 45), and the circulating library, one could argue that these circumstances were particularly conducive to a high number of female subscribers.

This does not challenge the importance of these libraries to the development of both a female readership and a demand for women's material. It does, however, cast doubt over the assumed primacy of women in the demand for library fiction, particularly if we accept that the novel was the main attraction to these establishments. It suggests that the contemporary preoccupation with female readers should not be interpreted literally as describing a numerical dominance. Rather, it should be seen as an expression of an apprehensive and at times openly hostile reaction to substantial changes in female behaviour. It is arguable that libraries attracted criticism because increasing numbers of women (and members of the poorer classes) used them as a source of literature, some of which had the potential to fill young minds with romantic delusions, but some of which could, equally, reveal areas of knowledge and ideas that had previously been inaccessible. As contemporaries were well aware, the reading habit had the potential to subvert the status quo.

Additionally, subscription to libraries could be seen as a further sign of the excessive leisure and genteel aspirations of women who would, in the minds of some contemporaries, be employed better in domestic or commercial activity. Therefore, it can be argued that, as a measure of social change, the critical response to women's use of these institutions belongs as much to the concurrent debates about 'Female Learning' and leisure as it does to disapproval of the novel and the increasingly commercial and pedestrian standards it was felt to represent.

The expansion in women's reading: further evidence

The proposition that a growing demand for fiction was only a part (albeit a major one) of a wider and more complex expansion in women's reading is supported by a scattering of evidence from subscription libraries and book clubs. Such clubs flourished in London and throughout the provinces from the 1730s and they probably gave rise to subscription libraries; between them they introduced reading facilities into many rural areas.[14] They were concerned primarily with lending and promoting the discussion of serious and didactic literature and occasionally they extended the scope of their activities to include public meetings and debates; for example, the management committee of Hull Subscription Library (founded in 1775) was empowered to 'suspend circulation of such books as are found to have an immoral tendency after admission', and to let the library room for 'lectures on literary or philosophical subjects' (*Catalogue* 1805, as quoted by Munby in his 'Index of Circulating Libraries', n.d.).

These libraries and clubs held less light fiction than commercial establishments, and in some cases they were founded in opposition to this type of literature.[15] The Lewes Society, for example, was formed in 1786 when, 'disgusted at the usual trash of Circulating Libraries, some gentlemen inhabitants of Lewes, conceived the design of establishing a Library' (*The Lewes Library Society; A Poem* 1804: Preface, as quoted by Munby).[16] The small amount of fiction stocked by these institutions usually consisted of works written by the major male authors but occasionally they held material by such better-known female novelists as Fanny Burney, Elizabeth Hamilton, and Hannah More. This was in addition to their holdings of women's nonfiction.[17] Membership was often controlled by ballot and, whilst details

137

are rare, extant lists show a persistent, although not as yet numerous, female presence. Five of the fifty-one subscribers to the Stamford Subscription Library (1787) were women, and in about 1790, the Clavering Society for Reading decided to admit female members at half rates.[18] The Lewes Library Society was evidently eager to receive women, celebrating their presence in verse:

Th' aspiring train eleven females join,
And crown with beauty's rays the hallow'd shrine,
Enchanted science joys to Hail the dames
And lengthen'd catalogues receive their names.

The polish'd mind, and virtuous heart they prize
More than their auburn locks, or beaming eyes,
Dearer to them is held th' instructive page
Than all the modish follies of the age.
(*The Lewes Library Society; A Poem* 1804, as quoted by Munby)

From his examination of twenty catalogues, Kaufman was able to calculate the number of female subscribers to nine book clubs (1967a: 26–8). These were in Birmingham, Bristol, Colne, Hull, Kendall, Liverpool, London, Manchester, and Sheffield, where women constituted 7 per cent, 3 per cent, 9 per cent, 7.6 per cent, 25 per cent, 4.3 per cent, 8.3 per cent, 2 per cent, and 10.6 per cent of their total membership, respectively. He noted that the societies expanded in number and size through the century, adding that by the late 1700s the total membership in Liverpool had risen to 950, with 'many ladies among its proprietors', including a Miss Twentyman, whose name appears in the lists of proprietors for seventy-eight years (ibid.: 30).

It is increasingly evident that by presenting the demand for women's fiction only in terms of female readers who were interested solely in fiction and who obtained the bulk of their reading matter from circulating libraries, historians have offered a reductive view of what was a more complex and interesting state of affairs. Although female readers were probably the largest general source of demand for women's novels, these works were read and enjoyed by men, who did not necessarily restrict themselves to authors of repute. Male subscribers to circulating libraries had ample opportunities to read widely amongst the many types and grades of women's fiction on offer, and there is no evidence to suggest that they did not.

As for the female readers, an interest in fiction was undoubtedly a major force (perhaps *the* major force) behind the growth of women's reading during the eighteenth century, but it is incorrect to view their demand exclusively in terms of the novel. The varied stock of circulating libraries, the publication of serious texts designed for female readers (for example, Charlton's *Ladies Astronomy and Chronology*, and *Newton's Theory of*

Light and Colours made familiar to the Ladies, both of which were offered to Bathoe's readers), the early participation of women in book clubs and subscription libraries, and (as will be shown later) the presence of articles in women's magazines on subjects like philosophy, natural history, and anthropology, all suggest the concurrent development of a wider thirst for knowledge. This was perhaps penumbral to their demand for fiction, but important none the less. These aspects of women's reading were not entirely separate. Certain novelists, including Sarah Scott, Elizabeth Hamilton, and Mary Wollstonecraft, used the genre for serious intellectual purposes, whereas the cultured Lady Mary Wortley Montagu preceded Boswell and Leigh Hunt in her cheerful acknowledgement of a lively interest in literary 'Trash' and 'Trumpery' (Letter to Lady Bute, 22 September 1755, in Montagu 1967: 88).

The social distribution of demand

Whilst crediting the novel with the creation of a niche in the literature market for women readers, historians have viewed the genre as central to a general broadening of the social and economic base of reading during the eighteenth century. Unfortunately, verification of this development is problematic. Literacy statistics, based upon signatures in marriage registers and on marriage licences (the usual indices in these studies), are an unreliable gauge for anything other than the most basic skills, and however formulaic some novels may have been, they demanded more than elementary literacy from their readership.[19] Furthermore, whatever such statistics may tell us about the ability of certain parts of the population to read, they reveal nothing of the extent to which these skills were put into practice.

The reading habit was dependent upon a range of factors other than literacy, including the length of the working day, the cost and availability of printed material, and the perceived value of the activity, either as an occupational requirement, or as a means of enhancing the quality of life. Therefore, other forms of evidence, such as the availability of schooling, changes in the quantity and character of publications, mechanisms that facilitated the distribution of printed material, and trends in public ideology which might have affected attitudes towards reading, are critical to our interpretation of the eighteenth-century reading public. Allowing for significant regional and social variations (for example, between urban and rural areas), these factors point to a significant spread of the reading habit during the eighteenth century so that by the late 1700s 'far more people in England were reading printed pages' (Wiles 1968: 65).

That this growing appetite for printed material included a vigorous demand for fiction has been demonstrated recently by David Vincent in his discussion of 'Imagination' within popular culture 1750–1914 (1989: 198–210).

No other category of popular culture covered by this study was so easily and completely invaded by print. If newly educated readers made the slightest attempt to employ for their own benefit their uncertain skills it would be to glance at a broadside or some later form of cheap fiction, and if newly equipped printers wanted to enter the popular market, fantasy rather than fact offered the most certain return on their investment. From as early as the mid seventeenth century, when the warehouses of wholesale chapbook merchants could contain as many as ninety thousand items, the publishers of fiction for the common people had been pioneers in the mass production of standardised articles for large-scale distribution. . . .

(ibid.: 197)

James Lackington's contemporary depiction of 'tales and romances' being read by the children of the rural poor (1792: 387) was not entirely without foundation. From the middle of the eighteenth century, Vincent argues, 'printed verses and tales' were common household possessions (1989: 198), and the widely distributed chapbooks and broadsides fed a taste for sensation that delighted in descriptions of extraordinary, scandalous, heroic, and violent scenes. The critical question for this study is whether or not the labourer's interest in the chapbook translated into a demand for the new 'polite' fiction of the novel, and particularly those written by women.

Assuming the requisite skills, time, and inclination, novels became available to the readership in forms that were cheaper than the standard volume publication, and the cost of access to libraries could be highly flexible. Additionally, communities had other means of overcoming the expense of books, from 'informal contact between individuals known in the neighbourhood as "readers", who would pool their random collections of battered volumes, to the growth of more structured self-improvement societies' (Vincent 1989: 209).

Furthermore, the thematic preferences of the novel-reading public, although characterized as more genteel, were not entirely removed from those of chapbook readers, particularly by the late eighteenth century. As the reviewer of *Isabella, or the Rewards of Good Nature* remarked: 'Death! duels! adulteries! fornications! burning livers, and breaking hearts! what would the present race of novelists do without you, ye horrid train?' (*Monthly Review* 1776: vol. 55, 157). It is not surprising, therefore, that Robert Mayo (1962) has identified a transference, in the early 1800s, of this new fiction into the older idiom of the serialized chapbook. Specializing in sensationalized material, these publications drew heavily upon the popular Gothic romances of the late eighteenth century and inevitably those by Ann Radcliffe were chosen frequently for their purposes. Mayo's recognition of the major role that redactions of women's fiction played in this development underlines, almost in passing, the importance of eighteenth-century female novelists to the 'revolution in popular literature' (Vincent 1989: 202) that occurred in the first half of the nineteenth century. According to Mayo, the serialized chapbooks demonstrated

> How far, by 1802–1803, prose fiction was now embraced by readers in the lower levels of the reading public. The degree of literacy demanded by the *London Spy* of 1698–1700 and the *Marvellous Magazine* of 1802–1804 was roughly the same, but the intervening one hundred years had seen a revolution in popular taste as a result of which the common reader now frankly accepted prose fiction as a medium of popular entertainment, . . . 'Rinaldo' in 'The Midnight Assassin' was only Mrs. Radcliffe's Schedoni, thinly disguised, but in the history of British journalism he was really a creature of the new age, an age in which a large popular audience could now interest itself in sensational fiction divested of its genteel trappings.
>
> (1962: 368–9)

Ironically, whilst chapbook proprietors made free with women's novels, one female author deliberately moved into this market and succeeded in appropriating its readers for her own reforming purposes. As a preliminary step towards fulfilling her desire to provide the literate poor with '*safe* books' (Letter to Bishop of Bath and Wells 1801, in More 1925: 185), Hannah More investigated her potential market and discovered the popularity of 'vulgar and indecent penny books' (Letter to Zachary Macaulay 1795, in ibid.: 456). With typical professionalism, she recognized the benefits of adopting the basic characteristics of this material and the resulting *Cheap Repository Tracts* (1795–8) were the same size, style, and price as chapbooks, and even included the customary woodcuts. The project was a massive success and for a while More succeeded in turning this particular section of the fiction market upon its head. The high numbers of subscribers in the first year enabled her to sell the *Tracts* at below cost and by March 1796 over two million copies had been bought.

More was exceptional in targeting fiction at the rural and urban labouring classes and although other works by women probably passed within their reach, factors such as literacy, leisure time, lighting, heating, and cost, meant that the demand from this social stratum was marginal. There are reasons for arguing, however, that a significantly higher level of consumption was possible amongst more affluent members of the lower strata. The academies that became so plentiful in certain areas of the country in the second half of the eighteenth century (considered in chapter 4) offered greater opportunties for education not only to the children of the more affluent middle ranks, but also to the families of traders and skilled artisans who could afford the lower school fees (Plumb 1975: 64–95). These people had a higher occupational requirement for literacy, and educated children could be seen as a means of enhancing their social as well as economic status. Furthermore, the slow

141

permeation through the social structure of a regard for empirical knowledge, particularly amongst the trading and manufacturing class (Plumb 1971: 1–26), argues for their increasing acceptance of the value of reading. The pursuit of useful knowledge might be the stimulus for acquiring literacy or fostering it in others, but once gained, the skill could be directed elsewhere. In this context the availability of women's fiction through relatively cheap alternatives to volume publication becomes increasingly important.

Within the lower strata, domestic servants were associated relatively frequently with the demand for fiction. Recipe books, instructional handbooks, and fiction (notably Richardson's *Pamela*), suggest that service was identified by the book trades as a particularly literate occupation. This is suggested by the response of the resourceful publisher depicted in *The Parallel*, who advised: 'As for Servant Wenches, there are three or four of them in some Families, and do but consider how much better Chance a Book has they can read, than one that is only fit for their Mistresses, who seldom read at all' ([Anon] 1748: 6). Although this evidence is hardly objective, it is supported by the fact that servants were drawn from diverse rural and urban backgrounds, including the families of farmers, merchants, shopkeepers, impecunious clerics, and 'decayed' gentry, all of which were likely to have offered some elementary education. Additionally, there were schools in London that specialized in training the young as a preliminary for service (Hecht 1956: 17), and once in employment, there were opportunities for learning from higher servants, or through the agency of the mistress of the household. Servants were noted also for their tendency to imitate their employers' behaviour and, within the restrictions of their working conditions, 'It is equally certain that the reading habits of employers were taken over in the same way' (ibid.: 216).

It is impossible to measure accurately the involvement of any particular occupational group or social stratum in the demand for women's fiction. Interpreting the relationship between literacy and the practice of reading, and between publications and the character of demand, is a complex matter and particularly so in the context of the eighteenth century where the evidence is often indirect or subjective. None the less, it is reasonable to conclude that the readers of women's novels were drawn principally from amongst the ranks of the middle classes, stretching downwards to embrace more affluent artisans, traders, and servants, and upwards into the aristocracy. This was the readership projected by the authors and the reviewers alike, and which had the greatest possibility of possessing the necessary attributes. However, it is important to note also the role played by women's fiction in extending the demand for reading amongst the poorer reaches of the population through the appropriation of the more sensational aspects of their novels by chapbook proprietors, and through Hannah More's appropriation of the chapbook for her own didactic purposes.

Access to women's fiction in book form

The retail price of publications was clearly a critical determinant of the spread of the demand for women's fiction. Novels were sold to the public in book form usually either bound or sewn in octavo or duodecimo size, and throughout the century most works were issued in more than one volume. Overall, the majority of women's novels during the 1700s were issued in two parts, with more single-volume works in the early decades, and large multi-volume productions of up to five parts appearing more frequently towards the end of the century.

We can deduce the level of retail prices through the period by reference to William McBurney's *Check List* (1960), which covers the first four decades of the century and includes the prices and the number of pages for most entries; and from price series in circulating library catalogues printed in the second half of the century. Catalogues by Bathoe (1757), Noble (1767), Bell (1778), and Lane (1796–1802) each record more than five hundred novels along with their retail prices and number of volumes. This exercise is facilitated by the fact that variations in the price per volume within individual catalogues decreased notably during the second half of the century.

The information provided by McBurney suggests that in the first half of the century the majority of novels cost the purchaser either 1s. (primarily for octavo works of between fifty and a hundred pages), or 1s. 6d. (for both octavo and duodecimo works of above a hundred pages). However, there were considerable variations in price, ranging from 6d. to 4s., primarily reflecting the number of pages in the publication and whether it was in octavo or duodecimo form. The retail cost of women's novels accords with this overall picture. Prices are available for six (duodecimo) novels by Penelope Aubin, five of which cost 1s. 6d. and one cost 2s.; and for thirty-one (predominantly octavo) novels by Eliza Haywood, of which eleven cost 1s., four cost 1s. 6d., and the remainder were between 6d. and 4s. Similar prices were charged for novels by Mary Davys, Jane Barker, Sarah Butler, Lydia Grainger, and Mary Hearne.[20]

The circulating library catalogue entries suggest that during the second half of the century octavo was the favoured size for novels. With numerous prices available, it is possible to restrict a discussion of the cost of fiction (in book form) to this size of publication. Information from Bathoe's catalogue (1757) reveals a price rise by the mid-century; nearly half his stock cost 3s. per volume and the majority of the remainder was priced at either 2s. or 2s. 6d. Many of these works were multi-volume publications. Noble's catalogue (1767) demonstrates that the trend towards a standard price continued. Over 75 per cent of his stock of more than 700 octavo novels cost 3s. per volume and he included only five works at 1s. 6d., thirty-six at 2s., and twenty-two at 2s. 6d. A large proportion of the novels were two-volume publications, particularly those that were priced at 3s. per volume. A similar pattern is discernible amongst Bell's library stock recorded a decade later. By the end of the century, however, prices were rising rapidly. The earliest section of Lane's catalogue (1796) contains over 1,000 works, the majority of which were priced at 3s. per volume. Subsequent sections reveal an increase to 4s. by 1800. Additionally, although two-volume publications continued to predominate and comprised approximately 55 per cent of the initial 1,000 books, three-volume novels were becoming relatively common and there were a few four-, five- and six-volume works. Single-volume editions were recorded only occasionally and many of these were older publications.

J.M.S. Tompkins, noting the rise in the price of novels during the 1790s, suggests that 'costs increased, but books on the whole became more substantial. The little duodecimo or small octavo volumes are packed closer, and broad margins and wide spacing disappear' (1932 [1962]: 11). An increase in the cost of production would undoubtedly have affected the retail price of novels and may explain the increase through the century. Unfortunately, without elaboration (and Tompkins goes no further with her assertion), we can only speculate about which of the constituent costs was responsible: raw materials, fees paid to authors (which do not appear to have risen with equivalent rapidity), transport costs (which arguably should have been decreasing), or changes in technology and fiscal policy. However, the behaviour of novel prices parallels overall price trends for the century which (notwithstanding a notable rise in the cost of some commodities, like provisions, after 1760) remained broadly stable until the rapid inflation of the final decade. By comparison with basic goods, for which demand was inelastic, the rise in the price of novels was slight. This reflects the behaviour of prices for comparable commodities during this period:

> The further removed the commodity was from being a sheer necessity, the smaller the rate of increase. This meant that it was the poorest workers . . . who were hardest hit, but it also meant that the growing number of artisans and factory operatives whose earnings commanded something more than a bare subsistence were beginning to enjoy a range of comforts and luxuries hitherto unattainable.
>
> (Burnett 1969: 139)

The evidence that emerges from these catalogues suggests that women's novels were at least as expensive as those by men (including works by such authors as Richardson, Fielding, Smollett, and Sterne), and in some cases they cost significantly more than the norm. Fanny Burney's five-volume *Camilla* (1796: £1. 5s.) and Ann Radcliffe's four-volume *Mysteries of Udolpho* (1794: £1. 4s.) were both at least one shilling per volume dearer than the current average price. High prices (per volume) could indicate either an inelastic demand for the work of popular writers (which would apply to these two highly successful novelists), or it could be a sign of a segmented market. It is likely that better-quality, costly editions of particular novels were produced but, given the essentially ephemeral nature of the material, it seems probable that the demand for luxury editions was highly restricted. On the whole, it seems probable that high retail prices reflect the publishers' exploitation of a resilient interest in certain authors.

Regardless of the author or any other exceptional considerations, novels in book form were relatively expensive items. The cost of a mid-eighteenth-century volume was roughly equivalent to the prices we have for a whole pig (2s. 6d.), a bushel of flour (3s. 4d. to 4s.), or a pair of women's shoes (2s. 6d. to 3s.), and the later works by Burney and Radcliffe compare unfavourably with the price James Woodforde paid (in 1789) for a mahogany wash-stand (10s. 6d.), a wig from his barbers (£1. 1s.), or '4 handsome Glass Salt-Cellars cut Glass' (16s.).[21] Throughout most of the century even the most pedestrian offering (bought new) would probably cost the purchaser at least 6s., and in many cases 9s. or considerably more. With the possible exception of certain works by major authors, novels were not consumer durables to be bought and then reused over time by the purchaser (this clearly does not preclude works being passed on to other readers or buyers). For many consumers, the essence of the novel's attraction was its novelty and therefore one would expect to find that novel buyers characteristically made frequent rather than single or occasional purchases.

Frequent novel buying, for example once a month, was within the financial capacity of the landowning aristocracy, gentry, squires (even decayed squires), wealthier freeholders and large farmers, wealthier merchants, industrialists, shopkeepers, and members of the professions. All these groups might expect to receive at least £100 to £200 per annum, and in many cases substantially more. There were numerous groups within the lower-middle and upper working classes, such as poorer farmers, curates, schoolteachers, skilled artisans, and small masters, on incomes of around £50 per annum, for whom an occasional purchase was possible. Below this stratum, the incomes of semi-skilled and unskilled industrial and agricultural workers (although affected considerably by a number of variables including their geographical location and the size and earning potential of their families) could not accommodate the price of the average two-volume, 6s. work, even assuming that they had acquired the necessary literacy and inclination to buy.

The wages of domestic servants were also highly variable, ranging from an approximate minimum of £30 per annum for upper male servants, between £8 to £20 for lady's maids, housekeepers, and footmen (rising gradually through the century), to about five guineas for the lowest female employees.[22] These could be supplemented by small additional sums from various sources and, since their basic living costs were often covered as part of their conditions of service and their wages were paid throughout the year, domestic servants probably had the economic advantage over equivalently paid industrial workers. None the less, these income levels did not permit anything other than an occasional (new) novel purchase, and, if we are to believe contemporary comment, these would have to compete with clothing, theatres, pleasure gardens, servants' clubs, and parties.

It is worth noting that the propensity of these marginal groups to consume was increased by the availability of cheaper second-hand copies through bookshops and auctions. The latter had been popular since the late seventeenth century and according to John Lawler in his study of these sales:

> The method immediately commended itself to collectors and persons wishing to dispose of their libraries; and so from 1676 to 1700 upwards of a hundred auctions were held, which meant the disposal of some 350,000 works, realising a round sum of about £250,000. . . . Encouraged by their success in London, we soon see them spreading into the provinces. . . . Auctions of books were held in booths at country fairs.
>
> (1898: xvii)

This suggests that the circulation of women's fiction published in book form could have been far greater than the retail prices would lead us to expect. Well-thumbed, second-hand editions of popular favourites may indeed have found their way eventually into the dwellings of agricultural workers or artisans.

The role of ephemeral publications

Since Watt (1957) highlighted the discrepancy between the income levels of some of the new constituents of the novel-reading public (notably domestic servants) and the retail price of novels, historians have rightly identified the bridging role of circulating libraries. In the same year, R.M. Wiles exposed another inexpensive source of fiction that was probably available more easily to provincial readers. In his study of *Serial Publication in England Before 1750*, he argued that 'between 1710 and 1750 the proprietors of many English newspapers gave to their subscribers, either in instalments printed in the columns of the papers themselves, or as detachable supplements, a wide variety of "literary" works', including prose fiction (1957: 73). He focused particularly upon the growth of 'numbers', a method of publication which, he asserted, became increasingly common after 1725. Number books were issued in weekly or monthly parts wrapped in blue covers and priced at between a few pence and 1s. each, making this a relatively accessible means of spreading the cost of reading. The method became very popular. Editions could be as large as 2,000–3,000 copies, and the numbers issued grew rapidly during and after 1732 (ibid.: 5). By the mid-eighteenth century the numbers trade was well established, potentially very profitable, and many works issued in fascicules were owned jointly by the *Congers*, or on a share basis by temporary associations and partnerships.

Of direct significance to this study is the fact that Wiles's information shows that early fiction by women was published in all these forms. For example: an unacknowledged reprint of Haywood's *Fatal Secret* (1724) appeared in instalments in Heathcote's *Original London Post* in 1724, as did Mary Hearne's *The Lover's Week* (1718) and its sequel *The Female Deserters* (1719) (1957: 27–8). Other works by Haywood were issued in this fashion, including her first novel, *Love in Excess*, which was reprinted in the *Generous London Morning Advertiser* (1957: 43); and a 'fifth' edition of her translation of Madeline de Gomez's *La Belle Assemblée* which was reprinted serially in the *General London Evening Mercury* (1957: 42). Both Behn's *Love-letters* (1684) and Manley's *New Atlantis* (1709) were reissued in parts costing a few pence each. Women's non-fiction was also published in fascicules, including Elizabeth Blackwell's *Curious Herbal* (issued three times), Phillips's notorious *Apology* (1957: 305, 312, 326, and 355), and Charke's *Narrative* (1755). It is clear from the text that the latter was issued in this form with the author's permission, which, as Wiles suggests, seems less likely with Heathcote's earlier ventures. These involved altering the works and failing to acknowledge the authors, probably in an attempt to avoid copyright payments. In a subsequent study, Wiles (1968) maintained that 'for the second half of the eighteenth century the list [of titles] becomes much more extensive', and that the 'range of subject matter is as wide as one finds in books published in the regular way' (ibid.: 56–7).

The continued popularity of fascicules was part of a sustained expansion in the production of cheap literature that occurred during the eighteenth century. This development included also the emergence of the periodical press, which played a major role in the percolation of the reading habit through the social structure – the 'democratization' of reading (Shevelow 1989: 22) – and in the distribution of fiction to the poorer sections of the potential demand. Robert Mayo's 'Catalogue of Magazine Novels and Novelettes 1740–1815' (1962) includes 1,375 titles which, he claims, is less than a tenth of those available. Fiction published in this way was inexpensive, circulated widely, and evidently very popular: Mayo uncovered fictive pieces of some sort in 470 different periodicals published between 1740 and 1815:

> Some, it is true, published only an occasional story, or the summary of a new novel, but others devoted as much as one-half of their contents to fiction, at the same time they enjoyed circulations of anything from one hundred copies to fifteen thousand monthly. Much of this fiction was borrowed from books and other outside sources, but about half was original, and was never reprinted in volume form.
>
> (ibid. 2)

Mayo's research has exposed a substantial quantity of women's fiction that was issued through this medium. His 'Catalogue' contains at least sixty-eight fictive pieces by female authors for the period 1740 to 1796, each one consisting of a minimum of 5,000 words. Twenty-three of the writers concerned are amongst the novelists listed in Appendix A, and there are a further five women who apparently never published fiction in book form, at least under their own names: E. Caroline Litchfield, Charlotte King, Hester Mulso, Anne Blower, and Eleanor Tatlock.[23] We can add to this list Mrs B. Finch, who has been identified subsequently by Edward Pitcher (1976: 26).

Women's fiction offered in these periodicals took various forms: résumés of novels, sometimes several thousand words long, incorporated into reviews; abridgements, sometimes with direct quotation merged with the text; episodes extracted from novels and sketches taken from prose miscellanies which were presented as self-contained short stories, or cameos; unacknowledged reprints of extracts from the novels presented under different titles; and original fiction. The use of redactions and the desire to avoid copyright payments meant that the original writers often went unacknowledged but, none the less, thirty-seven of the sixty-eight pieces were attributed to their female authors when they first appeared, and in many cases when they were reproduced elsewhere.

Twenty of the pieces listed by Mayo do not appear in Appendix A. Of these, eight were by the 'new' authors cited above, and twelve were the productions of known novelists, most notably Eliza Haywood. Perhaps more suggestive of the as yet unknown reserves of women's fiction are Anna Maria Porter's two pieces: 'The Delusions of the Heart', published initially in the *Lady's Magazine* in 1795, in *The Hibernian Magazine* from December 1795 to January 1796,[24] and in the *Scots Magazine* a month later; and 'The Exile', which appeared in the *Lady's New and Elegant Pocket Magazine* in 1796. These are a significant addition to the one novel, published by subscription, by which she is represented in Appendix A.

Most notable amongst the seven authors who do not appear in Appendix A is Anne Blower. She published three pieces through periodicals: 'The Maid of Switzerland', which was issued from January to February in 1789 in the *General Magazine*, and subsequently in four other magazines; a substantial work of 8,000 words entitled 'Adelaide, or Filial Affection', which appeared from March to May, 1789, in the *General*, and over a decade later in the *Britannic Magazine* (1798); and 'Memoirs of Mrs. Herbert', which also made an initial appearance in the pages of the *General* (its 14,000 words were distributed between February and October, 1790), and only a month after the first part was issued, serialization had started in the *Hibernian Magazine* and the *Universal Magazine and Review*.

Reappearances of women's fiction, often in rapid succession, were not uncommon. Thirty-two of the sixty-eight pieces by women were printed in at least one other magazine, and in some cases this occurred several times. For example, acknowledged and pirated extracts from three of Charlotte Smith's novels and one of her translations were published as magazine pieces during this period. Of these, two were reissued by other periodicals, most notably 'The Affecting History of Caroline Montgomery' (a substantial, attributed passage from *Ethlinde*), which appeared in the *Universal Magazine* during December 1789, the same year that the complete novel was published in volume form. By December 1791 the extract had been reprinted by at least seven other periodicals under virtually the same title and the author had been credited in all cases.

By issuing women's fiction in serialized form proprietors hoped to exploit the popularity of certain authors or novels. Substantial abridgements of Frances Brooke's *The Excursion* appeared in 1777, the year in which it was published in volume form. The *Universal Magazine* and the *Hibernian Magazine* each carried large portions of the work in four parts, and in both cases Mrs Brooke was acknowledged along with citations of her earlier novels. Equally, this was a means of capitalizing upon the proven popularity of earlier writers. It is not surprising to find that Harrison's influential *Novelists Magazine*, which was a source of material for provincial miscellanies, reprinted two of Sarah Fielding's novels, two by Charlotte Lennox, three by Haywood, two by Sheridan, and Collyer's *Letters from Felicia to Charlotte*; and in all but two cases, the writers were named. The *Ladies Magazine* even offered Behn's *Oroonoko: or, The Royal Slave* (1688) in its entirety, entitled 'The History of the Royal Slave', as 'the first of a projected series of classics in the novel form' (Mayo 1962: 528). Women's non-fiction was also a fruitful source of derived material for the miscellany proprietors. The most outstanding example is Helen Maria Williams's *Letters Written in France, in the Summer of 1790* (1790) which, within slightly more than a year of appearing in volume form, had supplied eight periodicals with a substantial extract (10,000 words) reprinted under variations of the title 'History of Monsieur Du F———' (Mayo 1962: 521). Six of the magazines acknowledged Williams's authorship.[25]

Despite the public's obvious taste for tried and tested favourites, a number of the complete pieces of magazine fiction by better-known women authors were original. The major contributors were probably Eliza Haywood and Charlotte Lennox, both of whom were 'dependent professionals', and who, as part of the range of their material, actually initiated and edited the periodicals that contained their stories. Haywood's *Female Spectator* (1744–6) was allegedly written by a group of women including: Mira, who was 'married to a gentleman'; a 'widow of quality'; and Euphrosine, the 'Daughter of a wealthy Merchant'. These and any other contributors were to be regarded as 'only the several Members of one Body' of which Haywood was the 'Mouth' (1744: vol. 1, 7–8). These transient contributors were probably fictitious and perhaps a projection of her intended readership.

As was noted in chapter 3, although Haywood's expressed aims in the periodical were didactic, the style was frequently reminiscent of her earlier fiction, as we find in her exemplary story of the adulterous 'fair and talented Martesia' and her lover 'Clitander', who are introduced to the reader 'entertaining each other without witness' (ibid.: 17). Her enumeration of the dire consequences of such liaisons, and the topics raised in the magazine's correspondence column, led her into long animadversions on arranged marriages, excessive parental restraint, masquerades, pleasure gardens, and numerous other aspects of her main theme: the effects of love and the dangers attendant upon ignorance and too great a susceptibility to 'softer feelings'. Overall, the *Spectator* accounted for a substantial proportion of her output of fiction in the form of allegedly autobiographical anecdotes, illustrative stories, and a long, sustained prose piece, 'The Triumph of Fortitude and Patience over Barbarity and Deceit'. At least five of her stories were reissued by other periodicals.

Like the *Spectator*, Charlotte Lennox's *Lady's Monthly Museum* (1760–1) had a professedly didactic purpose, although of a rather different character. This essay-miscellany sought to educate the readers as well as entertain them in accordance with her wish 'to render the ladies though learned not pedantic, conversable rather than scientific'. She undertook to 'avoid entering into any of those minutiae, or diving into those depths of literature, which may make their study dry to themselves, or occasion its becoming tiresome to others' (1760: vol. 1, 130).[26] Despite these laudable objectives, the main feature of the *Museum* was her 'Story of Harriot and Sophia', a heavily didactic romance which is remarkable for being written specifically for the periodical, and for its extraordinary length. It was published in the first eleven issues in instalments of several thousand words each. This substantial piece was supplemented by an eight-part translation of Madame de Tencin's 'Count de Comminge'; the 'History of Bianca Capello' in three parts; and 'The Tale of Geneura' from Ariosto. The educative element of the periodical was clearly ameliorated by the generous helping of fiction, and as the project failed shortly after the end of her serialized novel, this was probably the key to its survival.

As we saw in chapter 6, the opportunities for publication offered by magazines extended to amateurs as well as professionals, which was a double-edged sword for women writers. On the one hand, magazines offered new writers a welcome opportunity to reach large audiences with their material and to test their publication prospects whilst, if they chose, retaining complete anonymity. For example, Mayo has suggested that between 1775 and 1815 above a third of the original fiction in *The Lady's Magazine* may have been provided by its mostly female readership (1962: 307). On the other hand, flourishing amateurism inevitably undermined the earning potential of professional writers.

Despite their mixed influence upon the fortunes of women writers, it is clear that magazines made a considerable contribution to the growth of the market for their novels, particularly amongst the poorer sections of the potential readership. When this repository of their work is considered in conjunction with their fiction issued in fascicules, the number of their novels published in book form, and the circulation of their material in reprints and through second-hand purchases, the remarkable scale of the growth of women's fiction during the eighteenth century and of its permeation of the contemporary literature market becomes increasingly apparent.

For a number of years now we have understood that nineteenth-century women writers had an impressive inheritance upon which to build their own outstanding contributions to the novel. It is now clear that this consisted not only of the literary achievements of such authors as Burney and Radcliffe but also of an approach which viewed writing as an occupation and publication as a source of income. The dedication and resilience of Fanny Trollope's efforts in the 1800s to support her family through authorship continued the thread of hard-pressed professionalism exemplified earlier by Charlotte Smith. Equally, the extraordinarily productive careers of writers like Gore and Oliphant, and the remarkable commercial (as well as critical) successes of Edgeworth and Eliot, can be seen within the context of a well-established market for women's fiction where the routes towards profitable publication had been well travelled and defined by their female predecessors. When we examine the lives of those eighteenth-century pioneers and glimpse the circumstances that both propelled them towards authorship and fashioned how they wrote, when we identify the extent to which they engaged with the book trades in order to achieve publication, demonstrating both their understanding of the vicissitudes of the market and their ability to exploit its potential, and when we get a measure of their perseverence, failures, and successes, the development of women's fiction through the 1700s becomes ever more complex and intriguing.

APPENDIX A

A Catalogue of women's fiction published in book form 1696–1796

INTRODUCTION

This appendix lists 446 works of prose fiction that were published in Britain in book form and 174 British women authors who worked either alone or with female collaborators. The Catalogue is arranged alphabetically by author with a chronological listing of book titles against each name. Relevant alternative names, such as maiden, married, and colloquial names or pseudonyms are given, and those writers known to have worked professionally are identified by the notation (P). The novel entries consist of the date of the first edition (unless stated otherwise), and whenever possible, the name(s) of the publisher(s), including a reference to subscription where appropriate, the place of publication, and the number of volumes. A single asterisk by an author's name indicates that she published prose fiction after 1796. A double asterisk by a novel title denotes that the work has been excluded from the statistical analysis in chapter 3 and the reasons for this are provided in a reference.

The information for the Catalogue was obtained from over forty secondary and primary sources. Principal amongst them are bibliographies by McBurney (1960), Block (1961), Summers (1940 [1969]), and Hardy (c.1982), the *Dictionary of National Biography* (1922), and a study of subscription lists by F.J.G. Robinson and P.J. Wallis (1975).[1] Supplementary details have been gathered from Todd's *Dictionary* (1987), *Eighteenth-Century British Books* by G. Averley *et al.* (1979), Blain *et al.* (1990), the catalogues of the Bodleian and British Libraries, specialist literary and biographical studies, and contemporary novels, periodicals, and autobiographical materials. Specific details of the sources for the majority of the entries are given in Turner (1985).[2] Many of the novels can be found in more than one of the texts consulted and occasionally there are differences in the transcriptions and publication dates. Where it has not been possible to resolve such contradictions the relevant information is given in a reference.

The criteria used in the compilation of the Catalogue have been touched upon already in chapter 3, which discusses the relatively restrictive approach taken here to seemingly autobiographical material. The following are also excluded from Appendix A: works by continental female authors; direct translations by British women; short pieces of fiction published with poetry and other miscellaneous material;[3] novels written jointly with male authors or where some authorities have attributed the work to a male writer;[4] and anonymous publications. The latter embraces many novels that were ostensibly written by women. Copies of 'Complete Works', including those claiming to contain previously unpublished fiction are omitted also, although novels that were published later on their own are included and the second date of separate publication is recorded.[5]

Two conventions for recording novels in the Catalogue should be noted. Publications advertised as containing several original novels are entered as a single work and treated as such in the statistical analysis. Novels published over a number of years are regarded in the same way and the publication date is taken from the first year of issue, although details of any title alterations and the span of years for publication are recorded.

AUTHOR	YEAR OF PUBLICATION	TITLE	PUBLISHER PLACE OF PUB. NO. OF VOLS
ALEXANDER, Judith	1789	THE YOUNG LADY OF FORTUNE, or Her Lover gained by stratagem. A novel.	Printed for the Author by L. Alexander. (London) 2 Vols
ATKYNS, Lady	1769	THE HERMIT. A novel. By a lady. In two volumes.	Printed for H. Gardner. (London) 2 Vols
(P) AUBIN, Penelope	1721	THE LIFE OF MADAM DE BEAUMONT, A FRENCH LADY; who lived in a cave in Wales above fourteen years undiscovered, being forced to fly France for her religion; and of the cruel usage she had there. Also her Lord's adventures in Muscovy, where he was a prisoner some years. With an account of his returning to France, and her being discover'd by a Welsh gentleman who fetch'd her Lord to Wales; and of many strange accidents which befel them, and their daughter Belinda, who was stolen away from them; and of their return to France in the year 1718. By Mrs. Aubin.	Printed for E. Bell, J. Darby, A. Bettesworth, F. Fayram, J. Pemberton, J. Hooke, C. Rivington, F. Clay, J. Batley, and E. Symon. (London)
	1721	THE STRANGE ADVENTURES OF THE COUNT DE VINEVIL AND HIS FAMILY. Being an account of what happen'd to them whilst they resided at Constantinople. And of Madamoiselle Ardelisa, his daughter's being shipwreck'd on the uninhabited island Delos, in her return to France, with Violetta, a Venetian lady, the captain of the ship, a priest, and five sailors. The manner of their living there, and strange	Printed for E. Bell, J. Darby, A. Bettesworth, F. Fayram, J. Pemberton, J. Hooke, C. Rivington, F. Clay, J. Batley,

deliverance by the arrival of a ship commanded by Violetta's father. Ardelisa's entertainment at Venice, and safe return to France. By Mrs. Aubin.

and E. Symon. (London)

1722

THE LIFE AND AMOROUS ADVENTURES OF LUCINDA, AN ENGLISH LADY, her courageous and undaunted behaviour at sea, in an engagement wherein she was taken by a rover of Barbary, and sold a slave at Constantinople. An account of her treatment there, with several particular customs of the Turks. Her unexpected deliverance, with the lucky meeting of her first love, their return and settlement in their own country, where she at present resides. Written by her self. Intermixed with two diverting novels, the one call'd Conjugal duty rewarded, or, The rake reform'd. The other, Fortune favours the bold, or, The happy Milanese.

Printed for
E. Bell, J. Darby,
A. Bettesworth,
F. Fayram,
J. Pemberton,
J. Hooke,
C. Rivington,
F. Clay, J. Batley,
and E. Symon.
(London)

1722

THE NOBLE SLAVES: or, The lives and adventures of two lords and two ladies, who were shipwreck'd and cast upon a desolate island near the East-Indies in the year 1710. The manner of their living there: the surprizing discoveries they made, and strange deliverance thence. How in their return to Europe they were taken by two Algerine pirates near the Straits of Gibraltar. Of the slavery they endured in Barbary; and of their meeting there with several persons of quality, who were likewise slaves. Of their escaping thence, and arrival in their respective countries, Venice, Spain and France, in the year 1718. With many extraordinary accidents that befel some of them afterwards. Being a history full of most remarkable events. By Mrs. Aubin.

Printed for
E. Bell, J. Darby,
A. Bettesworth,
F. Fayram,
J. Pemberton,
J. Hooke,
C. Rivington,
F. Clay, J. Batley,
and E. Symon.
(London)

AUTHOR	YEAR OF PUBLICATION	TITLE	PUBLISHER PLACE OF PUB. NO. OF VOLS
	1723	LIFE OF CHARLOTTA DU PONT, AN ENGLISHLADY; Taken from her own memoirs. Giving an account how she was trepan'd by her stepmother to Virginia, how the ship was taken by some Madagascar pirates, and retaken by a Spanish man of war. Of her marriage in the Spanish West-Indies, and adventures whilst she resided there, with her return to England. And the history of her several gentlemen and ladies whom she met withal in her travels; some of whom had been slaves in Barbary, and others cast on shore by shipwreck on the barbarous coasts up the great river Oroonoko: with their escape thence, and safe return to France and Spain. A history that contains the greatest variety of events that ever was publish'd. By Mrs. Aubin.	Printed for A. Bettesworth. (London)
	1726	THE LIFE AND ADVENTURES OF LADY LUCY, the daughter of an Irish lord, who marry'd a German officer, and was by him carry'd into Flanders, where he became jealous of her and a young nobleman his kinsman, whom he kill'd, and afterwards left her wounded and big with child in a forest. Of the strange adventures that befel both him and her afterwards, and the wonderful manner in which they met again, after living eighteen years asunder. By Mrs. Aubin.	Printed for J. Darby, A. Bettesworth, F. Fayram, J. Pemberton, C. Rivington, J. Hooke, F. Clay, J. Batley, and E. Symon. (London)
	1728	THE LIFE AND ADVENTURES OF THE YOUNG COUNT ALBERTUS, the son of Count Lewis	Printed for J. Darby,

Author	Date	Title	Publisher
		Augustus, by the Lady Lucy: who being become a widower, turn'd monk, and went a missionary for China, but was shipwreck'd on the coast of Barbary. Where he met with many strange adventures, and return'd to Spain with some persons of quality, who by his means made their escape from Africa. After which he went a missionary again to China, where he arriv'd and ended his life a martyr for the christian faith. By Mrs. Aubin.	A. Bettesworth, F. Fayram, J. Osborn and T. Longman, J. Pemberton, C. Rivington, J. Hooke, F. Clay, J. Batley, and E. Symon. (London)
AUSTIN, Mrs	1771	THE NOBLE FAMILY. A novel, in a series of letters.	Pearch.
BALLIN, Rossetta	1790	THE STATUE ROOM; an historical tale.	H.D. Symonds. (London) 2 Vols
BARKER, Jane	1713	LOVES INTRIGUES; or, The history of the amours of Bosvil and Galesia, as related to Lucasia, in St. Germain's garden. A novel written by a young lady.	Printed for E. Curll, and C. Crownfield. (Cambridge)
	1715	EXILIUS: or, The banish'd Roman. A new romance. In two parts. Written after the manner of Telemachus, for the instruction of some young ladies of quality. By Mrs. Jane Barker.	Printed for J. Roberts. (London) [Also known to have been printed for E. Curll.]
	1723	A PATCH-WORK SCREEN FOR THE LADIES; or, Love and virtue recommended: in a collection of instructive novels, related after a manner intirely new, and interspersed with rural poems, describing the innocence of a country-life. By Mrs. Jane Barker of Wilsthorp, near Stamford, in Lincolnshire.	Printed for E. Curll and T. Payne.

AUTHOR	YEAR OF PUBLICATION	TITLE	PUBLISHER PLACE OF PUB. NO. OF VOLS
	1726	THE LINING FOR THE PATCH-WORK SCREEN; design'd for the farther entertainment of the ladies. By Mrs. Jane Barker.	Printed for A. Bettesworth. [Also included in a list of E. Curll's publications.]
BARRY, Mrs	1753	THE AMOROUS MERCHANT: or, Intriguing husband. Being a curious and uncommon process of love and law founded on facts. Written by Mrs. Graham, now Mrs. Barry, in the manner of Constantia Phillips.	(London)
(P) * BENNETT, Agnes Maria	1785	ANNA; or, Memoirs of a Welch heiress. Interspersed with anecdotes of a nabob. In four volumes.	Printed for W. Lane. (London) 4 Vols
	1786	JUVENILE INDISCRETIONS. A novel. In five volumes. By the author of Anna, or The Welch heiress.	Printed for W. Lane. (London) 5 Vols
	1789	AGNES DE COURCI. A domestic tale. In four volumes. Inscrib'd with permission to Col. Hunter. By Mrs. Bennett, author of The Welch heiress, and Juvenile indiscretions.	Printed and Sold, for the Author, By S. Hazard. (Bath) 4 Vols
	1794	ELLEN, COUNTESS OF CASTLE HOWEL, a novel, in four volumes. By Mrs. Bennett.	Printed for W. Lane. (London) 4 Vols
BERRY, Miss	1775	THE CORRESPONDENTS, an original novel; in a series of letters.	T. Becket. (London)

(P) BLOWER, Elizabeth	1780	THE PARSONAGE HOUSE. A novel. By a young lady. In a series of letters.	Macgowan. 2 Vols
	1782	GEORGE BATEMAN: a novel.	J. Dodsley. (London) 3 Vols
	1785	MARIA. A novel. By the author of George Bateman.	J. Dodsley. (London) 2 Vols
	1788	FEATURES FROM LIFE; or, A summer visit.	J. Dodsley. (London) 2 Vols
* BONHOTE, Elizabeth	1772 [1]	THE RAMBLES OF MR. FRANKLY. Published by his sister. In two volumes.	Printed for T. Becket and P.A. De Hondt. (London) 2 Vols
	1773	THE FASHIONABLE FRIEND. A novel.	Becket and De Hondt. (London)
	1777	HORTENSIA. A novel.	W. Lane. (London) 2 Vols
	1787	OLIVIA, or, Deserted bride. By the author of Hortensia, The rambles of Frankly, and The fashionable friend. In three volumes.	Printed for W. Lane. (London) 3 Vols
	1789	DARNLEY VALE; or, Emelia Fitzroy. A novel, by Mrs. Bonhote. Author of Parental monitor, &c. In three volumes.	Printed for W. Lane. (London) 3 Vols
	1790	ELLEN WOODLEY. A novel. By Mrs. Bonhote.	Printed for W. Lane. (London) 2 Vols

AUTHOR	YEAR OF PUBLICATION	TITLE	PUBLISHER PLACE OF PUB. NO. OF VOLS
	1796	BUNGAY CASTLE: a novel. By Mrs. Bonhote. Author of The parental monitor, &c. In two volumes.	Printed for W. Lane. (London) 2 Vols
BOUVERIE, Georgina (pseudonym?)	1787	GEORGINA: or, Memoirs of the Bellmour family. By a young lady. In four volumes.	Printed for the Author; and Sold by R. Baldwin. (London) 4 Vols
(P) BOYD, Elizabeth	1732	THE HAPPY-UNFORTUNATE; or, The female-page: a novel. In three parts. By Elizabeth Boyd.	Printed for Tho. Edlin. [Published by subscription.]
BOYS, Mrs S.	1785	THE COALITION; or Family anecdotes.	Logographic Press. (London) 2 Vols
(P) BRISCOE, Sophia	1771	MISS MELMOTH or The new Clarissa.	Lowndes.
	1772	THE FINE LADY. A novel. By the author of Miss Melmoth.	T. Lowndes. (London) 2 Vols
BROMLEY, Eliza (née NUGENT)	1784	LAURA AND AUGUSTUS, an authentic story; in a series of letters. By a young lady. In three volumes.	Printed [sic] for W. Cass. (London) 3 Vols
(P) * BROOKE, Frances (née MOORE, for publications before c.1756)	1763	THE HISTORY OF LADY JULIA MANDEVILLE. In two volumes. By the translator of Lady Catesby's letters.	Printed for R. and J. Dodsley. (London) 2 Vols

160

Author	Title	Date	Publisher
	THE HISTORY OF EMILY MONTAGUE. In four volumes. By the author of Lady Julia Mandeville.	1769 [2]	Printed for J. Dodsley. (London) 4 Vols
	THE EXCURSION. In two volumes. By Mrs. Brooke; author of The history of Lady Julia Mandeville, and of Emily Montague.	1777	Printed for T. Cadell. (London) 2 Vols
	THE HISTORY OF CHARLES MANDEVILLE. In two volumes. A sequel to Lady Julia, by Mrs. Brooke.	1790	Printed for W. Lane. (London) 2 Vols
BROOKS, Indiana	ELIZA BEAUMONT AND HARRIET OSBORNE: or, The child of doubt.	1789	Robinson. (London) 2 Vols
BULLOCK, Mrs	SUSANNA; or, Traits of a modern miss; a novel. In four volumes.	1795	Printed for W. Lane. (London) 4 Vols
* BURKE, Mrs	ELA; or The delusions of the heart. A tale, founded on facts.	1787	Robinsons. (London) 2 Vols
	EMILIA DE ST. AUBIGNE. By the author of Ela.	1788	Elliot and Co.
	ADELA NORTHINGTON, a novel.	1796	W. Cawthorne. (London) 3 Vols
	THE SORROWS OF EDITH; or, The hermitage of the cliffs: A Descriptive Tale, Founded on Facts.	1796	Crosby. 2 Vols
(P) * BURNEY, Frances (D'ARBLAY, Madame, after 1793)	EVELINA; or, The history of a young lady's entrance into the world.	1778	T. Lowndes. (London) 3 Vols

AUTHOR	YEAR OF PUBLICATION	TITLE	PUBLISHER PLACE OF PUB. NO. OF VOLS
	1782	CECILIA; or, Memoirs of an heiress. By the author of Evelina.	T. Payne and T. Cadell. (London) 5 Vols
	1796	CAMILLA; or, A picture of youth. By the author of Evelina and Cecilia.	Printed for T. Payne, and T. Cadell Jun; & W. Davies. [Published by subscription.] (London) 5 Vols
* BURNEY, Sarah Harriet	1796	CLARENTINE. A novel. In three volumes.	Printed for G.G. & J. Robinson. (London) 3 Vols
BUTLER, Sarah	1716 Posthumous	IRISH TALES: or, Instructive histories for the happy conduct of life. Containing the following events. Viz. I. The captivated monarch. II. The banish'd prince. III. The power of beauty. IV. The distrest lovers. V. The perfidious gallant. VI. The constant fair-one. VII. The generous rival. VIII. The inhuman father. IX. The depos'd usurper. X. The punishment of generous love. By Mrs. Sarah Butler.	Printed for E. Curll, and J. Hooke. (London)
CARTWRIGHT, Mrs H.	1779	MEMOIRS OF LADY ELIZA AUDLEY.	Richardson and Urquhart (London) 2 Vols
	1780	THE GENEROUS SISTER. In a series of letters.	Bew. 2 Vols

1785	THE DUPED GUARDIAN: or, The amant malade. A novel. In a series of letters.	Cass. (London) 2 Vols
1787	THE PLATONIC MARRIAGE: a novel, in a series of letters.	(Dublin) 2 Vols
1787	RETALIATION; or, The history of Sir Edward Oswald, and Lady Frances Seymour. A Novel. In a series of letters.	F. Noble. (London) 4 Vols
1789	THE POOR SOLDIER; an American tale, founded on a recent fact. Inscribed to Mrs. C.	(London)
1796	THE PAVILION. A novel. In four volumes.	Printed for W. Lane. (London) 4 vols

CHAMPION DE CRESPIGNY, Lady Mary

1755	THE MERCER; or Fatal Extravagance: being a true narrative of the life of Mr. Wm. Dennis, Mercer, in Cheapside, etc.	Bailey. (London)
1756	THE HISTORY OF HENRY DUMONT, ESQ., and Miss Charlotte Evelyn.	H. Slater, H. Slater jun., & S. White. (London) [Details are for third edition.]
1758	THE LOVER'S TREAT; Or, Unnatural Hatred. Being a true narrative as deliver'd to the author by one of the family, etc.	Bailey's Printing Office. (London)
No date [3]	**THE HISTORY OF CHARLES AND PATTY	

(P) CHARKE, Charlotte

164

	Date	Title	Publisher
	1749	A CHRISTMAS BOX, consisting of moral stories, adapted to the capacities of little children and calculated to give them early impressions of piety and virtue.	2 Vols
* COOPER, Maria Susanna	1789 [4] Posthumous	**THE DEATH OF CAIN, in five books; after the manner of The death of Abel. By a lady.	B. Crosby. (London)
	1762 [5]	LETTERS BETWEEN EMILIA AND HARRIET.	Dodsley. (London)
	1763	THE SCHOOL FOR WIVES. In a series of letters.	R. and J. Dodsley. (London)
	1769	THE EXEMPLARY MOTHER: or, Letters between Mrs. Villars and her family. Published by a lady from the originals in her possession. In two volumes.	Printed for T. Becket and P.A. De Hondt. (London) 2 Vols
	1775	THE HISTORY OF FANNY MEADOWS. In a series of letters. By the author of The exemplary mother.	T. Becket. (London) 2 Vols
COURTNEY, Mrs	1796	ISABINDA OF BELLEFIELD, a sentimental novel. In a series of letters.	Bagster. 3 Vols
COWLEY, Mrs	1789	BELINDA, or The fair fugitive. A novel. By Mrs. C———.	Allen. (London) 2 Vols
(P) * COX, Anna Maria. This author also published under the names of JOHNSON, Mrs (by 1789), and MACKENZIE, Mrs (by 1795)	1783	BURTON WOOD. In a series of letters. By a lady.	(Dublin) 2 Vols

165

AUTHOR	YEAR OF PUBLICATION	TITLE	PUBLISHER PLACE OF PUB. NO. OF VOLS
	1785	RETRIBUTION.	
	1786	THE GAMESTERS: a novel. By the authoress of Burton-wood and Joseph.	R. Baldwin. (London) 3 Vols
	1789	CALISTA. A novel. By Mrs. Johnson, author of Retribution, Gamesters, &c.	Minerva. (London) 2 Vols
	1790	MONMOUTH: a tale, founded on historic facts. Inscribed to His Grace the Duke of Buccleugh. By Anna Maria Johnson, author of Calista, a novel, &c. In three volumes.	Printed for W. Lane. (London) 3 Vols
	1791	THE DANISH MASSACRE, an historical fact. By the author of Monmouth.	Printed for W. Lane. (London) 2 Vols
	1792	SLAVERY, or, The times. By the author of Monmouth, The Danish massacre, &c.	Robinsons. (London) 2 Vols
	1792	ORLANDO AND LAVINIA.	W. Lane. (London) 3 Vols
	1795	MYSTERIES ELUCIDATED, a novel. In three volumes. By the author of Danish massacre, Monmouth, &c.	Printed for W. Lane. (London) 3 Vols
Written under the pseudonym of 'ELLEN OF EXETER'	1796	THE NEAPOLITAN; or, The test of integrity. A novel. In three volumes. By Ellen of Exeter.	Printed for W. Lane. (London) 3 Vols

* CRAIK, Helen	1796	JULIA DE ST. PIERRE. A novel. In three volumes.	Printed for W. Lane. (London) 3 Vols
* CRAVEN, Lady Elizabeth (ANSPACH, Margravine of, after 1791)	1779	MODERN ANECDOTES OF THE ANCIENT FAMILY OF THE KINKVERVANKOTSDAR-SPRAKENGOTCHDERNS: a tale for Christmas 1779. Dedicated to the Honorable Horace Walpole, Esq.	Printed for the Author; And Sold by M. Davenhill. (London)
(P) DAVYS, Mary	1704	THE AMOURS OF ALCIPPUS AND LEUCIPPE. A Novel. Written by a Lady.	James Round. (London)
	1705	THE FUGITIVE. Containing several very pleasant passages and surprizing adventures, observ'd by a lady in her country ramble; being both useful and diverting for persons of all ranks. Now first published from her manuscript.	Printed for G. Sawbridge and sold by J. Nutt.
	1724	THE REFORM'D COQUET; a novel. By Mrs. Davys, author of The humours of York.	Printed By Henry Woodfall, for the Author, and sold by J. Stephens. [Published by subscription.]
	1727	THE ACCOMPLISH'D RAKE: or, Modern fine gentleman. Being an exact description of the conduct and behaviour of a person of distinction.	Printed for the Author and sold by the Booksellers of London and Westminster.

AUTHOR	YEAR OF PUBLICATION	TITLE	PUBLISHER PLACE OF PUB. NO. OF VOLS
(P) DAWE, Anne	1732	THE FALSE FRIEND: or, The treacherous Portugueze. A novel. Interspersed with the adventures of Lorenzo and Elvira. Carlos and Leonora. Octavia and Clara. Written by a lady.	Printed for T. Astley.
	1770	THE YOUNGER SISTER: or, History of Miss Somerset.	(London) 2 Vols
* DE ACTON, Eugenia (pseudonym?)	1794	VICISSITUDES IN GENTEEL LIFE. In four volumes.	Printed by Arthur Morgan, and sold by T.N. Longman. (Stafford) 4 Vols
DEVONSHIRE, Georgiana, Duchess of	1773	EMMA; or The unfortunate attachment. A sentimental novel.	Hookham. (London) 3 Vols
	1779	THE SYLPH. A novel	T. Lowndes. (London) 2 Vols
(P) DRAPER, Sarah	1796	MEMOIRS OF THE PRINCESS OF ZELL, consort to King George the first.	Printed for the author by W. Lane. [Published by subscription.] (London) 2 Vols
(P) DUBOIS, Lady Dorothea	1770	THEODORA, a novel.	Nicoll. (London) 2 Vols

	EDEN, Anne	CONFIDENTIAL LETTER OF ALBERT; from his first attachment to Charlotte to her death. From the Sorrows of Werter.	1790	(London)
*	EDGEWORTH, Maria	LETTERS FOR LITERARY LADIES.	1795	J. Johnson. (London) 6 Vols
		THE PARENT'S ASSISTANT, or Stories for children.	1796—	
	EDWARDS, Miss	OTHO AND RUTHA, a dramatic tale.	1780	(Edinburgh)
	ELFORD, Sophia	THE CONSTANT COUPLE, or, the tragedy of love: being a true . . . relation of one Mrs. S.E., a young lady near St. James's, that poyson'd her self for love of a captain in Flanders, etc.	1709	
[*?]	ELLIOTT, Miss	THE RELAPSE.	1780	(London)
		HISTORY OF THE HON. MRS. ROSEMONT AND SIR HENRY CARDIGAN, in a series of letters.	1781	Hookham.
		THE MASQUED WEDDINGS, a novel, in a series of letters.	1781	T. Hookham. (London) 2 Vols
		THE ORPHAN.	1783	
		THE PORTRAIT, a novel.	1783	(London) 2 Vols
	EYTON, Elizabeth	THE FAULT WAS ALL HIS OWN. A novel, in a series of letters. By a lady.	1771	G. Riley. (London) 2 Vols
	FELL, Mrs	THE PEASANT; or, Female philosopher.	1792	Minerva. (London) 2 Vols
*	FENN, Lady Eleanor	FABLES IN MONOSYLLABLES.	1783	
		SKETCHES OF LITTLE BOYS.	c.1783	

AUTHOR	YEAR OF PUBLICATION	TITLE	PUBLISHER PLACE OF PUB. NO. OF VOLS
	1789	THE FAIRY SPECTATOR; or, The invisible monitor, by Mrs. Teachwell and her family.	Marshall. (London)
	c.1789	LILLIPUTIAN SPECTACLE DE LA NATURE.	J. Newbery. (London)
	No date [6]	**MRS. LOVECHILD'S GOLDEN PRESENT.	
* FENWICK, Eliza	1795	SECRESY; or, The ruin on the rock. In three volumes. By a woman.	Printed for the Author and sold by W. Lane . . . [and others]. (London) 3 Vols
(P) FIELDING, Sarah	1744	THE ADVENTURES OF DAVID SIMPLE: containing an account of his travels through the cities of London and Westminster in search of a real friend. By a lady. In two volumes.	A. Millar. (London) 2 Vols
	1747	FAMILIAR LETTERS BETWEEN THE PRINCIPAL CHARACTERS IN DAVID SIMPLE, and some others. To which is added, A vision. By the author of David Simple. In two volumes.	Printed for the Author: And sold by A. Millar. [Published by subscription.] (London) 2 Vols
	1749	THE GOVERNESS, or the little female academy, being the history of Mrs Teachum and her nine girls. By the author of David Simple.	(London)

FIELDING, Sarah in collaboration with COLLIER, Jane	1753	THE HISTORY OF BETTY BARNES.	D. Wilson and T. Durham. (London) 2 Vols
	1753	THE ADVENTURES OF DAVID SIMPLE, Volume the last, in which his history is concluded.	Printed for A. Millar. (London) 1 Vol.
	1757	THE LIVES OF CLEOPATRA AND OCTAVIA. By the author of David Simple.	Printed for the Author, And sold by A. Millar. [Published by subscription.] (London)
	1759	THE HISTORY OF THE COUNTESS OF DELLWYN. In two volumes. By the author of David Simple.	Printed for A. Millar. (London) 2 Vols
	1760	THE HISTORY OF OPHELIA. Published by the author of David Simple.	R. Baldwin. (London) 2 Vols
	1754	THE CRY: a new dramatic fable. In three volumes.	R. and J. Dodsley. (London) 3 Vols
FINGLASS, Esther	1790	THE RECLUSE; or, History of Lady Gertrude Lesley.	Barker. (London) 2 Vols
FITZJOHN, Matilda (Pseudonym ?)	1796	JOAN!!! A novel. By Matilda Fitzjohn. In four volumes.	Printed for Hookham and Carpenter. (London) 4 Vols
(P) FOGERTY, Mrs	1773	THE FATAL CONNEXION, Colonel Digby and Miss Stanley.	

AUTHOR	YEAR OF PUBLICATION	TITLE	PUBLISHER PLACE OF PUB. NO. OF VOLS
* FOSTER, Mrs E.M.	1795	THE DUKE OF CLARENCE. An historical novel. In four volumes. By E.M.F.	Printed for W. Lane. (London) 4 Vols
(P) FULLER, Anne	1786	THE CONVENT: or The history of Sophia Nelson. By a young lady.	T. Wilkins. (London) 2 Vols
	1786	ALAN FITZ-OSBORNE, an historical tale.	P. Byrne. (Dublin) 2 Vols [Also Robinson (London)]
	1789	THE SON OF ETHELWOLF: an historical tale. In three volumes	G.G.J. and J. Robinson. (London) 3 Vols
FURGUSS, Miss	1777	THE THOUGHTLESS WARD. By a lady.	
GALES, Winifred Marshall	1787	THE HISTORY OF LADY EMMA MELCOMBE, AND HER FAMILY. By a female. In three volumes.	Printed for G.G.J. and J. Robinson. (London) 3 Vols
(P) * GIBBES, Phebe	1764	THE LIFE AND ADVENTURES OF MR FRANCIS CLIVE. In two volumes.	Printed for T. Lowndes. (London) 2 Vols
	1767	THE WOMAN OF FASHION: or, The history of Lady Diana Dormer. In two volumes.	Printed for J. Wilkie. (London) 2 Vols
	1778	FRIENDSHIP IN A NUNNERY: or, The American Fugitive.	

	1788	THE NIECE: or, The history of Sukey Thornby.	F. Noble. (London) 3 Vols
	1789	HARTLY HOUSE, CALCUTTA.	Walter. (London) 2 Vols
(P) GOMERSALL, Ann	1789	ELEONORA, a novel. In a series of letters; written by a female inhabitant of Leeds in Yorkshire.	Scatcherd and Whitaker. [Published by subscription.] (London) 2 Vols
	1790	THE CITIZEN, a novel.	
	1796	THE DISAPPOINTED HEIR; or, Memoirs of the Ormond family.	Richardson. (London) 2 Vols
(P) * GOOCH, Elizabeth Sarah (née VILLA-REAL)	1795	THE CONTRAST. A novel.	3 Vols
	1796	THE WANDERINGS OF THE IMAGINATION. By Mrs. Gooch. In two volumes.	Printed for B. Crosby. (London) 2 Vols
(P) GOSLING, Jane	1794	ASHDALE VILLAGE: A moral work of fancy.	Robinsons. [Only Vols I & II published].
GRAINGER, Lydia	1733	MODERN AMOURS: or, A secret history of the adventures of some persons of the first rank. Faithfully related from the author's own knowledge of each transaction. With a key prefixed.	Messrs. Parker, Jackson, and Joliffe.
* GREEN, Sarah	1790	CHARLES HENLY; or, The fugitive restored.	Minerva. (London) 2 Vols

AUTHOR	YEAR OF PUBLICATION	TITLE	PUBLISHER PLACE OF PUB. NO. OF VOLS
(P) GRIFFITH, Elizabeth	1769 [7]	THE DELICATE DISTRESS. By "Frances."	Printed for T. Becket and P.A. De Hondt. (London) 2 Vols
	1771	THE HISTORY OF LADY BARTON, a novel in letters.	T. Davies & T. Cadell. (London) 3 Vols
	1776	THE STORY OF LADY JULIANA HARLEY. A novel. In letters. By Mrs. Griffith.	Printed for T. Cadell. (London) 2 Vols
* GUNNING, Elizabeth (afterwards Mrs PLUNKETT)	1794	LORD FITZHENRY. A novel.	Byrne. (Dublin) 2 Vols
	1794	THE PACKET: a novel. By Miss Gunning.	Printed for J. Bell. (London) 4 Vols
(P) * GUNNING, Susannah (née MINIFIE, for publications before 1768)	1764	FAMILY PICTURES, a novel, containing curious and interesting memoirs of several persons of fashion in W——re, By a lady.	(Dublin) 2 Vols
	1770 [8]	THE HERMIT.	(Dublin)
	1792	ANECDOTES OF THE DELBOROUGH FAMILY. A novel. In five volumes. By Mrs. Gunning.	Printed for W. Lane. (London) 5 Vols
	1793	MEMOIRS OF MARY: a novel. By Mrs. Gunning. In five volumes.	Printed for J. Bell. (London) 5 Vols

174

GUNNING, Susannah (written under her maiden name MINIFIE, in collaboration with her sister Margaret: see also MINIFIE)	1796	DELVES: A Welch tale.	Lackington. (London) 2 Vols
	1763	THE HISTORIES OF LADY FRANCES S—— AND LADY CAROLINE S—— Written by the Miss Minifies.	R. & J. Dodsley. [Published by subscription]. (London) 4 Vols
	1766	THE PICTURE. A novel. By Miss Minifies of Fairwater in Somerset.	J. Johnson. (London) 3 Vols
GWYNN, Albinia	1784	THE RECONTRE; or, Transition of a moment. A novel. In a series of letters. By a lady.	Minerva. (London) 2 Vols
	1785	THE HISTORY OF THE HONOURABLE EDWARD MORTIMER. By a lady.	Printed for C. Dilly. (London) 2 Vols
* HAMILTON, Elizabeth	1796	TRANSLATION OF THE LETTERS OF A HINDOO RAJAH. Written previous to, and during the period of his residence in England, to which is prefixed a preliminary dissertation on the history religion and manners of the Hindoos.	G.G. and J. Robinson. (London) 2 Vols
HARDING, Elizabeth	1734	THE MASTERPIECE OF IMPOSTURE: or, The adventures of John Gordon and the Countess of Gordon, alias Countess Dalco, alias Madam Dallas, alias Madam Kempster . . . Being an answer to the late Memoirs of the said John Gordon of Glencat. Done from authentic accounts. . . .	Printed for the author.

AUTHOR	YEAR OF PUBLICATION	TITLE	PUBLISHER PLACE OF PUB. NO. OF VOLS
(P) * HARLEY, M. (known later as HUGILL, Mrs)	1786	ST. BERNARD'S PRIORY. An old English tale; being the first literary production of a young lady.	Printed for the authoress, and sold at Swifts Circulating Library, Charles Street, St James's Square. [Published by subscription.] (London)
	1788	THE CASTLE OF MOWBRAY, an English Romance. By the author of St. Bernard's priory.	Stalker. (London)
	1789	THE COUNTESS OF HENNEBON. An historical novel. By the author of The priory of St. Bernard.	Minerva. (London) 3 Vols
	1793	JULIANA ORMISTON; or, The fraternal victim. By Mrs. Harley author of the Countess of Hennebon, Castle Mowbray, St. Bernard's Priory, &c.	Wogan, Byrne, Stone, Jones and Rice. (Dublin)
	1795	THE PRINCE OF LEON.	
HARVEY, Mrs	1753	THE MEMOIRS OF FIDELIS AND HARRIOT: wherein the contrast between virtue and vice is fully exhibited from a real fact. Transacted in the year 1720. Preserved in the original manuscript of Mrs. Harvey.	(Dublin)
HAWKE, Lady Cassandra	1788	JULIA DE GRAMONT. By the Right Honourable Lady H* * * *. In two volumes.	Printed by T. Bensley: for B. White and Son. (London) 2 Vols

* HAYS, Mary	**MAUSOLEUM OF JULIA.	No date [9]	(London) 2 Vols
	MEMOIRS OF EMMA COURTNEY.	1796	
(P) HAYWOOD, Eliza	LOVE IN EXCESS; or, The fatal enquiry. A novel.	1719–20 [10]	Pt. I: Printed for W. Chetwood and R. Francklin, and sold by J. Roberts. Pts. II and III for W. Chetwood and sold by J. Roberts.
	THE BRITISH RECLUSE: or, The secret history of Cleomira, suppos'd dead. A novel. By Mrs. Eliza Haywood.	1722	Printed for D. Browne, W. Chetwood, and S. Chapman.
	IDALIA: or, The unfortunate mistress. A novel. Written by Mrs. Eliza Haywood.	1723	Printed for D. Browne, Jun., W. Chetwood, and S. Chapman.
	THE INJUR'D HUSBAND: or, The mistaken resentment.	1723	Printed for D. Browne, Jun., W. Chetwood and J. Woodman, and S. Chapman.
	LASSELIA: or, The self-abandon'd. A novel. By Mrs. Eliza Haywood.	1723	Printed for D. Browne.
	THE ARRAGONIAN QUEEN: a secret history.	1724	Printed for J. Roberts.

AUTHOR	YEAR OF PUBLICATION	TITLE	PUBLISHER PLACE OF PUB. NO. OF VOLS
	1724	THE FATAL SECRET; or, Constancy in distress. By the author of The masqueraders, or Fatal curiosity.	Printed for J. Roberts. (London)
	1724-5	THE MASQUERADERS; or, Fatal curiosity; being the secret history of a late amour.	Printed for J. Roberts. 2 Vols
	1724	THE RASH RESOLVE: or, The untimely discovery. A novel. In two parts. By Mrs. Eliza Haywood.	Printed for D. Browne, Jun., and S. Chapman. (London)
	1724	A SPY UPON THE CONJURER: or, A collection of surprising stories, with names, places, and particular circumstances relating to Mr. Duncan Campbell . . . Written to my Lord —— by a lady, who for more than twenty years past, has made it her business to observe all transactions in the life and conversation of Mr. Campbell.	Sold by Mr. Campbell . . . and at Burton's Coffee House.
	1724	THE SURPRISE: or Constancy rewarded.	Printed for J. Roberts.
	1725	BATH – INTRIGUES: In four letters to a friend in London.	Printed for J. Roberts.
	1725	THE DUMB PROJECTOR: being a surprising account of a trip to Holland made by Mr. Duncan Campbell. . . .	Printed for W. Ellis, J. Roberts, Mrs. Billingsly, A. Dod, & J. Fox.

1725	FANTOMINA; or, Love in maze, being a secret history of an amour between two persons of condition.	Printed for D. Browne, Jun., and S. Chapman.
1725	FATAL FONDNESS: or, Love its own opposer. (Being the sequel of The unequal conflict.) A novel.	Printed for J. Walthoe and J. Crokatt.
1725	THE FORCE OF NATURE: or, The lucky disappointment: a novel. By Mrs. Eliza Haywood.	
1725	MEMOIRS OF THE BARON DE BROSSE, who was broke on the wheel in the reign of Lewis XIV. Containing, an account of his amours. With several particulars relating to the wars in those times. Collected from authentick authors, and an original manuscript.	Printed for D. Browne, Jun., and S. Chapman. (London)
1725	MEMOIRS OF A CERTAIN ISLAND ADJACENT TO THE KINGDOM OF UTOPIA. Written by a celebrated author of that country. Now translated into English.	Printed and sold by the Booksellers of London and Westminster. 2 Vols
1725	THE TEA-TABLE: or, A conversation between some polite persons of both sexes, at a lady's visiting day. Wherein are represented the various foibles, and affectations, which form the character of an accomplish'd beau, or modern fine lady. Interspersed with several entertaining and instructive stories. By Mrs. Eliza Haywood.	Pt. I. printed and sold by J. Roberts and the Booksellers of London and Westminster. Pt. II printed for J. Roberts.

AUTHOR	YEAR OF PUBLICATION	TITLE	PUBLISHER PLACE OF PUB. NO. OF VOLS.
	1725	THE UNEQUAL CONFLICT; or, Nature triumphant: a novel. By Mrs. Eliza Haywood.	Printed for J. Walthoe and J. Crokatt.
	1725	DALINDA; or, The double marriage.	
	1726	THE CITY JILT; or, The alderman turn'd beau. A secret history.	Printed for J. Roberts.
	1726	THE DISTRESS'D ORPHAN; or, Love in a mad house.	Printed for J. Roberts.
	1726	THE DOUBLE MARRIAGE: or, The fatal release. A true secret history.	Printed for J. Roberts.
	1726	THE MERCENARY LOVER: or, The unfortunate heiresses. Being a true, secret history of a city amour, in a certain island adjacent to the kingdom of Utopia. Written by the author of Memoirs of the said island. Translated into English.	Printed for N. Dobb and sold by the Booksellers of London and Westminster.
	1726	REFLECTIONS ON THE VARIOUS EFFECTS OF LOVE . . . . Collected from the best ancient and modern histories. Intermix'd with the latest amours and intrigues of persons of the first rank of both sexes, of a certain island adjacent to the kingdom of Utopia.	Printed for N. Dobb and sold by the Booksellers of London and Westminster.
	1727	CLEOMELIA: or, The generous mistress. Being the secret history of a lady lately arriv'd from Bengall, a kingdom in the East-Indies. By Mrs. Eliza Haywood. To which is add'd, I. The lucky rape: or, Fate the best	Printed for J. Millan and sold by J. Roberts, T. Astley,

	disposer. II. The capricious lover: or, No trifling with a woman.	W. Meadows, J. Mackeuen, and H. Northcock.
1727	THE FRUITLESS ENQUIRY. A collection of several entertaining histories and occurrences, which fell under the observation of a lady in her search after happiness.	Printed for J. Stephens.
1727	LETTERS FROM THE PALACE OF FAME. Written by a first minister in the regions of air, to an inhabitant of this world. Translated from an Arabian manuscript.	Printed for J. Roberts.
1727	THE PERPLEX'D DUTCHESS: or, Treachery rewarded: being some memoirs of the court of Malfy. In a letter from a Sicilian nobleman, who had his residence there, to his friend in London.	Printed for J. Roberts.
1727	PHILIDORE AND PLACENTIA: or, L'amour trop delicat. Parts I and II. By Mrs. Haywood.	Printed for T. Green and sold by J. Roberts.
1727	THE SECRET HISTORY OF THE PRESENT INTRIGUES OF THE COURT OF CARAMANIA.	Printed: and sold by the Booksellers of London and Westminster.
1728	THE AGREEABLE CALEDONIAN: or, Memoirs of Signiora di Morella, a Roman lady, who made her escape from a monastery at Viterbo, for the love of a Scots nobleman. Intermix'd with many other entertaining little histories and adventures which presented themselves to her in the course of her travels.	Printed for R. King and sold by W. Meadows, T. Green, J. Stone, J. Jackson, and J. Watson.

AUTHOR	YEAR OF PUBLICATION	TITLE	PUBLISHER PLACE OF PUB. NO. OF VOLS
	1728	IRISH ARTIFICE: or, The history of Clarina. A novel. By Mrs. Eliza Haywood. Included in the female dunciad.	Printed for T. Read and sold by the Booksellers of London and Westminster.
	1728	PERSECUTED VIRTUE: or, The cruel lover. A true secret history writ at the request of a lady of quality.	Printed for J. Brindley, and sold by W. Meadows and H. Whitridge, T. Worrall, R. Francklin, and J. Watson.
	1729	THE FAIR HEBREW: or, A true, but secret history of two Jewish ladies, who lately resided in London.	Printed for J. Brindley, W. Meadows and J. Walthoe, A. Bettesworth, T. Astley, T. Worrall, J. Lewis, J. Penn, and R. Walker.
	1730	LOVE-LETTERS ON ALL OCCASIONS LATELY PASSED BETWEEN PERSONS OF DISTINCTION. Collected by Mrs. Eliza Haywood.	Printed for and sold by J. Brindley, R. Willock, J. Jackson, J. Penn, and F. Cogan.

1736	ADVENTURES OF EOVAAI, PRINCESS OF IJAVEO. A pre-adamitical history. Interspersed with a great number of remarkable occurrences, which happened and may again happen, to several empires, kingdoms, republicks, and particular great men. Written originally in the language of nature, (of later years but little understood.) First translated into Chinese, at the command of the Emperor, by a cabal of seventy philosophers; and now retranslated into English, by the son of a mandarin, residing in London.	Printed for S. Baker.
1744	THE FORTUNATE FOUNDLINGS; being the genuine history of Colonel M——rs, and his sister Madame Du P——y, the issue of the Hon. Ch——es M——————d.	(London)
1748	LIFE'S PROGRESS THROUGH THE PASSIONS: or, The adventures of Natura. By the author of The fortunate foundlings.	Printed for T. Gardner. (London)
1751	THE HISTORY OF MISS BETSY THOUGHTLESS.	T. Gardner. (London) 4 Vols
1753	THE HISTORY OF JEMMY AND JENNY JESSAMY. In three volumes. By the author of The history of Betsy Thoughtless.	Printed for T. Gardner. (London) 3 Vols
1753	MODERN CHARACTERS: Illustrated by histories in real life, and address'd to the polite world.	Printed for T. Gardner. (London) 2 Vols
1755	THE INVISIBLE SPY. By Exploralibus.	T. Gardner. (London) 4 Vols

AUTHOR	YEAR OF PUBLICATION	TITLE	PUBLISHER PLACE OF PUB. NO. OF VOLS
HEARNE, Mary	1718	THE LOVER'S WEEK: or, The six days adventures of Philander and Amaryllis. Written by a young lady.	Printed for E. Curll and R. Francklin.
	1719	THE FEMALE DESERTERS. A novel. By the author of The lover's week.	Printed for J. Roberts and sold by E. Curll, R. Francklin, and J. Roberts.
* HELME, Elizabeth	1787	LOUISA; or, The cottage on the moor. In two volumes.	Printed for G. Kearsley. (London) 2 Vols
	1788	CLARA AND EMMELINE; or, The maternal benediction. A novel. By the author of Louisa; or, The cottage on the moor.	G. Kearsley. (London) 2 Vols
	1794	DUNCAN AND PEGGY: A Scottish tale.	J. Bell. (London) 2 Vols
	1796	THE FARMER OF INGLEWOOD FOREST, a novel. In four volumes. By Elizabeth Helme.	Printed for W. Lane. (London) 4 Vols
HERBERTS, Mary	1727	THE ADVENTURES OF PROTEUS, etc. A sett of novels never before publish'd.	Printed for Tho. Combes, J. Lacy, and J. Clarke.

HERON, Mary	1790	THE CONFLICT. A sentimental tale in a series of letters.	Printed by Hall and Elliot. (Newcastle) 2 Vols
(P) * HERVEY, Elizabeth	1788	MELISSA AND MARCIA; or, The sisters: a novel. In two volumes.	Printed for W. Lane. (London) 2 Vols
	1790	LOUISA: or, The reward of an affectionate daughter. By the author of Melissa and Marcia, or The sisters.	Hookham. (London) 2 Vols
	1796	THE HISTORY OF NED EVANS.	Robinson. 4 Vols
* HOLFORD, Margaret	1785 [11]	FANNY. A novel; in a series of letters. Written by a lady.	(London) 3 Vols
* HOWELL, Ann (née HILDITCH)	1787	ROSA DE MONTMORIEN, A novel. By Miss Ann Hilditch. In two volumes.	Printed for W. Lane. (London) 2 Vols
	1789	MOUNT PELHAM. A novel. By the author of Rosa de Montmorien.	Minerva. (London) 2 Vols
	1789	ROSENBERG. A legendary tale. By a lady. In two volumes.	Printed for W. Lane. (London) 2 Vols
	[1794] [12]	**MORTIMORE CASTLE. A Cambrian tale. By Mrs. Howell.	Minerva. (London) 2 Vols

AUTHOR	YEAR OF PUBLICATION	TITLE	PUBLISHER PLACE OF PUB. NO. OF VOLS
	1796	ANZOLETTA ZADOSKI. A novel. In two volumes. By Mrs. Howell, author of Georgina, &c. &c.	Printed for W. Lane. (London) 2 Vols
	1796	GEORGINA; or, The advantages of grand connections. A novel. By Mrs. Howell.	Minerva. (London) 2 Vols
HUGHES, Anne Rice	1786	ZORAIDA, or, Village Annals. A novel.	Minerva (London)
	1787	CAROLINE; or, The diversities of fortune: a novel. In three volumes.	Printed for W. Lane. (London) 3 Vols
	1788	HENRY AND ISABELLA; or, A traite through life. By the author of Caroline, or, The diversities of fortune. In four volumes.	Printed for W. Lane. (London) 4 Vols
	1795	JEMIMA. A novel. By the author of Zoraida, or Village annals, &c.	Printed for W. Lane. (London) 2 Vols
* HUNTER, Maria	1792	FITZROY; or, Impulse of the moment. A novel. In two volumes. By Maria Hunter.	Printed for W. Lane. (London) 2 Vols

* HURRY, Mrs Ives	1795	TALES OF INSTRUCTION AND AMUSEMENT, written for the use of young persons.	E. Newbery, (London) 2 Vols
(P) INCHBALD, Elizabeth	1787 [13]	**EMILY HERBERT; or Perfidy punished. A novel. In a Series of letters.	White etc. (Dublin)
	1791	A SIMPLE STORY. In four volumes. By Mrs. Inchbald.	Printed for G.G.J. and J. Robinson. (London) 4 Vols
	1796	NATURE AND ART. In two volumes. By Mrs. Inchbald.	Printed for G.G. and J. Robinson. (London) 2 Vols
JOHNSON, Mrs	1786	FRANCIS, THE PHILANTHROPIST; an unfashionable tale. In three volumes.	Printed for W. Lane. (London) 3 Vols
	1786	JULIANA: a novel. By the author of Francis, the philanthropist. In three volumes.	Printed for W. Lane. (London) 3 Vols
	1787	THE PLATONIC GUARDIAN; or, The history of an orphan. By a lady.	Minerva. (London) 3 Vols
	1789	THE INNOCENT FUGITIVE; or, Memoirs of a lady of quality. By the author of the Platonic guardian.	T. Hookham. (London) 2 Vols
KEIR, Susanna	1785	INTERESTING MEMOIRS. By a lady.	
	1787	THE HISTORY OF MISS GREVILLE. In three volumes. By the author of Interesting memoirs.	Printed and sold for the Author at Mr. Carruthers's. (London) 3 Vols

AUTHOR	YEAR OF PUBLICATION	TITLE	PUBLISHER PLACE OF PUB. NO. OF VOLS
(P) * KELLY, Isabella (known later as HEDGELAND, Mrs)	1794	MADELEINE; or, The castle of Montgomery, a novel. In three volumes.	Printed for W. Lane. (London) 3 Vols
	1795	THE ABBEY OF ST. ASAPH. A novel. In three volumes. By the author of Madeline, or The castle of Montgomery.	Printed for W. Lane. (London)
	1796	THE RUINS OF AVONDALE PRIORY, a novel, in three volumes, by Mrs. Kelly, author of Madeline, Abbey St. Asaph, &c.	Printed for W. Lane. (London) 3 Vols
* KILNER, Dorothy (pseudonyms: 'M. P.' and 'M. PELHAM')	1781	THE HISTORY OF A GREAT MANY LITTLE BOYS AND GIRLS OF FOUR AND FIVE YEARS OF AGE.	J. Marshall & Co. (London) 2 Vols
	c.1785	THE LIFE AND PERAMBULATIONS OF A MOUSE. [The address to the reader is signed M. P.]	(London) 2 Vols
	c.1790	ANECDOTES OF A BOARDING SCHOOL; or, an antidote to the Vices of those establishments. By M. P.	
	c.1795	THE HISTORIES OF MORE CHILDREN THAN ONE; or, goodness better than beauty. (By M. P.)	J. Marshall & Co. (London)
* KILNER, Mary Ann (pseudonym 'S. S.')	c.1780	THE ADVENTURES OF A PINCUSHION. Designed chiefly for the use of young ladies. With woodcuts.	J. Marshall & Co. (London)
	1782	MEMOIRS OF A PEG-TOP.	J. Marshall & Co. (London)

*	KNIGHT, Ellis Cornelia	c.1783	WILLIAM SEDLEY; or, the evil day deferred.	J. Marshall & Co. (London)
		1790	DINARBAS; a tale: being a continuation of Rasselas, Prince of Abissinia.	Printed for C. Dilly. (London)
		1792	MARCUS FLAMINIUS; or, A view of the military, political and social life of the Romans: in a series of letters from a young patrician to his friend, in the year 762 from the foundation of Rome, to the year 769, in two volumes.	C. Dilly. (London) 2 Vols
	LANSDELL, Sarah	1796	MANFREDI, BARON ST. OSMUND. An old English romance. In two volumes. By Sarah Lansdell, Tenterden.	Printed for W. Lane. (London) 2 Vols
	LARA, Catherine	1796	DURVAL AND ADELAIDE. A novel.	Ridgway.
		1796	LEWIS DE BONCOEUR.	2 Vols
(P)	LATTER, Mary	1771	PRO AND CON; or, The opinionists, an ancient fragment.	8 Vols
*	LEE, Harriet	1786	THE ERRORS OF INNOCENCE, in five volumes.	Printed for G.G.J. and J. Robinson. (London) 5 Vols
(P) *	LEE, Sophia	1783–5 [14]	THE RECESS; or A tale of other times. By the author of the Chapter of Accidents.	T. Cadell. (London) 1 Vol. [Reissued with two further volumes in 1785; Printed for T. Cadell (London).]

AUTHOR	YEAR OF PUBLICATION	TITLE	PUBLISHER PLACE OF PUB. NO. OF VOLS
(P) LENNOX, Charlotte (née RAMSAY for publications before c.1748)	1750	THE LIFE OF HARRIOT STUART. Written by herself. In two volumes.	Printed for J. Payne and J. Bouquet. (London) 2 Vols
	1752	THE FEMALE QUIXOTE; or, The adventures of Arabella. In two volumes.	Printed for A. Millar. (London) 2 Vols
	1758	HENRIETTA. By the author of The female quixote. In two volumes.	Printed for A. Millar. (London) 2 Vols
	1762	SOPHIA.	J. Fletcher. (London) 2 Vols
	1790 [15]	EUPHEMIA.	T. Cadell and J. Evans. (London) 4 Vols
McCARTHY, Charlotte	1745	THE FAIR MORALIST; or, Love and virtue. By a Gentlewoman . . . To which is added, several occasional poems, by the same.	(London)
(P) MANLEY, Delarivière	1696	LETTERS, TO WHICH IS ADDED A LETTER FROM A SUPPOSED NUN IN PORTUGAL.	
	1705	THE SECRET HISTORY, OF QUEEN ZARAH AND THE ZARAZIANS; being a looking-glass for ―――― in the Kingdom of Albigion. Faithfully translated from the Italian copy now lodg'd in the Vatican at Rome, and never before printed in any language.	Published in 2 separate parts.

1709	SECRET MEMOIRS AND MANNERS OF SEVERAL PERSONS OF QUALITY, OF BOTH SEXES FROM THE NEW ATLANTIS, AN ISLAND IN THE MEDITERANEAN. Written originally in Italian.	Printed for J. Morphew and J. Woodward. (London) [Published in 2 separate parts.]
1710	MEMOIRS OF EUROPE, TOWARDS THE CLOSE OF THE EIGHTH CENTURY. Written by Eginardus, secretary and favourite to Charlemagne; and done into English by the translator of the New Atlantis.	Printed for J. Morphew. (London) [Published in 2 separate parts.]
1711 [16]	COURT INTRIGUES, in a collection of original letters, from the island of the New Atlantis, &c. By the author of those Memoirs.	Printed for J. Woodward and J. Morphew.
1720	THE POWER OF LOVE: in seven novels. viz. I. The fair hypocrite. II. The physician's stratagem. III. The wife's resentment. IV–V. The husband's resentment In two examples. VI. The happy fugitives. VII. The perjur'd beauty. Never before published. By Mrs. Manley.	Printed for John Barber and John Morphew. (London)

(P) MARISHALL, Jean

1766	THE HISTORY OF CLARINDA CATHCART AND MISS FANNY RENTON.	J. Noble. (London) 2 Vols
1767	THE HISTORY OF ALICIA MONTAGUE.	Robinson and Roberts. [Published by subscription]. [Also Irish imprint for 1767, J. Murphy etc. (Dublin) 2 Vols]

AUTHOR	YEAR OF PUBLICATION	TITLE	PUBLISHER PLACE OF PUB. NO. OF VOLS
* MATHEWS, Charlotte	1793	SIMPLE FACTS; or, The history of an orphan. In two volumes. By Mrs. Mathews.	Printed by S. Low, for the Author. 2 Vols
	1794	PERPLEXITIES, or The fortunate elopement. A novel. By Mrs. Mathews of the Theatre Royal, York and Hull.	(London) 3 Vols
MATHEWS, Eliza	1785	CONSTANCE: a novel. The first literary attempt of a young lady. In four volumes.	Printed at the Logographic Press, for Thomas Hookham. (London) 4 Vols
	1789	ARGUS, THE HOUSE-DOG AT EADLIP. Memoirs in a family correspondence, by the author of Constance and The Pharos. In three volumes.	Printed for T. Hookham. (London) 3 Vols
	1790 [17]	ARNOLD ZULIG: a Swiss story. By the author of Constance, Pharos, and Argus.	(Dublin)
	1791	MEMOIRS OF A SCOTS HEIRESS addressed to the Right Honourable Lady Catherine ***** By the author of Constance, &c.	T. Hookham. (London) 3 Vols
	1792	THE COUNT OF HOENSDERN, a German tale.	3 Vols
(P) MEADES, Anna	1757	THE HISTORY OF CLEANTHES, AN ENGLISHMAN OF THE HIGHTEST QUALITY, AND CELEMENE, THE ILLUSTRIOUS AMAZONIAN PRINCESS. Written by a person well acquainted with all the principal characters from their original.	

(P) * MEEKE, Mary (used the pseudonym 'GABRIELLI' for some later works)	THE HISTORY OF SIR WILLIAM HARRINGTON. Written some years since, and revised and corrected by the late Mr. Richardson, author of Sir Charles Grandison, Clarissa, &c. Now first published, in four volumes.	1771	Printed for John Bell. (London) 4 Vols
	COUNT ST. BLANCARD, or, The prejudiced judge, a novel. In three volumes. By Mrs. Meek [sic].	1795	Printed for W. Lane. (London) 3 Vols
	THE ABBEY OF CLUGNY. A novel. By Mrs. Meeke.	1795	Minerva. (London) 3 Vols
(P) MEZIERE, Harriet (née CHILCOT)	ELMAR AND ETHLINDA; a legendary Tale.	1783	[Published by subscription].
	MORETON ABBEY; or, The fatal mystery. A novel, in two volumes. By the late Miss Harriet Chilcot of Bath. (Afterwards Mrs. Meziere.) Authoress of Elmar and Ethlinda, a legendary tale, &c. &c.	1786	Printed and sold by T. Baker. (Southampton) 2 Vols
(P) MINIFIE, Margaret	BARFORD ABBEY, a novel: in a series of letters.	1768.	T. Cadell and J. Payne. (London) 2 Vols
	THE COTTAGE; a novel: in a series of letters. By Miss Minifie, author of Barford-Abbey. In three volumes.	1769	Printed for T. Durham. (London) 2 Vols
	THE COUNT DE POLAND, by Miss Minifie, one of the authors of Lady Frances and Lady Caroline S———.	1780	Published for the Author, and sold by J. Dodsley. (London) 4 Vols

193

AUTHOR	YEAR OF PUBLICATION	TITLE	PUBLISHER PLACE OF PUB. NO. OF VOLS
MINIFIE, Margaret in collaboration with her sister Susannah	1783	COOMBE WOOD, a novel in a series of letters: by the author of Barford-Abbey and The cottage. See GUNNING, Susannah.	Baldwin. 2 Vols
(P) * MORE, Hannah	1792	VILLAGE POLITICS by Will Chip.	
MORRIS, Mrs	1784	THE RIVAL BROTHERS; a novel. In a series of letters founded on facts. By a lady.	Printed for the authoress and Sold by Symonds.
	1791	ILLICIT LOVE: a novel. By Mrs. Morris, author of The rival brothers, a novel; &c.	Symonds.
* MUSGRAVE, Agnes	1795	CICELY, or The rose of Raby. An historic novel.	Printed for W. Lane. (London) 4 Vols
NOAKE, Dorothy	1735	THE LIFE AND ADVENTURES OF THE MARCHIONESS URBINO. Containing several remarkable passages in England, Spain, Turkey, Italy, France, and Holland.	Printed for T. Cooper and sold by the Booksellers of London and Westminster.
NORMAN, Elizabeth	1789	THE CHILD OF WOE. A novel.	Symonds. 3 Vols
NUGENT, Miss in collaboration with TAYLOR, Miss	1779	THE INDISCREET MARRIAGE; or, Henry and Sophia Sommerville. In a series of letters.	J. Dodsley. (London)

* OPIE, Amelia (née ALDERSON, for publications before 1798)	1790	THE DANGERS OF COQUETRY. A novel. In two volumes.	Printed for W. Lane. (London) 2 Vols
* PALMER, Charlotte	1780	FEMALE STABILITY: or, The history of Miss Belville. In a series of letters.	F. Newbery. (London) 5 Vols
	1792	INTEGRITY AND CONTENT, AN ALLEGORY.	
	1792	IT IS AND IT IS NOT, a novel.	2 Vols
(P) PARKER, Mary Elizabeth	1795	ORWELL MANOR. A novel, by Mary Elizabeth Parker, in three volumes.	Printed for the author at the Minerva Press. [Published by subscription.] (London) 3 Vols
PARRY, Catherine	1784	EDEN VALE. A novel. In two volumes. Dedicated, by permission, to Lady Shelburne. By Mrs. Catherine Parry.	Printed for John Stockdale. (London) 2 Vols
(P) * PARSONS, Eliza (née PHELP)	1790	THE HISTORY OF MISS MEREDITH; a novel. Dedicated by permission, to the Most Noble the Marchioness of Salisbury. By Mrs. Parsons. In two volumes	Printed for the Author; and sold by T. Hookham. [Published by subscription.] (London) 2 Vols
	1791	THE ERRORS OF EDUCATION. By Mrs. Parsons.	Printed for W. Lane. (London) 3 Vols

AUTHOR	YEAR OF PUBLICATION	TITLE	PUBLISHER PLACE OF PUB. NO. OF VOLS
	1793	WOMAN AS SHE SHOULD BE; or, Memoirs of Mrs. Menville. A novel. In four volumes. By Mrs. Parsons, author of Errors of education, Miss Meredith, and Intrigues of a morning.	Printed for W. Lane. (London) 4 Vols
	1793	THE CASTLE OF WOLFENBACH; a German story. In two volumes. By Mrs. Parsons, author of Errors of education, Miss Meredith, Woman as she should be, and Intrigues of a morning.	Printed for W. Lane. (London) 2 Vols
	1793	ELLEN AND JULIA. By Mrs. Parsons.	Minerva. (London) 2 Vols
	1794	LUCY: a novel, in three volumes. By Mrs. Parsons.	Printed for W. Lane. (London) 3 Vols
	1795	THE VOLUNTARY EXILE, in five volumes, by Mrs. Parsons, author of Lucy, &c. &c.	Printed for W. Lane. (London) 5 Vols
	1796	THE MYSTERIOUS WARNING, a German tale. In four volumes. By Mrs. Parsons. Author of Voluntary exile, &c.	Printed for W. Lane. (London) 4 Vols
	1796	WOMEN AS THEY ARE. A novel, in four volumes, by Mrs. Parsons. Author of Mysterious warnings, &c.	Printed for W. Lane. (London) 4 Vols

PAUL, Sarah (pseudonym?)	1760	THE LIFE AND IMAGINATIONS OF SALLY PAUL.	Printed for S. Hooper. (London)
(P) * PEACOCK, Lucy	1785	THE ADVENTURES OF THE SIX PRINCESSES OF BABYLON, in their travels to the temple of virtue; an allegory.	Printed for the Author by T. Bensley. [Published by subscription.] (London)
	1786	THE RAMBLES OF FANCY; or, Moral and interesting tales. Containing, The Laplander, The ambitious mother, Letters from – Lindamira to Olivia, Miranda to Elvira, Felicia to Cecilia, The American Indian, The fatal resolution, The Creole. By the author of The six Princesses of Babylon. In two volumes.	Printed by T. Bensley, for the Author; And Sold by J. Buckland. (London) 2 Vols
	1793	THE KNIGHT OF THE ROSE. An allegorical narrative.	(London) 1 Vol.
	1794	THE VISIT FOR A WEEK; or Hints on the improvement of time. Containing original tales, anecdotes from natural and moral history, &c. Designed for the amusement of youth. By the author of The six Princesses of Babylon, Juvenile magazine, and Knight of the rose.	Printed for Hookham and Carpenter; and for the Author.
	1796	AMBROSE AND ELEANOR; or, the Adventures of two children deserted on an uninhabited island. Translated from the French with alterations . . . by the author of the Adventures of the Six Princesses of Babylon, etc.	R. & L. Peacock. (London)

AUTHOR	YEAR OF PUBLICATION	TITLE	PUBLISHER PLACE OF PUB. NO. OF VOLS
PEARSON, Susanna	1794	THE MEDALLION, a novel.	Robinsons. (London) 3 Vols
(P) PEDDLE, M.	1785	THE LIFE OF JACOB. In Ten Books.	[Published by subscription.] (Dorset)
* PILKINGTON, Miss or Mrs	1790	DELIA, a pathetic and interesting tale. In four volumes.	Printed for W. Lane. (London) 4 Vols
	1793	ROSINA: a novel. In five volumes. By the author of Delia, an interesting tale, in four volumes.	Printed for W. Lane. (London) 5 Vols
* PINCHARD, Elizabeth	1791	THE BLIND CHILD; or Anecdotes of the Wyndham family, written for the use of young people, by a lady.	E. Newbery. (London)
	1794	THE TWO COUSINS, a moral story, for the use of young persons. In which is exemplified the necessity of moderation and justice to the attainment of happiness. By the author of The blind child and Dramatic dialogues.	E. Newbery. (London)
(P) PIX, Mary	1696 [18]	THE INHUMANE CARDINAL, or: Innocence betrayed.	
* PLUMPTRE, Anne or Anna	1796	ANTOINETTE; a novel.	Minerva. (London) 2 Vols

* PLUMPTRE, Annabella	1796	MONTGOMERY; or, Scenes in Wales. In two volumes.	Printed for W. Lane. (London) 2 Vols
(P) * PORTER, Anna Maria	1793–5	ARTLESS TALES.	[Published by subscription.] (London) 2 Vols
* PURBECK, Elizabeth in collaboration with PURBECK, Jane	1789	HONORIA SOMMERVILLE: a novel. In four volumes.	Printed for G.G.J. and J. Robinson. (London) 4 Vols
	1790	RAYNSFORD PARK, a novel.	G. Kearsley. (London) 4 Vols
	1791	WILLIAM THORNBOROUGH, The benevolent quixote.	Robinsons. 4 Vols
	1796	MATILDA AND ELIZABETH, a novel. By the authors of Honoria Sommerville, Rainsford Park, The benevolent quixote, &c.	Sampson Low. (London) 4 Vols
* PURBECK, Jane (see above)			
PYE, Jael Henrietta	1786 Posthumous	THEODOSIUS AND ARABELLA. A novel. In a series of letters. By the late Mrs. Hampden Pye.	Minerva. (London) 2 Vols
(P) * RADCLIFFE, Ann (née WARD)	1789	THE CASTLES OF ATHLIN AND DUNBAYNE. A highland story.	Printed for T. Hookham. (London)
	1790	A SICILIAN ROMANCE. By the authoress of The castles of Athlin and Dunbayne. In two volumes.	Printed for T. Hookham. (London) 2 Vols

AUTHOR	YEAR OF PUBLICATION	TITLE	PUBLISHER PLACE OF PUB. NO. OF VOLS
	1791	THE ROMANCE OF THE FOREST: interspersed with some pieces of poetry. By the authoress of "A Sicilian romance," &c. In three volumes.	Printed for J. Carpenter. (London) 3 Vols
	1794	THE MYSTERIES OF UDOLPHO, a romance; interspersed with some pieces of poetry. By Ann Radcliffe, author of The romance of the forest, &c. In four volumes.	Printed for G.G. and J. Robinson. (London) 4 Vols
* RADCLIFFE, Mary Anne	1790	THE FATE OF VELINA DE GUIDOVA. A novel.	Minerva. (London) 3 Vols
	1790	RADZIVIL, a romance. Translated from the Russ of the celebrated M. Wocklow. In three volumes.	Printed for W. Lane. (London) 3 Vols
(P) * REEVE, Clara	1777	THE CHAMPION OF VIRTUE. A gothic story. By the editor of The Phoenix; a translation of Barclay's Argenis.	Printed for the Author, By W. Keymer, Colchester, and sold by him.
	1783	THE TWO MENTORS: a modern story. By the author of the old English Baron.	Printed for C. Dilly. (London) 2 Vols
	1788	THE EXILES: or, Memoirs of the Count de Cronstadt. By Clara Reeve, author of The old English Baron, Two mentors, &c. &c. In three volumes.	T. Hookham. (London) 3 Vols

	1791	THE SCHOOL FOR WIDOWS. By Clara Reeve. Author of The old English Baron, &c.	T. Hookham. (London) 3 Vols
	1792	PLANS OF EDUCATION; with remarks on the systems of other writers. In a series of letters between Mrs. Darnford and her friends.	T. Hookham and J. Carpenter. (London)
	1793	MEMOIRS OF SIR ROGER DE CLARENDON, the natural son of Edward Prince of Wales, commonly called the Black Prince; with anecdotes of many other eminent persons of the fourteenth century. By Clara Reeve.	Printed for T. Hookham and J. Carpenter. (London) 3 Vols
ROBERTS, Miss R.	1783	ALBERT, EDWARD AND LAURA, AND THE HERMIT OF PRIESTLAND; three legendary tales.	(London)
	1789	JULIA ST. LAWRENCE.	
(P) * ROBINSON, Mary 'Perdita' (née DARBY)	1792	VANCENZA; or, The dangers of credulity. In two volumes. By Mrs. M. Robinson, authoress of The poems of Laura Maria Ainsi va le monde, &c. &c.	Printed for the Authoress; and sold by Mr. Bell. (London) 2 Vols
	1794	THE WIDOW, or, A picture of modern times. A novel. In a series of letters.	Hookham. 2 Vols
	1796	ANGELINA. A novel.	T. Hookham and J. Carpenter. (London) 3 Vols
	1796	HUBERT DE SEVRAC, a romance, of the eighteenth century; by Mary Robinson, author of Poems, Angelina, The Sicilian lover, The widow, &c. &c. In three volumes.	Printed for the Author, by Hookham and Carpenter. (London) 3 Vols

AUTHOR	YEAR OF PUBLICATION	TITLE	PUBLISHER PLACE OF PUB. NO. OF VOLS
	1796	THE WANDERINGS OF THE IMAGINATION.	
* ROBINSON, Maria Elizabeth (daughter of above)	1794	THE SHRINE OF BERTHA. A novel. In a series of letters. By Miss M.E. Robinson.	Minerva. (London) 2 Vols
* ROCHE, Regina Maria (née DALTON, for publications before c.1793)	1789	THE VICAR OF LANSDOWNE; or, Country Quarters: A tale. By Regina Maria Dalton.	Printed for the Author. (London) 2 Vols
	1793	THE MAID OF THE HAMLET. A tale. By Regina Maria Roche. Author of The Vicar of Landsdowne.	Long. 2 Vols
	1796	THE CHILDREN OF THE ABBEY, a tale. In four volumes. By Regina Maria Roche.	Printed for W. Lane. (London) 4 Vols
ROGERS, Miss A.	1777	THE HISTORY OF MISS TEMPLE. In two volumes. By a young lady.	Printed for the Author; And sold by Wallis. (London) 2 Vols
ROWE, Elizabeth (née SINGER)	1728–32 [19]	FRIENDSHIP IN DEATH: in twenty letters from the dead to the living. To which are added, Letters moral and entertaining in prose and verse in three parts by the same author. Part I	H. Lintot. [Pt. III by T. Woral]
(P) * ROWSON, Susanna (née HASWELL)	1786	VICTORIA. A novel. The characters taken from real life, and calculated to improve the morals of the female	Printed by J.P. Cooke for the

	sex by impressing them with a just sense of the merits of filial piety. By Susannah Haswell.	Author. [Published by subscription]. (London) 2 Vols
1788	THE INQUISITOR; or, Invisible rambler.	G.G.J. and J. Robinson. (London) 3 Vols
1789	MARY, or, The test of honour. By a lady.	Abraham. (London) 2 Vols
1791	CHARLOTTE. A tale of truth.	Minerva. (London) 2 Vols
1791	MENTORIA: or, The young lady's friend: in two volumes. By Mrs. Rowson, author of Victoria, &c. &c.	Printed for W. Lane. (London) 2 Vols
1792	REBECCA, or The fille de chambre, in three volumes. By the author of The Inquisitor, &c.	Printed for W. Lane. (London) 3 Vols
1795 [20]	**TRIALS OF THE HUMAN HEART, a novel.	Printed for the Author by Wrigley and Berriman. (Philadelphia) 4 Vols
1789	THE BELLE WIDOWS: with characteristic sketches of real personages and living characters. A novel, inscribed to the Beau-Monde. With a preface by the editor of The letters of Charlotte during her connexion with Werter.	Printed for J. Kerby. (London) 2 Vols

(P) RUDD, Margaret Caroline

AUTHOR	YEAR OF PUBLICATION	TITLE	PUBLISHER PLACE OF PUB. NO. OF VOLS
(P) RYVES, Elizabeth	1789	THE HERMIT OF SNOWDEN; or Memoirs of Albert and Lavinia. Faithfully taken from the original manuscript found in the hermitage.	(London)
* SANDERS [SAUNDERS], Charlotte Elizabeth	1787	EMBARRASSED ATTACHMENT.	(London)
SANDHAM, Elizabeth	1788–9 [21]	THE TWIN SISTERS; or The effects of education: a novel; in a series of letters. By a lady.	Printed for T. Hookham. 4Vols
SCOTT, Sarah (née ROBINSON)	1750	THE HISTORY OF CORNELIA.	Printed for A. Millar. (London)
	1754	AGREEABLE UGLINESS; or, The triumphs of the Graces, exemplified in the real life and fortunes of a young lady of some distinction.	R. & J. Dodsley. (London) 1 Vol.
	1754	A JOURNEY THROUGH EVERY STAGE OF LIFE, described in a variety of interesting scenes, drawn from real characters. By a person of quality.	Printed for A. Millar. (London) 2 Vols
	1762	A DESCRIPTION OF MILLENIUM HALL, AND THE COUNTRY ADJACENT: together with the characters and inhabitants, and such historical anecdotes and reflections, as may excite in the reader proper sentiments of humanity, and lead the mind to the love of virtue. By a gentleman on his travels.	Printed for J. Newbery. (London)
	1765 [22]	THE MAN OF REAL SENSIBILITY; or, The history of Sir George Ellison.	

Author	Title	Date	Publisher
	THE TEST OF FILIAL DUTY. In a series of letters between Miss Emilia Leonard, and Miss Charlotte Arlington. A novel.	1772	Printed for the Author. (London) 2 Vols
SEWARD, Anna	**LOUISA.	1782	
SEYMOUR, Mrs	THE CONDUCT OF A MARRIED LIFE. In a series of letters.	1753	
SHERIDAN, Frances	MEMOIRS OF MISS SIDNEY BIDULPH, extracted from her own journal & now first published.	1761	Dodsley. (London) 3 Vols
	CONCLUSION OF THE MEMOIRS OF MISS SYDNEY BIDDULPH, as prepared for the press by the late editor of the former part.	1767 Posthumous	(Dublin)
	THE HISTORY OF NOURJAHAD. By the editor of Sidney Bidulph.	1767 [24] Posthumous	Printed for J. Dodsley. (London)
(P) * SHERWOOD, Mary Martha (née BUTT)	THE TRADITIONS, a legendary tale. In two volumes. Written by a young lady.	1795	Printed for W. Lane. [Published by subscription.] (London) 2 Vols
(P) SKINN, Ann Emelinda (née MASTERMAN)	THE OLD MAID; or, History of Miss Emily Ravenscroft. In a series of letters. By Mrs. Skinn late Miss Masterman of York.	1771	Bell. (London) 3 Vols
(P) * SMITH, Charlotte	EMMELINE, the orphan of the castle.	1788	T. Cadell. (London) 4 Vols
	ETHELINDE, or The recluse of the lake. By Charlotte Smith. In five volumes.	1789	Printed for T. Cadell. (London) 5 Vols

AUTHOR	YEAR OF PUBLICATION	TITLE	PUBLISHER PLACE OF PUB. NO. OF VOLS
	1791	CELESTINA. A novel. In four volumes. By Charlotte Smith.	Printed for T. Cadell. (London) 4 Vols
	1792	DESMOND. A novel, in three volumes. By Charlotte Smith.	Printed for G.G.J. and J. Robinson. (London) 3 Vols
	1793	THE OLD MANOR HOUSE. A novel.	J. Bell. (London) 4 Vols
	1793	D'ARCY. A novel.	(Dublin)
	1794	THE WANDERINGS OF WARWICK. By Charlotte Smith.	Printed for J. Bell. (London)
	1794	THE BANISHED MAN. A novel.	T. Cadell Jnr, and W. Davies. (London) 4 Vols
	1795	MONTALBERT. A novel. By Charlotte Smith. In three volumes.	Printed by S. Low for E. Booker. (London) 3 Vols
	1796	MARCHMONT: a novel. By Charlotte Smith. In four volumes.	Printed for S. Low. (London) 4 Vols
SMYTHIES, [Susan]	1753 [25]	THE STAGE-COACH: containing the character of Mr. Manly, and the history of his fellow-travellers.	Printed for T. Osborne. (London) 2 Vols

206

	1754	THE HISTORY OF LUCY WELLERS. Written by a lady. In two volumes.	Printed for R. Baldwin. (London) 2 Vols
	1758	THE BROTHERS. In two volumes. By the author of The stage-coach, and Lucy Wellers.	Printed for R. and J. Dodsley. (London) 2 Vols
(P) SPENCER, Sarah Emma	1788	MEMOIRS OF THE MISS HOLMSBYS.	Smith. [Published by subscription.]
STRATTON, Jemima Maria	1794	THE MAID OF THE CASTLE. A legendary tale. In three cantos. By Jemima Maria Stratton.	Minerva. (London) 1 Vol.
STREET, Miss	1791	THE LAKE OF WINANDER MERE. A novel. By the editor of Maria.	Minerva. (London) 2 Vols
	1792	THE RECLUSE OF THE APPENINES, a tale, in two volumes. By the author of the lake of Windermere.	Printed for W. Lane. (London)
	1792	THEODORE: a domestic tale. In two volumes.	Printed for W. Lane. (London) 2 Vols
TAYLOR, Miss in collaboration with NUGENT, Miss		See NUGENT, Miss	
(P) THOMAS, Ann	1795	ADOLPHUS DE BIRON. A novel founded on the French Revolution.	Printed for the Authoress. [Published by subscription.] (Plymouth) 2 Vols

AUTHOR	YEAR OF PUBLICATION	TITLE	PUBLISHER PLACE OF PUB. NO. OF VOLS
* THOMSON, Harriet	1787	EXCESSIVE SENSIBILITY; or, The history of Lady St. Laurence. A novel.	Robinson. (London) 2 Vols
	1788	FATAL FOLLIES: or, The history of the Countess of Stanmore. In four volumes.	Printed for G.G.J. and J. Robinson. (London) 4 Vols
	1791	THE LABYRINTHS OF LIFE. By the author of Excessive sensibility and Fatal follies.	Robinsons. 4 Vols
(P) TIMBURY, Jane	1788	THE MALE COQUET.	
	1789	THE TRIUMPH OF FRIENDSHIP; or, The history of Charles Courtney, and Miss Julia Melville.	Fox. 2 Vols
	1790 [26]	THE PHILANTHROPIC RAMBLER.	Printed for, and sold by the Author, Petty France, Westminster. (London)
TODD, Elizabeth	1788	THE HISTORY OF LADY CAROLINE RIVERS. In a series of letters.	Printed for the Authoress. (London) 2 Vols
* TOMLINS, Elizabeth Sophia	1785	THE CONQUESTS OF THE HEART.	3 Vols
	1787	THE VICTIM OF FANCY, a novel. In two volumes. By a lady, author of The conquests of the heart.	Sold by R. Baldwin. (London) 2 Vols

		1792	MEMOIRS OF A BARONESS.	Griffith and Farran.
*	TRIMMER, Sarah	1786	FABULOUS HISTORIES. The history of the robins. For the instruction of children on their treatment of animals.	(London)
(P) *	WAKEFIELD, Priscilla	1787	THE SERVANT'S FRIEND, an exemplary tale.	(London)
		1787	THE TWO FARMERS, an exemplary tale, &c.	(London)
		1795–8 [27]	JUVENILE ANECDOTES, founded on facts.	(London) 2 Vols
(P) *	WALKER, Lady Mary (afterwards HAMILTON)	1776	LETTERS FROM THE DUCHESS DE CRUI AND OTHERS, on Subjects Moral and Entertaining.	
		1777	MEMOIRS OF THE MARCHIONESS DE LOUVOIS. In letters. By a lady.	Robson. (London) 3 Vols
		1778	MUNSTER VILLAGE. A novel. In two volumes.	Printed for Robson and Co. (London) 2 Vols
		1782	THE LIFE OF MRS. JUSTMAN.	
	WARTON, Jane	1783	PEGGY AND PATTY; or, The Sisters of Ashdale.	Dodsley. (London) 4 Vols
*	WATTS, Susanna	1794	WONDERFUL TRAVELS OF PRINCE FANFEREDIN, THE COUNTRY OF ARCADIA.	(Northampton)
(P) *	WEST, Jane (under the pseudonym 'PRUDENTIA HOMESPUN')	1793	THE ADVANTAGES OF EDUCATION, or The history of Maria Williams. A tale for misses and their mammas, by Prudentia Homespun.	Printed for W. Lane (London) 2 Vols
		1796	A GOSSIP'S STORY, AND A LEGENDARY TALE. By the author of Advantages of education.	T.N. Longman, and O. Rees. (London) 2 Vols

AUTHOR	YEAR OF PUBLICATION	TITLE	PUBLISHER PLACE OF PUB. NO. OF VOLS
(P) * WILLIAMS, Helen Maria	1790	JULIA, a novel; interspersed with some poetical pieces. By Helen Maria Williams. In two volumes.	Printed for T. Cadell. (London) 2 Vols
	1794 [28]	THE CASTLE OF COUNT RODERICK.	
(P) * WOLLSTONECRAFT, Mary	1788	MARY, A FICTION.	J. Johnson. (London)
	1788	ORIGINAL STORIES FROM REAL LIFE; with conversations calculated to regulate the affections, and form the mind to truth and goodness.	J. Johnson. (London)
WOODFIN, Mrs A.	1756	NORTHERN MEMOIRS, or, The history of a Scotch family. Written by a lady.	J. Noble.
	1758 [29]	HISTORY OF MISS SALLY SABLE. By the author of Memoirs of a Scotch family.	(London) 2 Vols
	1760	THE AUCTION: a modern novel. In two volumes.	Printed for T. Lownds. (London) 2 Vols
	1762	THE HISTORY OF MISS HARRIOT WATSON.	Lownds. (London) 2 Vols
	1764	THE DISCOVERY: or, Memoirs of Miss Marianne Middleton.	(London) 2 Vols

(P) YEARSLEY, Ann (known as the 'BRISTOL MILKWOMAN')	1795 [30]	THE ROYAL CAPTIVES: a fragment of secret history. Copied from an old manuscript.	(London) 4 Vols [Also Irish imprint for 1795, J. Stockdale (Dublin) 2 Vols]
* YOUNG, Mary Julia	1791	THE FAMILY PARTY. In three volumes.	Printed for W. Lane. (London) 3 Vols

211

APPENDIX B
A chronological list of women authors
1696–1796

Annual totals are given beside the names of those authors who published more than one novel in a year; an asterisk indicates that the writer worked collaboratively on the publication. It should be noted that this appendix does not record those novels listed in Appendix A that have been excluded from the statistical analysis.

DATES

1696	MANLEY, Delarivière; PIX, Mary
1704	DAVYS, Mary
1705	DAVYS, Mary; MANLEY, Delarivière
1709	ELFORD, Sophia; MANLEY, Delarivière
1710	MANLEY, Delarivière
1711	MANLEY, Delarivière
1713	BARKER, Jane
1715	BARKER, Jane
1716	BUTLER, Sarah
1718	HEARNE, Mary
1719	HAYWOOD, Eliza; HEARNE, Mary
1720	MANLEY, Delarivière
1721	AUBIN, Penelope (2)
1722	AUBIN, Penelope (2); HAYWOOD, Eliza
1723	AUBIN, Penelope; BARKER, Jane; HAYWOOD, Eliza (3)
1724	DAVYS, Mary; HAYWOOD, Eliza (6)
1725	HAYWOOD, Eliza (10)
1726	AUBIN, Penelope; BARKER, Jane; HAYWOOD, Eliza (5)
1727	DAVYS, Mary; HAYWOOD, Eliza (6); HERBERTS, Mary
1728	AUBIN, Penelope; HAYWOOD, Eliza (3); ROWE, Elizabeth
1729	HAYWOOD, Eliza
1730	HAYWOOD, Eliza
1732	BOYD, Elizabeth; DAVYS, Mary
1733	GRAINGER, Lydia
1734	HARDING, Elizabeth

1735	NOAKE, Dorothy
1736	HAYWOOD, Eliza
1744	COLLYER, Mary; FIELDING, Sarah; HAYWOOD, Eliza
1745	McCARTHY, Charlotte
1747	FIELDING, Sarah (2)
1748	HAYWOOD, Eliza
1749	COLLYER, Mary (2); FIELDING, Sarah
1750	LENNOX, Charlotte; SCOTT, Sarah
1751	HAYWOOD, Eliza
1752	LENNOX, Charlotte
1753	BARRY, Mrs; FIELDING, Sarah (2); HARVEY, Mrs; HAYWOOD, Eliza (2); SEYMOUR, Mrs; SMYTHIES, Miss
1754	COLLIER, Jane *; FIELDING, Sarah *; SCOTT, Sarah (2); SMYTHIES, Miss
1755	CHARKE, Charlotte; HAYWOOD, Eliza
1756	CHARKE, Charlotte; WOODFIN, Mrs A.
1757	FIELDING, Sarah; MEADES, Anna
1758	CHARKE, Charlotte; LENNOX, Charlotte; SMYTHIES, Miss, WOODFIN, Mrs A.
1759	FIELDING, Sarah
1760	FIELDING, Sarah; PAUL, Sarah; WOODFIN, Mrs A.
1761	SHERIDAN, Frances
1762	COOPER, Maria S.; LENNOX, Charlotte; SCOTT, Sarah; WOODFIN, Mrs A.
1763	BROOKE, Frances; COOPER, Maria S.; GUNNING, Susannah*; MINIFIE, Margaret*
1764	GIBBES, Phebe; GUNNING, Susannah; WOODFIN, Mrs A.
1765	SCOTT, Sarah
1766	GUNNING, Susannah*; MARISHALL, Jean; MINIFIE, Margaret*
1767	GIBBES, Phebe; MARISHALL, Jean; SHERIDAN, Frances (2)
1768	MINIFIE, Margaret
1769	ATKYNS, Lady; BROOKE, Frances; COOPER, Maria S.; GRIFFITH, Elizabeth; MINIFIE, Margaret
1770	DAWE, Anne; DUBOIS, Lady Dorothea; GUNNING, Susannah
1771	AUSTIN, Mrs; BRISCOE, Sophia; EYTON, Elizabeth; GRIFFITH, Elizabeth; LATTER, Mary; MEADES, Anna; SKINN, Anne
1772	BONHOTE, Elizabeth; BRISCOE, Sophia; SCOTT, Sarah
1773	BONHOTE, Elizabeth; DEVONSHIRE, Duchess of; FOGERTY, Mrs
1775	BERRY, Miss; COOPER, Maria S.
1776	GRIFFITH, Elizabeth; WALKER, Lady Mary

1777 BONHOTE, Elizabeth; BROOKE, Frances; FURGUSS, Miss;
REEVE, Clara; ROGERS, Miss A.; WALKER, Lady Mary
1778 BURNEY, Frances; GIBBES, Phebe; WALKER, Lady Mary
1779 CARTWRIGHT, Mrs H.; CRAVEN, Lady Elizabeth;
DEVONSHIRE, Duchess of; NUGENT, Miss*; TAYLOR, Miss*
1780 BLOWER, Elizabeth; CARTWRIGHT, Mrs H.; EDWARDS,
Miss; ELLIOTT, Miss; KILNER, Mary Ann; MINIFIE,
Margaret; PALMER, Charlotte
1781 ELLIOT, Miss (2); KILNER, Dorothy
1782 BLOWER, Elizabeth; BURNEY, Frances; KILNER, Mary Ann;
WALKER, Lady Mary
1783 COX, Anna M.; ELLIOT (2), Miss; FENN, Lady Eleanor (2);
KILNER, Mary Ann; LEE, Sophia; MEZIERE, Harriet;
MINIFIE, Margaret; REEVE, Clara; ROBERTS, Miss R.;
WARTON, Jane
1784 BROMLEY, Eliza Nugent; GWYNN, Albinia; MORRIS, Mrs;
PARRY, Catherine
1785 BENNETT, Agnes M.; BLOWER, Elizabeth; BOYS, Mrs S.;
CARTWRIGHT, Mrs H.; COX, Anna M.; GWYNN, Albinia;
HOLFORD, Margaret; KEIR, Susanna; KILNER, Dorothy;
MATHEWS, Mrs; PEACOCK, Lucy; PEDDLE, M.;
TOMLINS, Elizabeth S.
1786 BENNETT, Agnes M.; COX, Anna M.; FULLER, Anne (2);
HARLEY, M; HUGHES, Anne Rice; JOHNSON, Mrs (2);
LEE, Harriet; MEZIERE, Harriet; PEACOCK, Lucy; PYE, Jael
Henrietta; ROWSON, Susanna; TRIMMER, Sarah
1787 BONHOTE, Elizabeth; BOUVERIE, Georgina; BURKE, Mrs;
CARTWRIGHT, Mrs H. (2); GALES, Winifred M.; HELME,
Elizabeth; HOWELL, Ann; HUGHES, Anne; JOHNSON, Mrs;
KEIR, Susanna; SANDERS, Charlotte E.; THOMSON, Harriet;
TOMLINS, Elizabeth S.; TRIMMER, Sarah (2)
1788 BLOWER, Elizabeth; BURKE, Mrs; GIBBES, Phebe; HARLEY,
M.; HAWKE, Lady Cassandra; HELME, Elizabeth; HERVEY,
Elizabeth; HUGHES, Anne; REEVE, Clara; ROWSON,
Susanna; SANDHAM, Elizabeth; SMITH, Charlotte; SPENCER,
Sarah E.; THOMSON, Harriet; TIMBURY, Jane; TODD,
Elizabeth; WOLLSTONECRAFT, Mary (2)
1789 ALEXANDER, Judith; BENNETT, Agnes M.; BONHOTE,
Elizabeth; BROOKS, Indiana; CHAMPION DE CRESPIGNY,
Lady Mary; COWLEY, Mrs; COX, Anna M.; FENN, Lady
Eleanor (2); FULLER, Anne; GIBBES, Phebe; GOMERSALL,
Ann; HARLEY, M.; HOWELL, Ann (2); JOHNSON, Mrs;
MATHEWS, Mrs; NORMAN, Elizabeth; PURBECK,
Elizabeth*; PURBECK,

Jane*; RADCLIFFE, Ann; ROBINSON, Mary 'Perdita';
ROCHE, Regina M.; ROWSON, Susanna; RUDD, Margaret C.;
RYVES, Elizabeth; SMITH, Charlotte; TIMBURY, Jane

1790   BALLIN, Rossetta; BONHOTE, Elizabeth; BROOKE, Frances;
COX, Anna M.; EDEN, Anne; FINGLASS, Esther;
GOMERSALL, Ann; GREEN, Sarah; HERON, Mary;
HERVEY, Elizabeth; KILNER, Dorothy; KNIGHT, Ellis C.;
LENNOX, Charlotte; MATHEWS, Mrs; OPIE, Amelia;
PARSONS, Eliza; PILKINGTON, Miss; PURBECK,
Elizabeth*; PURBECK, Jane*; RADCLIFFE, Ann;
RADCLIFFE, Mary Anne (2); TIMBURY, Jane; WILLIAMS,
Helen M.

1791   CLARKE, Eliza; COX, Anna M.; INCHBALD, Elizabeth;
MATHEWS, Mrs; MORRIS, Mrs; PARSONS, Eliza;
PINCHARD, Elizabeth; PURBECK, Elizabeth*; PURBECK,
Jane*; RADCLIFFE, Ann; REEVE, Clara; ROWSON, Susanna
(2); SMITH, Charlotte; STREET, Miss; THOMSON, Harriet;
YOUNG, Mary J.

1792   COX, Anna M. (2); FELL, Mrs; GUNNING, Susannah;
HUNTER, Maria; KNIGHT, Ellis C.; MATHEWS, Mrs;
MORE, Hannah; PALMER, Charlotte (2); REEVE, Clara;
ROBINSON, Mary 'Perdita'; ROWSON, Susanna; SMITH,
Charlotte; STREET, Miss (2); TOMLINS, Elizabeth S.

1793   GUNNING, Susannah; HARLEY, M.; MATHEWS, Charlotte;
PARSONS, Eliza (3); PEACOCK, Lucy; PILKINGTON, Miss;
PORTER, Anna M.; REEVE, Clara; ROCHE, Regina M.;
SMITH, Charlotte (2); WEST, Jane

1794   BENNETT, Agnes M.; CHARLTON, Mary; DE ACTON,
Eugenia; GOSLING, Jane; GUNNING, Elizabeth (2);
HELME, Elizabeth; KELLY, Isabella; MATHEWS, Charlotte;
PARSONS, Eliza; PEACOCK, Lucy; PEARSON, Susanna;
PINCHARD, Elizabeth; RADCLIFFE, Ann; ROBINSON,
Mary 'Perdita'; ROBINSON, Maria E.; SMITH, Charlotte (2);
STRATTON, Jemima M.; WATTS, Susanna; WILLIAMS,
Helen M.

1795   BULLOCK, Mrs; COX, Anna M.; EDGEWORTH, Maria;
FENWICK, Eliza; FOSTER, Mrs E.M.; GOOCH, Elizabeth S.;
HARLEY, M.; HUGHES, Anne; HURRY, Mrs Ives; KELLY,
Isabella; KILNER, Dorothy; MEEKE, Mary (2); MUSGRAVE,
Agnes; PARKER, Mary E.; PARSONS, Eliza; SHERWOOD,
Mary M.; SMITH, Charlotte; THOMAS, Ann; WAKEFIELD,
Priscilla; YEARSLEY, Ann

1796   BONHOTE, Elizabeth; BURKE, Mrs (2); BURNEY, Frances;
BURNEY, Sarah H.; CHAMPION DE CRESPIGNY, Lady

Mary; COURTNEY, Mrs; COX, Anna M.; CRAIK, Helen; DRAPER, Sarah; EDGEWORTH, Maria; FITZJOHN, Matilda; GOMERSALL, Ann; GOOCH, Elizabeth S.; GUNNING, Susannah; HAMILTON, Elizabeth; HAYS, Mary; HELME, Elizabeth; HERVEY, Elizabeth; HOWELL, Anne (2); INCHBALD, Elizabeth; KELLY, Isabella; LANSDELL, Sarah; LARA, Catherine (2); PARSONS, Eliza (2); PEACOCK, Lucy; PLUMPTRE, Annabella; PLUMPTRE, Anne; PURBECK, Elizabeth*; PURBECK, Jane*; ROBINSON, Mary 'Perdita' (3); ROCHE, Regina M.; SMITH, Charlotte; WEST, Jane

NOTES

1 EARLIER INTERPRETATIONS OF THE DEVELOPMENT OF EIGHTEENTH-CENTURY WOMEN'S FICTION

1 See also: Littlewood 1921; Eshleman 1949; Donnelly 1949; Jones 1952 [1968]; and McBurney 1959.

2 For example, Singer 1933 [1963] includes the following novels which are not listed in any of the bibliographies consulted during the compilation of the appendices: Mrs Seymour, *The Conduct of a Married Life. In a Series of Letters* (1753) (1933: 127); and Mrs Morris, *Illicit Love* (1791) (1933: 132). Singer's chapter surveying 'The Epistolary Novel from Richardson to 1800' (1933: 99–155) mentions over thirty female authors.

3 For a discussion of anonymity and the work of eighteenth-century women prose-fiction writers, see ch. 2, pp. 27–8; ch. 3, p. 46; ch. 5, pp. 91–2 and pp. 94–5; and ch. 7, p. 134.

4 Séjourné 1966 does include a decade by decade arrangement (from 1740 to 1790) of an alphabetical list of the better-known writers with their works and the most important critical and biographical texts. However, he does not observe the decadal boundaries and authors are entered in the decade during which their first publication appeared, accompanied by all their subsequent publications. For example, we find Sarah Fielding listed within 1740 because of *David Simple* (1744), along with all her works up to 1760.

5 See Fetterley 1978 for an exposition of this concept. See also Schweickart 1989.

6 In the preface to *Incognita: or, Love and Duty Reconciled*, Congreve argued that romances

> are generally composed of the Constant Loves and invincible Courages of Hero's, Heroins [*sic*], Kings and Queens, Mortals of the first Rank, and so forth; where lofty Language, miraculous Contingencies and impossible Performances, elevate and surprize the Reader into a giddy Delight, which leaves him flat upon the Ground . . . when he is forced to be very well convinced that 'tis all a lye. Novels are of a more familiar nature; Come near us, and represent to us Intrigues in practice, delight us with Accidents and odd Events, but not such as are wholly unusual or unprecedented: . . .
> (1692 [1971]: ii–iii)

7 See, for example: Whicher 1915; Anderson 1935–36; Hilbish 1941; Palomo 1978; Koon 1978–9; Larson 1981 (ch. 2 for a study of Sarah Robinson Scott; ch. 3 for a study of Charlotte Ramsay Lennox); and Morgan 1987.

8 For example, although Showalter 1977 had a similar focus to that of this study, 'the

professional writer who wants pay and publication, not . . . the diarist or letter-writer' (1977: 12), she began her analysis with the Brontës, arguing that although nineteenth-century women novelists were familiar with the work of earlier authors like Burney, Edgeworth, Radcliffe, and Austen, 'as well as with scores of lesser writers such as Inchbald', there was relatively little direct influence between them, and almost 'no sense of communality and self-awareness . . . apparent among women writers before the 1840s'. She continued:

> More important than the question of direct literary influence, however, is the difference between the social and professional worlds inhabited by the eighteenth- and nineteenth-century women. The early women writers refused to deal with a professional role, or had a negative orientation towards it. . . . These women may have been less than sincere in their insistence that literary success brought them only suffering, but they were not able to see themselves as involved in a vocation that brought responsibilities as well as conflicts, and opportunites as well as burdens. Moreover, they did not see their writing as an aspect of their female experience, or as an expression of it.
>
> (ibid.: 18–19)

2 SEVENTEENTH-CENTURY FOUNDATIONS

1 For the second half of the century, Matthews 1950 includes diaries by: Elizabeth Mordaunt, Viscountess of County Down; Mary Rich, Countess of Warwick; an anonymous female relative of Oliver Cromwell; Elizabeth Bury of Clare in Suffolk; Sarah Savage; Elizabeth Freke; an anonymous French refugee; Mary Woodforde of Binstead; Celia Fiennes; and an anonymous business diary by a London midwife. We can add to this diaries by Jane Ward, whose record of her visions was published in 1699; and Margaret Blagge, later Mrs Godolphin (see Evelyn 1955: 152).

2 For the second half of the century, Matthews 1955 includes autobiographies by: Mary Rich, Countess of Warwick; Mrs William Veitch; Anne Jackson; Jane Turner (see also Hobby 1988: 68–9, who discusses Turner's *Choice Experiences* (1653) as a conversion narrative); Alice Thornton; Lady Ann Fanshawe; Lucy Hutchinson; and Margaret Cavendish, Duchess of Newcastle. We can add to these, autobiographical pieces by Anne, Lady Halkett (see Reynolds 1920 [1964]; and Hobby 1984); and Lady Anne Clifford (Hobby 1988). For a discussion of the range of the 'dozens' of extant autobiographical texts by seventeenth-century women, including conversion narratives and pamphlets by radical sectaries, see Graham *et al.* 1989: 1–27.

3 Matthews describes Jane Turner as the wife of a sea captain (1955: 310); Sarah Savage (1664–1732) as the Nonconformist daughter of the Reverend Philip Henry (1950: 49); and Alice Thornton as the wife of a Yorkshire gentleman (1955: 304).

4 See Morton (1970: 28) for the response of Katherine Chidley's supporters to her published replies to the hostile Presbyterian Thomas Edwards.

5 For example, in the 'Introduction' to *The Parental Monitor*, Elizabeth Bonhote stated that the sole initial motivation behind her writing was the desire to provide private guidance for her children in the event of her own early death. However, she went on to explain her decision to enter the public domain in terms of a larger mission:

> Another very interesting inducement for making them public arose from the pleasant reflection, that by so doing they might possibly be useful to others; that the orphan, the uninstructed, the thoughtless, neglected, or

distressed, might find, in the monitions of the mother and the friend, a
guide to direct their unguarded steps through the devious and dangerous
paths of life. The earnest desire of being serviceable to my fellow-creatures,
and in some degree supplying the place of a parent to those deprived of a
parent's tender care, armed me with trembling resolution to encounter
censure, rendered me indifferent to all illiberal reflections, and encouraged
me to hope I should meet with the indulgence of the generous and candid
for the attempt, however I may have failed in the execution of it.

(1788: vol. 1, viii-ix)

6 For details, see n. 5.

7 Hannah Wolley's impressive example was followed by other seventeenth-
century women who earned money by both writing about and teaching cookery
skills. The substantial interest in such matters, and the desire to record and read
about them, is further suggested by surviving recipes that were written privately, perhaps over years or even decades, to pass on accummulated knowledge
within a family. For example, Jane Mosley, the daughter of affluent Derbyshire
graziers, kept a small octavo notebook of her recipes (c.1669–1712). Her awareness of potential readers is suggested by the added literary flourishes of her own
love poem and, at least initially, a careful script and sub-headings; see Mosley
1979.

8 Elizabeth Cellier sought funding in 1687 for a royal hospital and college for
midwives. In 1688 she defended the scheme through the pamphlet *To Dr———:
An Answer to His Queries Concerning the Colledg of Midwives* in which she
asserted that it had received James II's consent. See Donnison 1977: 18–20; and
Hobby 1988: 187–9.

9 For example, the Duchess of Newcastle wrote twenty-six plays as part of her
considerable literary activity during this period. Unfortunately for someone who
acknowledged an ambition that was 'restless, and not ordinary, because it would
have an extraordinary fame', she can have had little hope of seeing her material
performed on the stage (Cavendish 1656: xi). For details of women's involvement
in the theatre during this period see Cotton 1980.

10 By comparison with Behn their achievements have remained obscure, but they
were well known to contemporary audiences. These dramatists had four, five,
twelve, and nineteen plays produced and published, respectively. Trotter's *The
Fatal Friendship* (1698) and Pix's *The Innocent Mistress* (1697) were performed at
Lincoln's Inn Fields with considerable success; whilst Centlivre's *The Busy Body*
(1709) and *The Wonder! A Woman Keeps A Secret* (1714) were both performed
several hundred times before 1800, and many times thereafter. Centlivre's most
outstanding comedy, *A Bold Stroke for a Wife* (1718), became a stock piece in the
first half of the century.

11 *The Female Wits or the Triumvirate of Poets at Rehearsal* is reprinted in Morgan
1981: 392–433; she dates the first performance to c.1697.

12 See ch. 3, p. 46.

13 Singer 1933 [1963] demonstrated that a substantial quantity of this type of prose
fiction was produced between the late seventeenth and early nineteenth centuries,
and that many women novelists chose this form. See also Day 1966; and Perry
1980.

14 Its considerable success, passing through at least sixteen editions by the end of the
eighteenth century, was due in part to the nature of the subject matter. This was
the real love affair between Lord Grey of Werk and his sister-in-law Lady
Henriette Berkley that had been reported in the *London Gazette* and which Behn
described through a series of imaginary letters between 'Philander' and 'Sylvia'.

3 THE GROWTH OF WOMEN'S FICTION

1 See also Spacks 1976; for a discussion of Manley's *Rivella* (1714), which is a good example of the close relationship between autobiography and fiction at this time, see Barash 1987.

2 Appendix A includes eight works that have been excluded from the analysis. Each one is indicated by a double asterisk beside the title and an explanation is given in a reference.

3 For each year in turn from 1698 to 1794, the mean average number of novels produced in the five-year period centred on that year has been calculated, thus producing the entry for that year. Based on the appendices, which cover the period 1696 to 1796, entries can only be calculated for the period 1698 to 1794 as information is required for the two years either side of the year of entry. However, since in the course of research no novels were uncovered for 1694 and 1695, it has been considered reasonable to regard the totals for these years as zero and to calculate the entries for 1696 and 1697 accordingly. The years 1797 and 1798 are outside the primary focus of this study and, although information about women's fiction published in those years has been compiled, the search was not exhaustive. Therefore, the entries for the years 1795 and 1796 have been projected in order to facilitate comparisons with the other figures. This has been achieved by assuming that the values for 1795 and 1796 increased annually by the average rate of increase for the previous ten entries.

4 The variations would be much more pronounced than occurred for the novel data since there are fewer novelists. Additionally, it is not possible to smooth out these variations meaningfully by using the five-year moving average technique. Since novelists can occur more than once during a five-year period a simple moving average would actually produce the number of different novelists writing in those five years multiplied by their average rate of production for that period, which is a statistic of little value.

5 For this calculation each novelist has been counted as a writer for each year between and including the years of her first and last publication. The total for any year is thus the number of women whose literary activities spanned that date.

6 Taking each year between 1696 and 1794 in turn, the number of different women with a five-year period spanning that year has been calculated. In effect this method means that if a novelist failed to publish for five years a gap appears in her literary career. For example, if a writer published a novel in 1765 and again in 1770, then no gap will occur since the five-year period centred on 1765 ends in 1767 and the period centred on 1770 begins in 1768. If, however, she published first in 1765 and again in 1771, then as the first five-year period ends in 1767 and the second begins in 1769, she is viewed as having a one-year gap in her career.

7 It is only possible to calculate these figures for the period 1696 to 1794 for reasons similar to those which applied to the five-year moving average of the novel data. These were outlined in n. 3. Projected entries for 1795 and 1796 are presented in Figure 4 and these have been calculated as outlined in n. 3.

8 The average rate of production has been obtained by dividing the total number of novels by the number of different novelists in each moving five-year period, producing the average rate of production for writers during those five years.

9 The growth in women's fiction continued into the nineteenth century. Approximately 40 per cent of the women in Appendix A published after 1796 (indicated by an asterisk beside their names) and a number of these authors produced in quantity. Most notable amongst them was Mary Martha Sherwood, who achieved the extraordinary total of eighty-five novels between 1799 and 1848. Furthermore, new women continued to enter in the market. According to

information in Blakey 1939, five appeared in William Lane's lists in 1797 (1939: 181–2), four in 1798 (ibid.: 184–6), followed by three more in 1799 (ibid.: 188–9). At least five of these new 'Minerva' writers produced more than one publication during these years. The early decades of the nineteenth century saw the emergence of yet more highly productive writers including Frances Trollope, Catherine Gore, Charlotte Yonge, and Margaret Oliphant.

10 Some literary historians have offered more dramatic conclusions. For example, Figes 1982: 11 and Rogers 1982: 22, echoing the comments of hostile or concerned eighteenth-century observers, claim that by the final decades of the century women novelists actually outnumbered their male competitors.

11 Lackington offered an interesting speculation as to why the cessation of hostilities might have influenced the sale of books. He argued

> that if there is any thing in the news-papers of consequence, that draws many to the coffee house, where they chat away the evenings, instead of visiting the shops of booksellers . . . or *reading* at home. The best time for bookselling, is when there is no kind of news stirring.
>
> (1792: 385)

12 During this period, numerous family businesses, in widely varying trades, were carried forward by widows. For example, Plomer *et al.* (1922; 1932) list substantial numbers of women engaged successfully in printing, bookselling, and publishing; witness the career of Mrs Anderson who succeeded to her husband's Edinburgh printing business after his death in 1676 and ran it for forty years. During this time she held a monopolistic position as the King's Printer, and printer to the town and college, and in 1712 she became printer to the General Assembly (1922: 6). Women were also apprenticed throughout the clothing trades, where large numbers worked as milliners, mantua makers, stay makers, embroiderers, and seamstresses. Pinchbeck (1930 [1981]: 287) suggests that this field 'offered greater scope than any other in which women were concerned, and therefore attracted women with capital and some social standing' who established their own businesses. For a discussion of the employment opportunities available to women from the middle ranks, see ch. 4, pp. 66–78.

13 For a discussion of sexual morality during this period, see also: O'Malley 1933; Thomas 1959; Benkovitz 1976; Laslett 1977; Stone 1979; Boucé 1982; Amussen 1987; Ingram 1988; and Jones 1990.

14 For example, according to Morgan

> Mrs Manley was not happy with the actors [who performed her comedy *The Lost Lover* in 1696], and the actors were not happy with her. Given this miserable situation, it is impossible to judge whether the play's failure was entirely due to the fact that it is not very good.
>
> (1987: 74)

15 The anonymous author of a preliminary address 'To the World' in *The Works of the Celebrated Mrs. Centlivre* recorded how the dramatist

> Was even ashamed to proclaim her own Genius, probably because the Custom of the Times discounted poetical Excellence in a Female. The Gentleman of the Quill published it not, perhaps envying her superior Talents; and her Bookseller, complying with national Prejudices, put a fictitious Name to her Love's Contrivance, thro' Fear that the Work shou'd be contemned if known to be Feminine. . . . Her play of the *Busy Body*, when known to be the work of a Woman, scarce defray'd the Expenses of the First Night.
>
> ([Anon] 1761: vol. 1, vii–viii)

221

16 The commercial potential of describing (and then condemning) thwarted and successful sexual assault is demonstrated not only by the trajectory of Haywood's career, but also by the inclusion of these powerful themes in the work of later novelists, most notably Samuel Richardson.

17 See the account of these exchanges in Morgan 1987: 115–17.

18 According to *Curll Papers. Stray Notes on The Life and Publications of Edmund Curll, From Notes and Queries* 1879: 79, 'The Author to Let' is 'more probably from the pen of the writer who prefixed to *The Dunciad* the Letter to the Publisher signed William Cleland – namely, Pope himself'. This attribution would help to explain an apparent *volte face* by Savage, who praised Haywood in verses prefixed to her *Love in Excess* (1719–20) and *The Rash Resolve* (1724).

19 Reeve's opinion of Manley's contribution was less favourable: 'She hoarded up all the public and private scandal within her reach, and poured it forth' (1785 [1930]: 119).

20 See Reeve 1785 [1930]: 111 for a later exposition of the distinction between 'The Romance' and 'The Novel'.

21 For details of Aubin's publications, including re-editions, see McBurney 1960.

22 Wollstonecraft's attack cites *The Platonic Marriage* (1787) by Mrs H. Cartwright amongst other 'interesting tales'. She continued her criticisms of the 'reveries of the stupid novelists' in *Vindication of the Rights of Woman* (1792 [1975]: 306). See also ch. 7, p. 129.

23 It can be perceived also in the tone of Anna Laetitia Barbauld's reponse to Wollstonecraft's *Vindication*, 'The Rights of Woman', which opens with the call:

> Yes, injured Woman! rise, assert thy right!
> Woman! too long degraded, scorned, opprest;
> O born to rule in partial Law's despite,
> Resume thy native empire o'er the breast!
>
> Go forth arrayed in panoply divine;
> That angel pureness which admits no stain;
> Go, bid proud Man his boasted rule resign,
> And kiss the golden sceptre of thy reign.

(1825: vol. 1, 185)

4 PROFESSIONAL AUTHORSHIP – THE ALTERNATIVES FOR WOMEN

1 There are women writers in Appendix A who are not eligible for consideration in this context because their professional activity belonged to a period outside the scope of this study. For example, Eliza Fenwick wrote in order to support herself and her two children after she separated from her alcoholic husband in 1800.

2 Hannah Cowley's career demonstrates that it was still possible for a late eighteenth-century professional woman writer to work almost exclusively in the theatre. Her thirteen plays included some of the most popular comedies of the period. Mary Barber, the wife of a Dublin-based woollen-draper, published several works of poetry during her career, the most famous being her *Poems on Several Occasions* (1734). This attracted a substantial and impressive list of subscribers, largely due to the persistent efforts of Swift, and the profit helped to support her in her widowhood. See ch. 6, p. 106 for further details of Swift's involvement with Barber and other literary women.

3 For an account of the case, see *The Gentleman's Magazine* 1766: vol. 36, 537–9.

4 Ch. 1, p. 14 refers to the recent reinterpretation by McKeon (1988) of the social and cultural context of the 'origins' of the novel and its relationship with the 'rising' middle class.

5 Habakkuk (1950) suggests that the prospect was slightly more favourable for mercantile heiresses.

6 Defoe in his *An Essay upon Projects* (1697) identified lack of education as a key cause of women's subjection. As Clinton (1974–5) demonstrates, such arguments were propounded also by a number of *philosophes* including Montesquieu, Diderot, Voltaire, Grimm, and Condorcet. These assaults upon notions of the 'natural' incapacity of women provided a context within which later eighteenth-century writers like M.A. Radcliffe, Wollstonecraft, and Hays could launch their own critiques.

7 Richardson was also known for his qualified support of women's education. For example, see his letter of February–March 1751 to Lady Bradshaigh (1964: 177–9); and his letter to Thomas Edwards of 25 July 1754 (1964: 309–10). See also Wilkes 1741.

For a reference to the possible identity of 'Sophia', see Rosenkrantz in Todd 1987: 292. *Woman Not Inferior to Man* was swiftly countered by *Man superior to Woman; containing a plain confutation of the fallacious arguments of Sophia in her late Treatise intitled Woman not Inferior to Man.* 'Sophia' responded in 1740 with *Woman's Superior Excellence over Men: or, A Reply to the Author of a Late Treatise, entitled, Men Superior to Woman, In which the excessive weakness of that Gentleman's answer to Woman not Inferior to Man is exposed.* The three pamphlets were published together a few years later as *Beauty's Triumph*.

8 Elizabeth Elstob published by subscription *An English-Saxon Homily on the Birth-day of St. Gregory . . . translated into modern English* (1709), and *Rudiments of Grammar for the English-Saxon-Tongue, First Given in English; With an Apology for the Study of Northern Antiquities* (1715). See Green 1980.

9 Kamm 1965 offers a wide-ranging discussion of girls' education in the eighteenth century; see also Schnorrenberg 1976.

10 See ch. 2, pp. 25–6; and Hobby 1988, ch. 8.

11 For these events to be successful an actress had to attract the attention of notable people. For example, see the letter from Mrs Bellamy to Dr Johnson seeking his patronage at her benefit, after she had been 'reduced to the greatest distress' by a 'long chancery suit, and a complicated train of unfortunate events' (11 May 1783, in Boswell 1799 [1927]: vol. 2, 512, n. 1).

12 Oldfield also left ten guineas to her aunt Jane Gourlaw, or an annuity of £30 for life if her mother died before her aunt. This was altered by a codicil bequeathing her aunt an annuity of £10 during her mother's lifetime. Details from 'A True Copy of the Last Will and Testament of Mrs Anne Oldfield', in Egerton 1731: Appendices 2 and 3.

13 Charke's account provides a fascinating glimpse into the hard and occasionally burlesque quality of this makeshift existence. For example, she described performing *The Beaux Strategem* before a less than appreciative audience:

> In the first Row of the Pit sat a Range of drunken Butchers, some of whom soon entertained us with the inharmonious Musick of their Nostrils: Behind them were seated, as I suppose, their unsizable Consorts, who seemed to enjoy the same State of Happiness their dear Spouses were possessed of; but, having more Vivacity than the Males, laugh'd *'and talk'd louder than the Players'*.
>
> (1755: 203–4)

14 Phebe Phillips, alias Maria Maitland, published an account of her life as a

courtesan under the title *Woman of the Town*; Lady Vane's *Memoirs of a Lady of Quality* (1751) recorded her life and amatory encounters (for an opinion of Lady Vane's conduct, see Lady Mary Wortley Montagu's letter to Lady Pomfret, 1739 in Montagu 1986: 163); whilst according to the *Gentleman's Magazine* (1766: vol. 36, 83–4) Teresia Constantia Phillips's notorious *An Apology for the Conduct of Mrs. Teresia Constantia Phillips* (1748–9) 'was a subject of universal conversation in *England*'.

15 Plomer *et al.* (1932: 121) record that on the verso of the last page of *The Virtuous Villager* (1742) there is an advertisement headed 'New Books, sold by Eliza Haywood, publisher, at the sign of Fame in Covent Garden'. It mentions only two books and the venture was apparently short-lived. Altogether, this source includes over 100 women who were engaged in the book trades during this period.

5 WOMEN NOVELISTS AND THEIR PUBLISHERS

1 For additional information for Scotland, see: Carnie and Doig 1959; Carnie 1961; and Bowers 1962.
2 It should be noted that these figures are only approximate since some individual entries in the sources may in fact refer to the same person. For example: Keinton (M) could also be K. Mary; Johnson, R. could also be Johnson (Roberts); or J (T) could be Thomas, James – all of which are recorded separately.
3 In addition to working as a housekeeper, Elizabeth Raffald helped to establish a newspaper and she produced the first Manchester directory. Her *Experienced English Housekeeper* (1769) was so successful that she is alleged to have sold the copyright for £1,400 in 1773.
4 The printer J. Miller advertised one of his pamphlets as being on sale at J. Almon's shop in Piccadilly. The pamphlet contained one of the notorious letters of Junius and Almon was charged with publishing seditious libel. The judges and witnesses agreed that he was guilty, regardless of his ignorance of the pamphlet's contents. See Plant 1974: 68.
5 Using this method, individual books were divided into shares. Each shareholder was responsible for their portion of the expenses and received a proportionate number of books at cost price or, in certain cases, a proportionate amount of the profits. The practice became sufficiently widespread in the eighteenth century for the records of the Stationers' Company to have a separate column for the registration of shares. These could be expensive; for example, a sixteenth part of Samuel Richardson's *Pamela* (1740) cost £18.
6 Apparently, women publishers were not very active in the production of women's fiction, or indeed fiction written by men. Exceptionally, Anne Ward, a printer at York between 1759 and 1789, is believed to have printed the first edition of Sterne's *Life and Opinions of Tristam Shandy* (1759). She was also responsible for the publication of the *York Courant* for thirty years. Anne Dodd's main commercial interests lay outside the novel market, primarily in the sale of pamphlets and news sheets in London between approximately 1726 and 1743. According to Plomer *et al.* (1932: 75) she was frequently prosecuted by the authorities and in one of her petitions said that she had been left a widow with a large family which she was just able to feed by selling papers.
7 These publishing partnerships issued, respectively: *The Lover's Week* (1718) by Mary Hearne; *Modern Amours* (1733) by Lydia Grainger; *The Exemplary Mother* (1769) by Maria S. Cooper; *Cecilia* (1782) by Fanny Burney; and *Joan !!! A Novel* (1796) by Matilda Fitzjohn.

8 Curll's *Catalogue of Poems, Plays and Novels* (1720) includes approximately sixty miscellaneous publications (mostly poetry), eleven 'Plays Printed on an *Elziver* Letter, in neat Pocket Volumes', nine 'Plays Printed in *Octavo*', and thirteen novels. Listed amongst the latter is *The entertaining Novels of Mrs. Jane Barker; Honour the Victory: and Love the Prize: . . . Written by Mrs. Hearne. Dedicated to Mrs Manley; Instructive Novels for the happy Conduct of Life. . . . Written by Mrs. Butler;* and *Memoirs of the Life of Mrs Manley. (Author of the Atlantis) Containing not only the History of her own Adventures, but likewise an Account of the most considerable Amours in the Court of King Charles the Second.* See Straus (1927) for an account of Curll's business ventures and a list of his publications; and McBurney (1958) for a discussion of the publisher's involvement with Jane Barker.

9 The *Minerva Literary Repository. . . . General Prospectus* (1798) as rpt. in Blakey (1939: 311–14) lists the following women: Ann [Agnes] Maria Bennett; Regina Maria Roche; Elizabeth Meeke; Agnes Musgrave; Ann Howell; Mary Charlton; Isabella Kelly; Eliza Parsons; Elizabeth Bonhote; and Anna Maria M'Kenzie [Cox]

10 Dunton 1818: 292. Plomer *et al.* (1922) note that Batley published several novels and romances between 1717 and 1737 (1922: 26), and describe Richard Bentley as a well-known publisher of novels, plays, and romances between 1675 and 1697 (ibid.: 31). Plomer *et al.* (1932: 127) state that C. Hitch in partnership with L. Hawes dealt primarily in novels between 1733 and 1764.

11 See Hobby 1988: 172–4 for an account of how, in the seventeenth century, Hannah Wolley's considerable success led a publisher to use her name to promote a publication based 'loosely' on her material, but which had been reworked by a hack. Women novelists who had achieved some commercial standing were similarly vulnerable to unlicensed trading upon their reputations. According to Bendixen in Todd 1987: 168, M. Hugill (née Harley) denied responsibility for *Augusta Fitzherbert* (1796), which purported to be written by the author of *St. Bernard's Priory* (1786), which was in fact Hugill. Her novel had been a critical and commercial success. See also Charlotte Smith's correspondence as quoted in McKillop (1951–2: 244) in which she disowns a novel entitled *D'Arcy* that had been published in Ireland with her name on the title page.

12 Other pseudonyms employed by women writers include: 'Mrs Crackenthorpe' -Delarivière Manley in the *Female Tatler*; 'Laura Maria', 'Sappho', and 'Tabitha Bramble' – Mary 'Perdita' Robinson in various magazines; 'Mary Singleton, Spinster' – Frances Brooke in *The Old Maid*; 'Mira' – Eliza Haywood in the *Female Spectator*; and 'The Muse' – Elizabeth Inchbald in the *World or Fashionable Gazette*.

13 Hannah More's biographer tells us that she came to dislike and distrust John Marshall, the publisher in charge of the London end of the highly lucrative *Cheap Repository Tracts* scheme. She disapproved of his treatment of the writer Sarah Trimmer as 'a mere bookseller's fag' (letter 10 May 1787 as quoted in Jones 1952 [1968]: 143), and dismissed him in November 1797, appointing Evans and Hatchard in his place. Marshall continued to profit from the connection by issuing his own series of tracts under the same title.

14 See Reynolds 1920 [1964]: 76–7, n. 1 for a discussion of the changing use of 'Miss' and 'Mrs' between 1660 and 1750.

6 PROFESSIONAL WOMEN NOVELISTS: EARNING AN INCOME

1 Eliza Parsons attached dedications to at least six of her novels: *The History of Miss Meredith. A Novel, Dedicated by permission, to the Most Noble the Marchioness of Salisbury* (1790); *The Errors of Education* (1791), dedicated to the Marchioness of Downshire; *Woman As She Should Be* (1793), dedicated to the Duchess of Gloucester, who was the dedicatee of a number of novels by women authors; *Ellen and Julia* (1793), dedicated to Mrs Crespigny, who was a novelist and a patron to both the playwright Mariana Stark and the biographer Ann Thicknesse; *The Mysterious Warning* (1796), dedicated to the Princess of Wales, who occurs relatively frequently as the subject of novel dedications by women writers; and *Women As They Are* (1796), dedicated to 'Mrs. Anson, of Shuckborough [*sic*] Manor, Staffordshire'.

2 Constantia Grierson was only eighteen years old when her much-praised edition of Virgil (1724) was published, and this was followed by editions of Terence (1727) and Tacitus (1730). She died at twenty-seven leaving an incomplete edition of Sallust. Swift had a high opinion of Laetitia Pilkington's abilities (for example, see his letter to Mrs Pilkington, 1 January [1732–3], in Swift 1965: vol. 4, 95–6). Indeed, according to Pilkington (1749: 249), Swift's preference for her literary talents over those of her husband caused jealousy within her marriage.

3 More explained her views on education for the poor in a letter to Sir W.W. Pepys in 1821 in which she described attempting to 'steer the middle way between the scylla of brutal ignorance and the charybdis of a literary education. The one is cruel and the other preposterous' (More 1925: 199).

4 Robinson and Wallis 1975 include the following women's novels for the period up to and including 1796: Sarah Fielding *Familiar Letters Twixt the Principal Characters of David Simple* (1747); Sarah Fielding *The Lives of Cleopatra and Octavia* (1757); Harriet Chilcot (later Meziere) *Elmar and Ethlinda* (1783); Lucy Peacock *The Adventures of the Six Princesses of Babylon* (1785); Mrs. M. Harley *St. Bernard's Priory. An Old English Tale* (1786); Ann Gomersall *The Citizen: A Novel* (1790); Eliza Parsons *The History of Miss Meredith: A Novel* (1790); Eliza Clarke *The Sword; Or Father Bertrand's History* (1791); Anna M. Porter *Artless Tales* (1793); Mary E. Parker *Orwell Manor* (1795); Mary M. Sherwood *The Traditions, A Legendary Tale* (1795); and Frances Burney *Camilla: Or, a Picture of Youth* (1796). They record also a number of anonymous novels by 'A Lady', and material by women published after 1796.

   The other novels in Appendix A known to have been published by subscription are: Mary Davys *The Reform'd Coquet* (1724) (Backscheider in Todd 1987: 99); M. Peddle *The Life of Jacob. In Ten Books* (1785) (Thompson in Todd 1987: 243); Margaret and Susannah Minifie *The Histories of Lady Frances S. . . . and Lady Caroline S. . . .* (1763) (Tompkins 1932 [1962]: 10); Susanna Rowson *Victoria. A Novel* (1786) (*Dictionary of National Biography* 1922: vol. 17, 368); Sara Draper *Memoirs of the Princess of Zell* (1796) (Blakey 1939: 176); Ann Thomas *Adolphus de Biron, A Novel* (1795) (Lonsdale 1989: 361); Jean Marishall *The History of Alicia Montague* (1767) (Marishall 1789: vol. 2, 193); Elizabeth Boyd *The Happy Unfortunate* (1732 [1972]); and Sarah Emma Spencer *Memoirs of the Miss Holmsbys* (1788) (Clark in Todd 1987: 294).

5 For example, see the ingratiating tone of Mary Barber's letter to the Earl of Oxford in which she sought his support for a subscription edition of her poetry (9 June 1731 in Swift 1913: 443–4).

6 For example, in the 'Preface' to *The Real Story of John Carteret Pilkington.*

Written by Himself Pilkington wondered how

> a young man, with so small a share of merit, and so much a smaller degree of interest, could have obtained such a number of noble adventurers to deposit half a guinea, for a work they had never seen, and of which, from the title, they could have but little conception; after having, as themselves repeatedly assured me, been considerable loosers [*sic*] by subscribing to books, which never were even written, much less intended for publication.
>
> (1760: iii)

7 For example, see Fanny Burney's letter to her father written in 1795 in which she recalled that

> the word *novel* was long in the way of 'Cecilia,' [1782] as I was told at the Queen's house; and it was not permitted to be read by the Princesses till sanctioned by a Bishop's recommendation, – the late Dr. Ross of Exeter.
>
> (Burney 1842–6: vol. 6, 47)

8 The edition in the British Library has the handwritten attribution '[By Pope]'. This is plausible as the piece describes, with relish, the result of a purgative allegedly given to Curll after Pope discovered that the publisher was involved in producing a controversial volume of poems (*Court Poems* 1716) which were falsely assigned to himself and Lady Mary Wortley Montagu. The reference to Centlivre indicates the extent to which the dramatist had become linked with Curll.

9 For example, Cadell's supplementary payment to Smith was probably an attempt to retain the interest of this highly promising new novelist. In her introduction to Smith's *Emmeline*, Ehrenpreis (1971) tells us that 1,500 copies of the first edition (1788) were sold, a second edition (probably of 500 copies) appeared before the end of the year, and a third was printed by June 1789. Smith, although pleased with this popularity, was unhappy with her share of Cadell's profit. Ehrenpreis quotes from a letter dated 18 June 1789 addressed to George Robinson which revealed that Smith was 'writing to a rival publisher in hopes of improving her financial position' (1971: viii). Although Cadell went on to publish her next two novels, *Ethlinde* (1789) and *Celestina* (1791), Smith was still complaining about their financial arrangements in 1798. See McKillop 1951–2: 245.

10 For example, as Hannah More revealed in a letter to the Bishop of Bath and Wells in 1801, she was in a position to donate the £200 plus profit from her written answer to Dupont, 'the atheistical orator of France', to the relief of French emigrant clergy (More 1925: 181).

11 Shevelow (1989: 149) suggests that The *Female Tatler*, edited by 'Mrs Crackenthorpe', and the *Whisperer*, edited by 'Mrs Jenny Distaff', 'falsely suggested associations with Steele', and 'exploited the feminine associations of gossip or scandal rather than including content specifically designed to attract women readers'.

12 Morgan (1987: 167–8) provides a list of Manley's publications; see also Needham 1948–9.

13 Popping, along with J. Roberts, J. Morphew, R. Burleigh, and J. Baker, published the anonymous anti-Curll satire *A Full and True Account of a Horrid and Barbarous Revenge* (1716); see ch. 6, p. 115. According to Plomer *et al.* (1922: 242), she was a printer and publisher between 1712 and 1723. Her name appeared on an edition of *An Account of the Tryal of the Earl of Winton* (1716), which was printed in violation of an Order granting exclusive rights to Tonson. She was imprisoned for printing and publishing the paper and later discharged after presenting a petition to the House, disclaiming knowledge of the publication (see

Curll Papers 1879: 37–9). Plomer *et al.* (1932) list Hester Farley, Sarah James, Cassandra Meere (Mears, Meeres, or Meres), and Anne Ward as also being involved with the production and distribution of newspapers during the eighteenth century.

14 For example, Trimmer's *The Guardian of Education* identified 'a *conspiracy against* CHRISTIANITY *and all* SOCIAL ORDER'. This was to be countered by 'the commencement of a CHRISTIAN EDUCATION from the very *cradle*' for which the periodical would provide guidance (June 1802: vol. 1, 2–3).

15 The Della Cruscan literature consisted largely of poetical epistles exchanged in Bell's *World* with Robert Merry, who was 'Della Crusca'. Bell published some of the material separately as *The Poetry of Anna Matilda* (1788), and *Diversity; A poem by Della Crusca* (1788) (First Edition Club 1931: 11–13).

16 Oliver Goldsmith alleged that the *Monthly Review* was in fact edited by a woman, Isabella Griffiths, who was the wife of its key reviewer, the bookseller Ralph Griffiths. Other female contributors to the *Monthly Review* are recorded in Nangle 1934 and 1955. These include Fanny Burney, whose obituary of William Seward was published in 1799; Mrs Barbauld, who submitted articles, mostly short reviews of fiction, from 1809 to 1815; and Mrs Elizabeth Moody, who wrote many reviews for the periodical between 1789 and 1808.

17 By writing for children or about education, a number of these writers were developing ideas that were rooted in their own domestic experience. For a discussion of the seventeenth-century antecedents of this area of women's writing see ch. 2, pp. 23–4.

18 See Grome in Todd 1987: 269–70 for details of Robertson's career.

19 See also the 'Advertisement' in Mary Jones's *Miscellanies in Prose and Verse* which explains that her eventual resort to publication, despite a modest 'dread of such an undertaking', was 'for the sake of a relation, grown old and helpless thro' a series of misfortunes; and whom she had no other methods of effectually assisting' (1750: v). She attracted a total of 1,505 subscribers, of whom 576 were women.

20 For an example of the favourable contemporary response to Fielding's translation, see the *Monthly Review* 1763: vol. 27, 171–2.

21 Earlier in her career Griffith had adapted Marmontel's *L'Heureux Divorce* for the English stage under the title *The Platonic Wife*, which ran for six nights at Drury Lane in 1765. She followed *The School for Rakes* with *A Wife in the Right*, which was produced at Covent Garden in 1772 and ran for one night only; it was later published by subscription. She was more successful with an adaption from Goldoni's *Bourru Bienfaisant*, at Garrick's suggestion, which was produced for six nights in 1779 under the title *The Times*.

22 Evidence suggests that from the early 1700s payments for popular dramatists could be relatively high. For example, the *Gentleman's Magazine* 1824: vol. 94, 319 quotes Susanna Centlivre as stating that in 1715 she received 'of Mr. Curll twenty guineas in full, for the copy of my play call'd The Wonder; a Woman Keeps a Secret. Rec'd the same sum for The Cruel Gift, and the same for The Artifice'. Later in the century, Elizabeth Ryves received £100 for *The Debt of Honour* even though it was never performed, whilst Hannah More's tragedy *Percy* (written and produced under Garrick's guidance) earned her £750. It ran for twenty-one nights at Covent Garden and 4,000 copies were sold within the first two weeks of publication.

7 ACCESS TO WOMEN'S FICTION

1 For example, *Poems by Eminent Ladies* includes material by Behn, Carter, Chudleigh, Cockburn, Grierson, Jones, Killigrew, Leapor, Madan, Masters, Montagu, Monk, Newcastle, Philips, Pilkington, Rowe, and Winchilsea. It is interesting to note that the 'Preface' suggests that 'most of their poems were first published by subscription' (1755: iv).

2 Manley remained the dedicatee when Hearne's *The Lover's Week* was reissued in 1720 as part of *Honour the Victory: and Love the Prize*. Boyd's *The Happy-Unfortunate; or the Female-Page: A Novel* (1732 [1972]) includes a poem entitled 'On Louisa's NOVEL, call'd The Happy-Unfortunate' which refers to 'Heywood' [*sic*], and the fact that 'A new Eliza writes'. Clearly, the novelist was attempting to link her writing with the work of her better-known contemporaries.

3 For example, Delarivière Manley ridiculed the poet Sarah Fyge Egerton in both the *New Atlantis* (1709) and her *Memoirs of Europe* (1710), and although the attack was upon Sarah's character, it did not spare her literary aspirations. See also Lady Mary Wortley Montagu's disparaging opinion of Sarah Scott's *The History of Cornelia* (1750) expressed in a letter to Lady Bute in 1752 (Montagu 1986: 232).

4 See ch. 3, p. 54 and n. 22. Wollstonecraft's review of Smith's *Emmeline* (1788) in *The Analytical Review* 1788: vol. 1 (May–August), 333 offered similar criticisms of the moral implications of the work. It is worth noting here that Wollstonecraft also promoted what she regarded as 'improving' material by women. For example, *The Female Reader; or Miscellaneous Pieces. In Prose and Verse; . . . For the Improvement of Young Women*, 'By Mr. Cresswick, Teacher of Elocution [Wollstonecraft]' (1789), includes pieces by Trimmer, Pennington, Chapone, Talbot, Aikin, Barbauld, Smith, Carter, Genlis, and Wollstonecraft herself.

5 From a review of Smith's *Emmeline* (1788) in the *Monthly Review* 1788: vol. 79, 242 in which the reviewer was relieved to commend the novel since 'almost every page of it breathes the purest and most benevolent affections'.

6 See Richardson's letter to Sarah Fielding 7 December 1756 (Richardson 1964: 330).

7 Information taken from Kaufman 1967a: 10. Details of these libraries are given in his 'Check List' (ibid.: 50–3).

8 These catalogues, listed in chronological order, are: Rev. Samuel Fancourt, *An Alphabetical Catalogue of Books and Pamphlets, in English, French and Latin, Belonging to the Circulating Library in Crane-Court*, London, 1748; William Bathoe, *A New Catalogue of the Curious and Valuable Collection of Books: (Both English and French) Consisting of Several Thousand Volumes by the Best Authors*, London, 1757; John Noble, *A New Catalogue . . . of John Noble's Circulating Library*, London, 1767; William Gray, *A Catalogue of Books. . . . To be lent by William Gray Bookseller*, Edinburgh, 1772; John Bell, *A New Catalogue of Bell's Circulating Library consisting of above 50,000 volumes*, London, 1778; Palmer and Merrick, *A New Catalogue of Palmer and Merrick's Circulating Library, High Street: Oxford, Consisting of Upwards of Seven Thousand Volumes*, Oxford, 1789; Harrods, *A Catalogue of Harrods Circulating Library: Comprising 700 Novels, etc. and 300 Plays*, Stamford, 1790; M. Heavisides, *A Catalogue of Books, Instructive and Entertaining which are to be lent out by M. Heavisides: Bookseller, Stationer, Bookbinder and Printer*, Darlington, 1790; [Thomas and Thomas Jordan] Hookham, *Nouveau Catalogue François de la Bibliothèque Circulaire de Messrs. Hookham*, London, 1791; Ann

Yearsley, *Catalogue of Books, Tracts, etc. Contained in Ann Yearsley's Public Library*, Bristol, 1793; William Lane, *A Catalogue of the Minerva General Library, Leadenhall Street, London: Containing upwards of Five Hundred Thousand Volumes, in all classes of Literature*, London, 1796–1802; J. Barratt, *A New Catalogue of Barratt's Public Library, Bond Street, Bath*, Bath, [c.1817 (based on contents)].

Kaufman (1967a) refers to the fact that 'more than twenty complete catalogues, widely distributed regionally, are available' (1967a: 11) and he notes briefly the location, range of material, and percentage of fiction contained in twenty-two (ibid.: 11–13). Five of the twelve catalogues examined for this study are not listed by Kaufman – for the libraries of William Gray, Palmer and Merrick, Harrods, Ann Yearsley, and J. Barratt – although Kaufman records the existence of both Yearsley's and Barratt's establishments in his 'Check List'.

9 The range of the material offered by the twelve libraries in the sample is indicated by the catalogue of Fancourt's Universal Circulating Library, at Crane Court, Fleet Street, which records that:

> The present Collection contains a Variety of Histories, ancient and modern, foreign and domestic; Lives, Memoirs, Travels, and Voyages; with several of the best Treatises in Anatomy, Architecture, Arithmetic, Astronomy, Botany, Chemistry, Chronology, Cookery, Dancing, Dictionaries of Words, Persons and Things, Divinity, practical and conversational; Essays and Fables, political, humorous, moral and divine; Geography, Law, Civil, Statute and Ecclesiastical; Logic, Mathematics, Medicine, Metaphysics, Music, Oeconomy, Philology, Philosophy, Physic, Poetry, Policy, Reports, Surgery etc. Together with a great variety of the best pieces of Amusement in French and English.
>
> (1748: i)

10 These institutions tended to be oriented towards more serious reading, debate, and study, and therefore we would expect to find less fiction amongst their stock and loans. For an analysis of such reading habits in Bristol, see Kaufman (1960); and Hapgood (1981).

11 Lane's entrepreneurial approach to the library business is reflected not only in his substantial establishment in Leadenhall Street, but also in his willingness to supply potential proprietors with 'several *Thousand Volumes*, ready bound, in HISTORY, VOYAGES, NOVELS, PLAYS', to compile and print their catalogues, and to provide training in library management (1796–1802: iv).

12 Several of the works in Bathoe's catalogue are listed by Gray, who also includes a 'modernization' of Sidney's *Arcadia* by Mrs Stanley, 'Mrs. Macaulay's history of England', and 'Chudleigh's (Lady) poems'. Bell lists a number of additional works including: the 'Countess of Montgomery's Urania', 'Lady Russell's Letters', poetry by Barker, Reeve, and Masters, letters by Lady Mary Wortley Montagu, Brooke's translation of Millot's *Elémens de l'histoire d'Angleterre*, 'Brumoy's Greek Theatre, by Mrs Lennox', 'Lady Chudleigh's Essays', and two memoirs. Additional works by women recorded in Palmer and Merrick's catalogue include: 'Craven (Lady) Travels through Spain and Portugal', Elizabeth Carter's *Epictetus*, 'Chapone's Letters on the Improvement of the Mind' and her 'Miscellanies, in Prose and Verse', 'Mrs. Charke's Narrative of her Life', 'Conduct of a Married Life, in Letters from Lady Seymour', and several memoirs. Yearsley's catalogue adds a number of other works to the list including *Sacred Dramas* by Genlis, *Letters written from France in the Summer of 1790* by Helen Maria Williams, and, naturally enough, three volumes of her own poetry.

13 Figures as quoted in Kaufman 1967a: 62, and in Kaufman 1967b [1969]: 224.

Kaufman states in the latter that the manuscript includes nearly 1,800 patrons, amongst whom were an 'appreciable number of spinsters'. He notes also that 'the married women entered their names without their husbands' (ibid.: 225).

14 A card catalogue of circulating libraries and book clubs compiled by Munby, and a 'Collection of Labels of Circulating Libraries', both of which are held in the John Johnson Collection, Bodleian Library, Oxford, indicate between them the extensive spread of these facilities during the eighteenth century, from Boston to Bury St Edmunds, and from Stoke to Stourbridge.

15 An anonymous correspondent writing to 'Mr. Urban' in the *Gentleman's Magazine* (1794: vol. 64, 47) put the contemporary case for private subscription libraries:

> Let us suppose such a library begun by a few reading, public-spirited men, in a market town, in any part of England. Any person above the state of penury, residing within five miles of that town, may, without inconvenience, become a member, inasmuch as he will always have, once or twice a week at the least, an opportunity of sending, or receiving, books; and the monthly subscription need not be more than one shilling. Within this circle we may reasonably expect to find fifty subscribers, whose yearly contribution for the purchase of books would amount to thirty pounds, without being felt by any member. Now, on this moderate scale, the society would, in twenty years, have insensibly laid out in the purchase of moral and instructive books, of its own choice, no less than £600.
>
> A valuable collection like this, would, in the family of every subscriber, prove a general luminary to the human mind, and effectually exclude all the corruptive trash of our common circulating libraries.

16 The poem, by John Button Jun. (1804), is quoted by Munby in his card catalogue. Munby records also that the Society was founded by seven members who each made an initial contribution of 2s. 6d. and a further payment of 1s. per month. By 1794 they had sixty members, and by April 1801 they had 1,342 volumes worth £546.

17 For example, see the letter on 'Country Book-Clubs Fifty Years Ago' in the *Gentleman's Magazine* 1852: vol. 37, 572, which describes the holdings of one such institution, noting that:

> Works of fiction were not numerous. We had neither Fielding, nor Richardson, nor, I think, Smollet. . . . we begun with Madame d'Arblay, with Madame de Genlis, and Dr. Moore. . . . Then came the whole series of Mrs. Opie's novels and tales. . . . Godwin, also, with his political speculations and his powerful novels, Miss Edgeworth, . . . with her exquisite fictions, Miss Hamilton, and Hannah More, and Miss Hawkins, and numerous other worthies.

See also the stock of the Bristol Library Society, as recorded by Kaufman 1960, in which women's non-fiction outweighed their fiction.

18 Information taken from *Rules for regulating the Subscription Library at Stamford*. The involvement of women members in decision making was given special attention under 'Rule IV' which stated that 'All questions which come before the Society at large, shall be determined by a majority of the Subscribers present; but Ladies, who are Members of the Society, shall have the privilege of voting by proxy, provided the proxy be a subscriber' ([Anon] 1787: 4). Information about the Clavering Society for Reading is taken from Kaufman 1964 [1969]: 53.

19 For discussion of the varying levels of literacy before and during this period, see: Stone 1969; Sanderson 1972; Schofield 1972–3; Cressy 1980; Spufford 1981; and

Vincent 1989. For analyses of the impact of such factors as ideology, schooling, and the rise of new forms of popular literature, see also: Wiles 1957; Cranfield 1962; Wiles 1968: 49–65; Plumb 1971: 1–26; Plumb 1975; and Shevelow 1989.

20 The novels by Davys, Barker, Butler, Grainger, and Hearne were priced as follows: Mary Davys's novels – *The Fugitive*, 1s. 6d. (duodecimo), *The Reform'd Coquet*, 3s. (duodecimo), *The Accomplish'd Rake*, 2s. 6d (duodecimo), *The False Friend*, 1s. (duodecimo); Jane Barker's novels – *Loves Intrigues*, 1s. & 1s. 6d. (octavo), *Exilius*, 3s. (2 pts, duodecimo), *A Patch-Work Screen*, 2s. 6d. (2 pts, duodecimo), *The Lining for the Patch-Work Screen*, 2s. 6d. (duodecimo); Sarah Butler's novel – *Irish Tales*, 1s. 6d. & 2s.; Lydia Grainger's novel – *Modern Amours*, 1s. 6d. & 2s. (duodecimo); Mary Hearne's novels – *The Lover's Week*, 1s. (octavo), *The Female Deserters*, 1s. 6d. (octavo), *Honour the Victory and Love the Prize*, 2s. 6d. & 3s.

21 Figures taken from Burnett 1969: 136–7; and Woodforde 1935 [1987]: 363.

22 Figures taken from Hecht 1956: 142–9.

23 The twenty-three authors included in Mayo 1962 are: Fielding, Smith, Peacock, Bennett, Burney, Reeve, Ann Radcliffe, Porter, Lennox, Frances Brooke, Palmer, Haywood, Hays, Ryves, Yearsley, Rowson, Williams, Sheridan, Collyer, Trimmer, Inchbald, Robinson, and Sophia Lee. He lists the following pieces of magazine fiction by Litchfield, King, Mulso, and Tatlock, respectively: *The Forest of Alstone* (1792) (1962: 496); *The Prater* (1794 and 1795) (ibid.: 574); [*The Mischiefs of Superstition and Infidelity*] (1753, 1774, and 1793) (ibid.: 557); and *The Unexpected Interview* (1793) (ibid.: 610). Anne Blower, who became a frequent contributor to the *General* (1787–92), was the only novelist that the proprietor '[Thomas] Bellamy ever brought forward by name', apart from himself (ibid.: 304–5).

24 The information concerning the reprinting of 'The Delusions of the Heart' in *The Hibernian Magazine* is taken from Pitcher 1976: 23.

25 With the exception of Pitcher 1976, I am indebted to Mayo's 'Catalogue' 1962 for the information used in the discussion on pp. 148–9.

26 For example, through the series 'Philosophy for the Ladies' the *Lady's Monthly Museum* introduced its readers to the 'Natural History' of such species as 'The Calamary or Ink Fish', and 'the Ephemeron, or Day-Fly'. 'Variety [is] our aim', Lennox declared (1760: vol. 1, 132), and other instructive series included the 'Natural History of the Islands of Amboyna', a detailed study of 'The Universe as considered under a general view', and 'An Essay on the Original Inhabitants of Great Britain'.

APPENDIX A

Introduction

1 Before using Block's bibliography, see the review of the revised edition in *The Times Literary Supplement*, 21 April 1961: 256.

2 Information obtained from Averley *et al.* 1979 and Todd 1987 is not included in Turner 1985. Twenty novels have been added subsequently to Appendix A, and Averley and Todd have contributed the following authors: Mary Ann Kilner, Miss Edwards, and Sophia Elford from Averley; and Charlotte Charke, Anne Eden, M. Peddle, Charlotte Elizabeth Sanders (Saunders), Charlotte McCarthy, and Jane Warton from Todd. Todd has also introduced or confirmed the professional status of the following writers: Aubin, Blower, Brooke, Collier, Cox, Gooch, Hervey, Kelly, Meades, Meeke, Pix, and Wakefield.

3 For example, *Captivity, a poem, and Celadon and Lydia a Tale* (1777) by Mrs M. Robinson; and *Letters and Essays Moral and Miscellaneous* (1793) by Mary Hays, which contains 'The Story of Melville and Cecilia'. This criterion also excludes the author Arabella Plantin, whose two works of fiction, *Love Led Astray: or, The Mutual Inconstancy* and *The Ingrateful: or, The Just Revenge*, were published in *Letters to the Lady Wharton* (1727) and later in *Whartoniana, or Miscellanies in Verse and Prose by the Wharton Family* (1727).

4 For example Hardy (c.1982: 78) records *Novellettes, selected for the use of young ladies and gentlemen; written by Dr. Goldsmith, Mrs. Griffith. etc. and illustrated by elegant engravings* (London: Fielding and Walker, 1780) as being by Oliver Goldsmith, Elizabeth Griffith, and Mr M'Millan; whilst according to the catalogue of the British Library, *The History of the Life and Adventures of Mr. Duncan Campbell* (1720) was a collaborative venture between Daniel Defoe, William Bond, and Eliza Haywood. Neither work has been included.

5 For example, *The Works of Mrs Mary Davys: Consisting of Plays, Novels, Poems, and Familiar Letters. Several of which never before Published. In Two Volumes* (1725) has been omitted although it contains the following previously unpublished fiction: *The Lady's Tale*; *The Cousins; A Novel*; and *Familiar Letters Betwixt a Gentleman and a Lady*. However, a version of *The Cousins* published in 1732 as *The False Friend: or, The Treacherous Portugues* has been included.

Catalogue

1 Two further volumes were published by T. Becket in 1776.

2 *The History of Emily Montague* was written in Quebec and has been described by McMullen (in Todd 1987: 60) as 'the first Canadian novel'. Brooke returned to England in 1768. A further novel, *All's Right at Last: or, The history of Miss West*, 2 vols (London: Printed for F. and J. Noble, 1774), is attributed to Brooke by Block (1961: 165) and this is given some support by McMullen (1987: 60–1). However, Hardy (c.1982: 10) treats it as an anonymous publication, and comments that it was 'incorrectly attributed to Frances Brooke in the French translation, HISTOIRE DE MISS WEST, ou l'Heureux denoument, par Mme, . . . auteur de "l'Histoire d'Emilie Montague" ' (1777).

3 The source, Strange (in Todd 1987: 83), describes the work as 'a 32-page undated tale, . . . also attributed to CC'.

4 This has been excluded from the statistical analysis in chapter 3 as it was not published until twenty-six years after Collyer's death.

5 This publication was revised and republished as *The Daughter: or The history of Miss Emilia Royston, and Miss Harriet Ayres; in a series of letters. By the authoress of The exemplary mother* (London: J. Dodsley, 1775).

6 This work has been excluded from the statistical analysis in chapter 3 due to the lack of a publication date.

7 This novel appeared originally as the first two volumes of a joint publication with her husband Richard Griffith, entitled *Two Novels. In letters. By the authors of Henry and Frances. In four volumes* (London: Printed for T. Becket and P.A. De Hondt, 1769). Therefore, according to my selection criteria, it is arguable that the work is ineligible for the appendix. However, evidence suggests that Elizabeth's novel was also published separately. A note on the fly-leaf of Frederick's *Catalogue* (1774), accompanying a transcription of a discussion of *The Delicate Distress* in Act I, scene 3 of Sheridan's *The Rivals*, states that this novel is the same as *Delicate Embarrassments*, which was also published in 1769. The latter is

listed as a separate publication by Frederick (1774: 74, no. 2713) and therefore the novel has been included in the statistical analysis in chapter 3.

8 Thaddeus (in Todd 1987: 144) is the source for the details of *The Hermit*. It should be noted that Lane's *Catalogue* (1796: pt. 1, 79, no. 2500) records this work as 'by the Miss Minifies'. Unfortunately, Lane's entry is undated.

9 This work has been excluded from the statistical analysis due to the lack of a publication date.

10 The first two parts of *Love In Excess* were published in 1719 and Part III in 1720.

11 Contradictory information complicates the attribution of Holford's publications. In an entry about her daughter, Mrs Margaret Hodson, the *DNB* (1922: vol.9, 968) states that in addition to two plays, Holford published 'a tale, "Fanny and Selina", with "Gresford Vale, and other poems", [in] 1798'. Summers (1940 [1969]: 67, attributes the following novels to Holford: *Fanny; or, The deserted daughter. Being the first literary attempt of a young lady* (1792); *Selima, or The Village tale. By the authoress of Fanny* (1793); *Gresford Vale* (1794); and *Calaf. A Persian tale* (1794). Block (1961: 112) allocates only *Calaf* to her, and he dates the work to 1798. The *Dictionary of Anonymous and Pseudonymous English Literature*: vol. 9, 101 attributes *Fanny. A novel; in a series of letters* (1785) to Holford, noting that 'the same author is said by Summers . . . to have written "Fanny; or the deserted daughter" '. However, *Selima* is attributed by both Block (1961: 244) and the *Dictionary of Anonymous and Pseudonymous English Literature*: (vol. 5, 219) to Harriet Ventum. Finally, Blain *et al.* (1990: 531) state that the latter attribution is incorrect and they give a publication date of 1798 for the work. They also record *Calaf* and *Gresford Vale* as being published in that year. I have accepted the conclusions of this source.

12 This work is included in Blakey's supplementary list of Minerva publications which she has 'not definitely dated'. Her source was a 1794 advertisement.

13 Whilst both the British Library catalogue and Smith (in Todd 1987: 175) note that Inchbald has been credited with this work, they point out that her name is not printed in the novel. As some doubt about the attribution remains, it has been excluded from the statistical analysis.

14 For the purposes of the statistical analysis in chapter 3 this has been treated as a single work published in 1783.

15 Lennox has been credited with two further novels. Shevelow (in Todd 1987: 197) notes that *The History of Eliza* (1766) has recently been attributed to her and this is echoed by Blain *et al.* (1990: 648); whilst Block (1961: 136) lists Lennox as the author of *Hermione; or, The Orphan Sisters* (1791). However, other sources either consider *Euphemia* to be Lennox's final publication, or they treat *Hermione* as an anonymous work. Neither has been included in the statistical analysis.

16 *Court-Intrigues* was first published in 1705 as *The Lady's Pacquet of letters*, which was included in a publication by Marie Catherine Jumelle de Berneville, Comtesse d'Aulnoy, entitled *Memoirs of the Court of England. In two parts. By the Countess of Dunois . . . Now made English. To which is added The Lady's pacquet of letters, taken from her by a French privateer in her passage to Holland. Suppos'd to be written by several men of quality. Brought over from St. Malo's by an English officer at the last exchange of prisoners* (Printed and sold by B. Bragg, 1705).

17 *Arnold Zulig* and *Memoirs of a Scots Heiress* have been attributed here to Mrs Mathews since it is clear that they were written by the author of *Constance* and *Argus, The House-Dog At Eadlip*. The attribution of *The Count of Hoensdern* is based on Tompkins (1932 [1962]: 47, n. 1), who states that the author of *Memoirs of a Scots Heiress* and *Constance* also wrote *Arnold Zulig*, *Argus*, and *The Count*.

18 Cotton (in Todd 1987: 256) refers to a second novel by Pix entitled *Violenta*

(1704). This is *Violenta, or the Rewards of Virtue: turn'd from Boccace [from the Decameron] into verse*. It has been excluded from the appendix, which is restricted (with the exception of Seward) to prose works.

19 Part II of *Letters Moral and Entertaining* was published in 1731 and Part III in 1732.

20 Susanna Rowson emigrated to America with her husband in 1793 and the publication details of the *Trials of the Human Heart* indicate that it was published in Philadelphia. It has therefore been excluded from the statistical analysis in chapter 3.

21 The first three volumes were published in 1788, the fourth in 1789.

22 A number of sources, for example Schnorrenberg (in Todd 1987: 280) and Blain *et al.* (1990: 960), credit Scott with *The History of Sir George Ellison* published in 1766, and not with *The Man of Real Sensibility* (1765). However, Hardy (c.1982: 133), whilst recording the first novel, comments that it was 'expanded from *The Man of Real Sensibility, or The History of Sir George Ellison*. 1765'. Therefore, only the earlier title has been included in the appendix.

23 This poetical novel has been excluded from the statistical analysis, which is restricted to prose fiction.

24 Frances Sheridan died in 1766. Another novel, *Eugenia and Adelaide, a novel* (London: C. Dilly, 1791), which was written when she was only fifteen, was also published posthumously. It has not been included in the analysis due to the considerable gap between the author's death and publication.

25 Summers (1940 [1969]: 194) is unsure as to whether this novelist is Susan Smythies (born 1720), Ann (born 1724) or Elizabeth (born 1727). Blain *et al.* attribute the novels to Susan (1990: 1003).

26 A second volume appeared in 1791 entitled: *The Philanthropic Rambler Part II. A sequel.*

27 In the statistical analysis this has been treated as one novel published in 1795.

28 Both Summers (1940 [1969]: 215) and Singer (1933 [1963]: 224) also attribute *Anecdotes of a Convent. By the author of Memoirs of Mrs. Williams* (London: T. Becket and P.A. De Hondt, 1771) to Helen Maria Williams. As Williams would have been about nine years old when the novel was published, it seems unlikely that she was the author. The work was probably written by the author of *Letters between an English Lady, and her friend at Paris, in which are contained the Memoirs of Mrs. William* (1770) (Tompkins 1932 [1962]: 156, n. 2).

29 MacCarthy (1947: 64) gives the publication date as 1758; Lenihan (in Todd 1987: 334) gives it as 1765; whilst both Block (1961: 256) and the British Library catalogue offer an approximate date of 1770. The earlier date has been accepted.

30 Two further volumes were published by Robinson in 1795.

WORKS CITED

PRIMARY SOURCES

Books and pamphlets

Allestree, Richard (1673) *The Ladies Calling. By the Author of the Whole Duty of Man*, Oxford: Printed at the Theater.

[Anon] (1716) *A Full and true Account of a Horrid and Barbarous Revenge by Poison, On the Body of Mr. Edmund Curll, Bookseller; With a faithful Copy of his Last Will and Testament. Publish'd by an Eye Witness*, London: Roberts, Morphew, Burleigh, Baker, & Popping.

—— (1739) 'Preface' to Penelope Aubin *A Collection of Entertaining Histories and Novels*, London: D. Midwinter *et al*.

—— (1748) *The Parallel; or, Pilkington and Phillips Compared. Being Remarks upon the Memoirs of those two Celebrated Writers. By an Oxford Scholar*, London: M. Cooper.

—— (1760–1) 'Address to the World' in *The Works of the Celebrated Mrs. Centlivre. In three Volumes. With a New Account of her Life*, London: J. Knapton *et al*.

—— (1787) *Rules for regulating the Subscription Library at Stamford and a list of the Committee, Subscribers etc. To Which is added a Catalogue of the Books in the Library at its first opening*, Stamford: Newcome & Peat.

—— (1797) *The Use of Circulating Libraries Considered: with Instructions for Opening and Conducting A Library Either upon a large or small plan*, Printed for J. Hamilton, Paternoster Row, and T. Wilson, Bookseller and Stationer, Bromley, Kent.

—— (1879) *Curll Papers. Stray Notes on The Life and Publications of Edmund Curll. From Notes and Queries*, Printed for Private Circulation.

Astell, Mary (1694) *A Serious Proposal To the Ladies, For the Advancement of their true and greatest Interest. By a Lover of Her Sex*, London: K. Wilkin.

Aubin, Penelope (1739) *A Collection of Entertaining Histories and Novels, Designed To promote the Cause of VIRTUE and HONOUR. Principally founded on FACTS, and interspersed with a Variety of beautiful and instructive Incidents. By Mrs. Penelope Aubin*, London: D. Midwinter, A. Bettesworth & C. Hitch, J. & J. Pemberton, R. Ware, C. Rivington, A. Ward, J. & P. Knapton, T. Longman, R. Hett, S. Austen, & J. Wood.

Austen, Jane (1818 [1906]) *Northanger Abbey*, London: J.M. Dent.

Barbauld, Anna Laetitia (1825) *The Works of Anna Laetitia Barbauld. With a Memoir By Lucy Aiken*, London: Longman, Hurst, Rees, Orme, Brown, & Green.

Barratt, J. (*c.*1817 [based on contents]) *A New Catalogue of Barratt's Public Library, Bond Street, Bath*, Bath: J. Barratt & Son.

Bathoe, William (1757) *A New Catalogue of the Curious and Valuable Collection of Books (Both English and French) Consisting of Several Thousand Volumes by the Best Authors. (Including all those that have been lately published) in almost every Branch of Polite LITERATURE . . . by William Bathoe, Bookseller, at the Original Circulating Library* (Being the first of its kind in London) *At the Blue Bible near Exeter-Exchange in the Strand*, London: Bathoe.

Beeton, Isabella (1865 [1984]) *Beeton's Every-day Cookery and Houskeeping Book*, New York: Gallery.

Behn, Aphra (1687 [1915]) 'Preface' to *The Lucky Chance; or, An Alderman's Bargain*, in *The Works of Aphra Behn*, vol. 3, ed. Montague Summers, London: Heinemann.

Bell, John (1778) *A New Catalogue of Bell's Circulating Library consisting of above 50,000 volumes*, London: John Bell.

Bonhote, Elizabeth (1788) *The Parental Monitor. In Two Volumes. By Mrs. Bonhote, of Bungay, Suffolk*, London: W. Lane.

Boswell, James (1950) *Boswell's London Journal, 1762–3: Now First published from the original manuscript*, ed. Frederick A. Pottle, London: Heinemann.

—— (1799 [1927]) *The Life of Samuel Johnson, LL.D*, 3rd edn, London: Oxford University Press.

Bowden, Samuel (1754) *Poems on Various Subjects; with some Essays in Prose, Letters to Correspondents, etc. And A Treatise on Health*, Bath: Printed by T. Boddely, for the Author.

Boyd, Mrs Elizabeth (1732 [1972]) *The Happy Unfortunate: or, the Female Page: a Novel. In Three Parts*, London: Garland.

Brereton, Jane (1744) *Poems on Several Occasions: By Mrs Jane Brereton. With Letters to her Friends, and an account of her life*, London: E. Cave.

Brontë, Charlotte (1847 [1969]) *Jane Eyre*, London: Oxford University Press.

Burney, Fanny (1778 [1909]) *Evelina; or The History of a Young Lady's Entrance into the World*, London: J.H. Dent.

—— (1842–6) *The Diary and Letters of Madame d'Arblay: 1778–1840. Author of Evelina, Cecilia, etc. Edited by her Niece* vols 6 and 7, ed. Charlotte Frances Barrett, London: Henry Colburn.

Cavendish, Margaret (Duchess of Newcastle) (1656) *Natures Pictures*, London.

—— (1664) *CCXI Sociable Letters . . . by M. Cavendish*, London: Wilson.

Centlivre, Susanna (1707) *The Platonick Lady. A Comedy. As it is Acted at the Queens Theatre in the Hay-Market*, London: J. Knapton.

Chapone, Hester Mulso (1808) *The Posthumous Works of Mrs. Chapone*, 2nd edn, vol. 2, London: J. Murray.

Charke, Charlotte (1755) *A Narrative of the Life of Mrs. Charlotte Charke, (Youngest Daughter of COLLEY CIBBER, Esq;). Written by HERSELF*, London: W. Reeve, A. Dodd, & E. Cook.

Chudleigh, Lady (1709) *The Ladies Defence: or The Bride-Woman's Counsellor Answered: A Poem. In a Dialogue between Sir John Brute, Sir Wm. Loveall, Mellissa, and a Parson*, London: Bernard Lintott.

Cibber, Theophilus (1753) *The Lives of the Poets of Great Britain and Ireland to the time of Dean Swift*, 2nd edn, 4 vols, London: Printed for R. Griffiths, at the Dunciad in St Paul's Churchyard.

Congreve, William (1692 [1971]) *Incognita : or, Love and Duty Reconciled*, Menston, Yorkshire: Scolar Press.

Curll, Edmund (1720) *A Catalogue of Poems, Plays, and Novels, Printed for, and Sold by E. CURLL next the Temple Coffee-House in Fleet-Street*, London: Curll.

Davys, Mary (1725 [1964]) 'Preface' to *The Works of Mrs. Davys . . . in Two Volumes*, in *Four Before Richardson: Selected English Novels, 1720–1727*, ed. William H. McBurney, Lincoln: University of Nebraska Press.

—— (1727 [1964]) *The Accomplished Rake: or, Modern Fine Gentleman*, in *Four Before Richardson: Selected English Novels, 1720–1727*, ed. William H. McBurney, Lincoln: University of Nebraska Press.

Defoe, Daniel (1697 [1969]) *An Essay upon Projects*, Menston, Yorkshire: Scolar Press.

—— (1719 [1869]) 'An Office for Marriages', *The Weekly Journal and Saturday's Post (Mist's Weekly Journal)* 4 April, in William Lee *Daniel Defoe: His Life, and Recently Discovered Writings: Extending from 1716 to 1729*, vol. 2, London: John Camden Hotten, Piccadilly.

—— (1720 [1869]) 'A Female distressed for a Fortune and a Husband', *The Weekly Journal and Saturday's Post (Mist's Weekly Journal)* 30 January 1720, in William Lee (1869) *Daniel Defoe: His Life, and Recently Discovered Writings: Extending from 1716 to 1729*, vol. 2, London: John Camden Hotten, Piccadilly.

—— (1727 [1969]) *The Complete English Tradesman in Familiar Letters: Directing him in all the several Parts and Progressions of Trade*, 2nd edn, vol. 1, New York: Augustus M. Kelley.

Dunton, John (1818) *The Life and Errors of John Dunton, Citizen of London*, vol. 1, London: J. Nichols, Son, & Bentley.

Egerton, William [E. Curll?] (1731) *Faithful Memoirs of the Life, Amours and Performances, of That justly Celebrated, and most Eminent Actress of her Time, Mrs. Anne Oldfield. Interspersed with several other Dramatical Memoirs*, London.

Enfield, William (1774) *Observations on Literary Property*, London: Joseph Johnson.

Evelyn, John (1955) *The Diary of John Evelyn: Now First Printed in Full from the Manuscripts Belonging to Mr. John Evelyn*, vol. 4 *Kalendarium, 1673–1689*, ed. E.S. De Beer, London: Oxford University Press.

Fancourt, Rev. Samuel (1748) *An Alphabetical Catalogue of Books and Pamphlets, in English, French and Latin, Belonging to the Circulating Library in Crane-Court*, London.

Fénelon, Archbishop of Cambray (1760–1) *Treatise on the Education of Daughters*, trans. 'by a Friend of the Author of the Museum'. Serialized in *Lady's Museum* 1–2.

Fielding, Henry (1907) *The Journal of a Voyage to Lisbon*, ed. Austin Dobson, London: Oxford University Press.

Fielding, Sarah (1744 [1987]) *The Adventures of David Simple, containing an Account of his Travels through the Cities of London and Westminster in the Search of a Real Friend*, Oxford: Oxford University Press.

—— (1749 [1987]) *The Governess or, Little Female Academy*, London: Pandora.

First Edition Club, London ([1931]) *A Catalogue of Books, Newspapers, etc., Printed by John Bell . . . and by John Browne Bell . . . Exhibited at the First Edition Club, London . . . 15 April–May 5, 1931*, [London: First Edition Club].

Frederick, William (1774) *Catalogue of Near Ten Thousand Volumes of Books: Being Part of the Stock of William Frederick, Bookseller in Bath*, Bath: Frederick.

Gray, William (1772) *A Catalogue of Books in History Ancient and Modern, Voyages and Travels, Philosophy and the Belles Lettres, Divinity and Church History, Plays and Poetry, Novels and Entertainments: To be lent by William Gray Bookseller*, Edinburgh: W. Gray.

Griffith, Elizabeth (1782) *Essays, Addressed To Young Married Women. By Mrs. Griffith*, London: T. Cadell & J. Robson.

—— (1786) *A Series of Genuine Letters, Between Henry and Frances. A New Edition*, London: J. Bew.

Harrods (1790) *A Catalogue of Harrods Circulating Library: Comprising 700 Novels, etc. and 300 Plays*, Stamford.

Haywood, Eliza (1719) *Love in Excess; or the Fatal Enquiry, A Novel*, London: W. Chetwood, R. Francklin, J. Roberts.

—— (1727 [1964]) *Philidore and Placentia; or, L'Amour trop Delicat*, in *Four Before Richardson: Selected English Novels, 1720–1727*, ed. William H. McBurney, Lincoln: University of Nebraska Press.

—— (1727) *The Secret History of the Present Intrigues of the Court of Caramania*, London: Printed and sold by the Booksellers of London and Westminster.

—— (1751 [1986]) *The History of Miss Betsy Thoughtless*, London: Pandora.

Heavisides, M. (1790) *A Catalogue of Books, Instructive and Entertaining which are to be lent out by M. Heavisides Bookseller, Stationer, Bookbinder and Printer*, Darlington.

Hookham, [Thomas and Thomas Jordan] (1791) *Nouveau Catalogue François de la Bibliothèque Circulaire de Messrs. Hookham*, London.

Hunt, Leigh (1891) *The Autobiography of Leigh Hunt*, new edn, London: Smith, Elder & Co.

Inchbald, Elizabeth (1791 [1987]) *A Simple Story*, London: Pandora.

Johnson, Samuel (1752) Review of Charlotte Lennox *The Female Quixote; or the Adventures of Arabella*, *Gentleman's Magazine* 22 (March): 146.

—— (1759 [1816]) 'The Idler, Number 55', *The Universal Chronicle, or Weekly Gazette* 5 May, in *The Works of Samuel Johnson LL.D.*, new edn, vol. 7, London: Nichols, Rivington [and others].

—— (1907) *The Essays of Samuel Johnson. Selected From The Rambler, 1750–1752; The Adventurer, 1753; and The Idler, 1758–1760*, ed. S.J. Reid, London: Walter Scott Publishing Company.

Jones, Mary (1750) *Miscellanies in Prose and Verse*, Oxford: Dodsley, Clements, & Frederick.

Lackington, James (1792) *Memoirs of The First Forty-Five Years of the Life of James Lackington, . . . Written by Himself*, London: Printed for the Author.

Lane, William (1796–1802) *A Catalogue of the Minerva General Library, Leadenhall Street, London: Containing upwards of Five Hundred Thousand Volumes, in all classes of Literature*, London: Minerva.

Leapor, Mary (1751) *Poems Upon Several Occasions. By the late Mrs. Leapor, of Brackley in Northamptonshire*, London: J. Roberts.

Lennox, Charlotte (1752 [1986]) *The Female Quixote; or, The Adventures of Arabella*, London: Pandora.

Lloyd, Robert (1774) 'The Puff', in *The Poetical Works of Robert Lloyd, A.M*, London: T. Evans.

Locke, John (1960) *Two Treatises of Government*, ed. P. Laslett, Cambridge: Cambridge University Press.

—— (1975) *An Essay Concerning Human Understanding*, abridged and ed. A.D. Woozley, London: Fontana.

—— (1989) *Some Thoughts Concerning Education*, ed. John W. Yolton and Jean S. Yolton, Oxford: Clarendon Press.

Macaulay, Catherine (1774) *A Modest Plea for the Property of Copyright*, London: Edward & Charles Dilly.

Macleod, Allan (1804) *Lackington's Confessions, Rendered Into Narrative. To Which Are Added Observations on the Bad Consequences of Educating Daughters at Boarding Schools*, London: B. Crosby & Co.

Makin, Bathsua (1673 [1980]) *An Essay to Revive the Antient Education of Gentlewomen, in Religion, Manners, Arts, and Tongues, with an Answer to the*

Objections against this Way of Education, Los Angeles: Clark Memorial Library.

Manley, Delarivière [Mary] (1725) *Mrs. Manley's History of Her Own Life and Times. Published from Her Original Manuscript*, 4th edn, London: E. Curll & J. Pemberton.

Marishall, Jean (1789) *A Series of Letters. By The Author of Clarinda Cathcart; Alicia Montague; and the Comedy of Sir Henry Gaylove. In Two Volumes*, Edinburgh: Printed for the Author.

Meeke, Mary (1802) *Midnight Weddings. A Novel. In Three Volumes. By Mrs. Meeke, Author of Anecdotes of the Altamont Family, Ellesmere, &c. &c.*, London: W. Lane.

Montagu, Lady Mary Wortley (1967) *The Complete Letters of Lady Mary Wortley Montagu*, vol. 3, ed. Robert Halsband, London: Oxford University Press.

—— (1986) *The Selected Letters of Lady Mary Wortley Montagu*, ed. R. Halsband, Harmondsworth: Penguin.

More, Hannah (1785) 'Prefatory Letter to Mrs Montagu. By a Friend', in Ann Yearsley *Poems on Several Occasions by Ann Yearsley A Milkwoman of Bristol*, London.

—— (1799) *Strictures on the Modern System of Female Education. With a View of the Principles and Conduct Prevalent among Women of Rank and Fortune*, London: T. Cadell Jun. & W. Davies.

—— (c.1810) *The Two Wealthy Farmers; or The History of Mr. Bragwell, in seven parts*, London: Sold by Howard & Evans (Printers to the Cheap Repository for Moral and Religious Tracts,) . . . & J. Hatchard, . . . London. By J. Binns, Bath; and by all Booksellers, Newsmen, and Hawkers, in Town and Country.

—— (1925) *The Letters of Hannah More*, ed. R.B. Johnson, London: John Lane, The Bodley Head.

Mosley, Jane (1979) *Jane Mosley's Derbyshire Recipes*, ed. Joan Sinar, Derby: Derbyshire Museum Service.

Munby, A.N.L. (n.d.) 'An Index of Circulating Libraries', John Johnson Collection, Bodleian Library.

[—— ?] (n.d.) 'A Collection of Labels of Circulating Libraries', John Johnson Collection, Bodleian Library.

Nichols, John Bowyer (1858) *Illustrations of the Literary History of the Eighteenth Century: Consisting of Authentic Memoirs and Original Letters of Eminent Persons. To which are appended additions to the literary anecdotes and literary illustrations*, vol. 8, London: J.B. Nichols.

Noble, John (1767) *A NEW CATALOGUE of the Large and Valuable Collection of BOOKS, (Both ENGLISH, and FRENCH) In JOHN NOBLE's Circulating LIBRARY: Consisting of Several Thousand VOLUMES, BY THE Best AUTHORS, In almost every Branch of Literature, Which are LENT to READ, BY THE YEAR, QUARTER, OR SINGLE BOOK, By JOHN NOBLE, BOOKSELLER, At DRYDEN's Head, in St Martin's Court, near Leicester Square.*, London.

Osborne, Dorothy (1928) *The Letters of Dorothy Osborne to William Temple*, ed. G.C. Moore Smith, London: Oxford University Press.

Palmer and Merrick (1789) *A New Catalogue of Palmer and Merrick's Circulating Library. High Street, Oxford: Consisting of Upwards of Seven Thousand Volumes*, Oxford.

Pennington, Lady [Sarah] (1784) *An Unfortunate Mother's Advice to her Absent Daughters; in a Letter to Miss Pennington*, 7th edition, London: J. Walter.

Pilkington, John Carteret (1760) *The Real Story of John Carteret Pilkington. Written by Himself*, London.

Pilkington, Laetitia (1749) *Memoirs of Mrs. Laetitia Pilkington, Wife to the Rev. Mr. Mathew Pilkington. Written by Herself. Wherein are occasionally interspersed, Her Poems, with Variety of Secret Transactions of Some Eminent Persons*, vol. 2, Dublin; rpt. London: R. Griffiths.

—— (1760) *A Collection of Letters, Between Mrs. Laetitia Pilkington, deceased, and the late Right Honourable Lord Kingsborough*, in J.C. Pilkington *The Real Story of John Carteret Pilkington. Written by Himself*, London.

Poems by Eminent Ladies (1755), 2 vols, London: R. Baldwin.

Pope, Alexander (1714 [1846]) *The Rape of the Lock*, in *The Poetical Works of Alexander Pope: From the Text of Dr. Warburton*, new edn, London: J.J. Chidley.

—— (1743 [1846]) *The Dunciad*, in *The Poetical Works of Alexander Pope: From the Text of Dr. Warburton*, new edn, London: J.J. Chidley.

Radcliffe, Ann (1791 [1986]) *The Romance of the Forest*, Oxford: Oxford University Press.

Radcliffe, Mary Ann (1810) *The Memoirs of Mrs Mary Ann Radcliffe; in Familiar Letters To Her Female Friend*, published with *The Female Advocate; or, An Attempt to Recover the Rights of Women From Male Usurpation*, Edinburgh: Printed for the Author.

Reeve, Clara (1785 [1930]) *The Progress of Romance, through Times, Countries, and Manners; with remarks on the good and bad effects of it, on them respectively; in a course of evening conversations*, in Clara Reeve, *The Progress of Romance and the History of Charoba, Queen of Egypt*, New York: The Facsimile Text Society.

Richardson, Samuel (1964) *Selected Letters of Samuel Richardson*, ed. John Carroll, London: Oxford University Press.

[Robinson, Mary] (1784) *The Memoirs of Perdita; Interspersed With Anecdotes of the Hon. Charles F———X; Lord M———; Col. T———; P———E of W———S; Col. St. L———R; Mr. S———N, and Many Other Well Known Characters*, London: G. Lister.

Savage, Richard (1777) 'Author to Let', in *The Works of Richard Savage Esq: Son of the Earl Rivers. With an Account of the Life and Writings of the Author by Samuel Johnson, LL.D.*, new edn, vol. 2, London: Printed for T. Evans in the Strand.

Scott, Sarah (1762 [1986]) *A Description of Millenium Hall and The Country Adjacent*, London: Virago.

Sheridan, Richard Brinsley (1775 [1975]) *The Rivals*, in *Sheridan's Plays*, ed. Cecil Price, London: Oxford University Press.

'Sophia' (1740) *Woman Not Inferior to Man: or, A short and modest Vindication of the natural Right of the FAIR-SEX to a perfect Equality of Power, Dignity, and Esteem, with the Men. By Sophia, A Person of Quality*, 2nd edn, London: J. Hawkins.

Sterne, Laurence (1935) *Letters of Laurence Sterne*, ed. Lewis P. Curtis, London: Oxford University Press.

Swift, Jonathan (1913) *The Correspondence of Jonathan Swift, D.D.*, vol. 5, ed. F. Elrington Ball, London: G. Bell.

—— (1963; 1965) *The Correspondence of Jonathan Swift*, vols 3 and 4, ed. H. Williams, London: Oxford University Press.

[Thomas, Elizabeth] (1722) *Miscellany Poems on Several Subjects*, London: Tho. Combes.

Trotter, Catharine (1737) 'Verses, occasion'd by the BUSTS in the Queen's Hermitage, and Mr DUCK being appointed Keeper of the Library in Merlin's Cave', *The Gentleman's Magazine* 7: 308.

Wakefield, Priscilla (1798) *Reflections on the Present Condition of the Female Sex: with Suggestions for its Improvement*, London: J. Johnson, and Darton & Harvey.

Warburton, Mr (1757) 'Advertisement' in *The Works of Alexander Pope, Esq. In Ten Volumes Complete. With his Last Corrections, Additions, and Improvements; . . . Printed verbatim from the Octavo Edition of Mr. Warburton*, vol. 1, London: A. Millar, J. & R. Tonson, H. Lintot, & C. Bathurst.

Wilkes, Wetenhall (1741) 'An Essay on the Pleasures and Advantages of Female Literature', *Godwyn Pamphlet* 398: 3–42.

Wollstonecraft, Mary (1788 [1980]) *Mary, A Fiction* in *Mary, A Fiction and The Wrongs of Woman*, ed. James Kinsley and Gary Kelly, Oxford: Oxford University Press.

[——] (1789) *The Female Reader; or Miscellaneous Pieces. In Prose and Verse; Selected from the Best Writers, And Disposed under Proper Heads; For the Improvement of Young Women. By Mr. Cresswick, Teacher of Elocution*, London: J. Johnson.

—— (1975) *Vindication of the Rights of Woman*, ed. Miriam Kramnick, Harmondsworth: Penguin.

—— (1798) *Posthumous Works of the Author of a Vindication of the Rights of Woman. In Four Volumes*, London: J. Johnson.

—— (1979) *Collected Letters of Mary Wollstonecraft*, ed. R.M. Wardle, London: Cornell University Press.

Woodforde, James (1935 [1978]) *The Diary of a Country Parson 1758–1802*, ed. John Beresford, Oxford: Oxford University Press.

Woolf, Virginia (1920 [1978]) 'The Intellectual Status of Women', *New Statesman* 16 October, in *The Diary of Virginia Woolf*, vol. 2, appendix 3, ed. Ann Olivier Bell, London: Hogarth Press.

—— (1929 [1977]) *A Room of One's Own*, London: Grafton.

Yearsley, Ann (1793) *Catalogue of the Books, Tracts, etc. Contained in Ann Yearsley's Public Library*, Bristol: Printed for the Proprietor.

Periodicals

The Analytical Review, or History of Literature, Domestic and Foreign, on an Enlarged Plan, London: J. Johnson.

The Annual Register, or a View of the History, Politics, and Literature, for the Year 1761 (1779) 4th edn, London: J. Dodsley.

The Critical Review: or, Annals of Literature. By A Society of Gentlemen, London: A. Hamilton.

The Gentleman's Magazine: and Historical Chronicle, London: F. Jefferies; D. Henry & R. Cave; E. Cave; E. Cave, Jun.; D. Henry; J. Nichols.

The Female Spectator (1744) 1, London: T. Gardner.

Lady's Monthly Museum, or Polite Repository of Amusement and Instruction, London: Vernor & Hood.

The Lady's Museum; By the Author of the Female Quixote, (1760–1) London: J. Newberry & J. Coote.

The Monthly Review; or, Literary Journal, London: R. Griffiths.

The Guardian of Education, A Periodical Work (1802) 1, London: J. Hatchard.

SECONDARY SOURCES

Adburgham, Alison (1972) *Women in Print: Writing Women and Women's Magazines from the Restoration to the Accession of Victoria*, London: Allen & Unwin.

Agress, Lynne (1978) *The Feminine Irony: Women on Women in Early-Nineteenth-Century English Literature*, Rutherford: Fairleigh Dickinson University Press.

Allen, Walter (1958) *The English Novel: A Short Critical History*, London: Penguin.

Amussen, S.D. (1987) 'Gender, Family and the Social Order, 1560–1725', in *Order and Disorder in Early Modern England*, ed. A. Fletcher and J. Stevenson, Cambridge: Cambridge University Press.

Anderson, Paul Bunyan (1935–6) 'Mistress Delarivière Manley's Biography', *Modern Philology* 33: 261–78.

Averley, G., Flowers, A., Robinson, F.J.G., Thompson, E.A., Wallis, P.J., and Wallis, R.V. (1979) *Eighteenth-Century British Books: A Subject Catalogue Extracted from the British Museum General Catalogue of Printed Books*, Project for Historical Biobibliography, University of Newcastle-upon-Tyne: Dawson.

Barash, Carol L. (1987) 'Gender, Authority and the "Life" of an Eighteenth-century Woman Writer: Delarivière Manley's *Adventures of Rivella*', *Women's Studies International Forum* 10 (2): 165–9.

Beasley, Jerry C. (1972) *A Check List of Prose Fiction Published in England, 1740–1749*, Charlottesville: University Press of Virginia.

—— (1978) *English Fiction, 1660–1800: A Guide to Information Sources*, Detroit: Gale Research Company.

Beilin, Elaine V. (1987) *Redeeming Eve: Women Writers of the English Renaissance*, Princeton, N.J.: Princeton University Press.

Benkovitz, Miriam J. (1976) 'Some Observations on Women's Concept of Self in the 18th Century', in *Woman in the 18th Century and Other Essays*, ed. Paul Fritz and Richard Morton, Toronto: Samuel Stevens Hakkert.

Blain, Virginia, Clements, Patricia, and Grundy, Isobel (1990) *The Feminist Companion to Literature in English: Women Writers from the Middle Ages to the Present*, London: Batsford.

Blakey, Dorothy (1939) *The Minerva Press 1790–1820*, London: Bibliographical Society.

Block, Andrew (1961) *The English Novel 1740–1850: A Catalogue Including Prose Romances, Short Stories, and Translations of Foreign Fiction*, new and revised edn, London: Dawson.

Boucé, Paul-Gabriel (ed.) (1982) *Sexuality in Eighteenth-Century Britain*, Manchester: Manchester University Press.

Bowers, Fredson (1962) 'Scottish Printers and Booksellers 1668–1775. A Second Supplement (II)', *Studies in Bibliography: Papers of the Bibliographical Society of the University of Virginia* 15: 105–20.

Brink, Jeanie R. (ed.) (1980) *Female Scholars: A Tradition of Learned Women Before 1800*, Montreal: Eden Press.

Burnett, John (1969) *A History of the Cost of Living*, London: Penguin.

The Cambridge Bibliography of English Literature (1940), ed. F.W. Bateson, 4 vols, Cambridge: Cambridge University Press.

The Cambridge History of English Literature vols 10 and 11 (1913; 1914) ed. A.W. Ward and A.C. Waller, Cambridge: Cambridge University Press.

Capp, Bernard [Stuart] (1979) *Astrology and the Popular Press: English Almanacs 1500–1800*, London: Faber.

Carnie, Robert Hay (1961) 'Scottish Printers and Booksellers 1668–1775. A Second Supplement (I)', *Studies in Bibliography: Papers of the Bibliographical Society of the University of Virginia* 14: 81–96.

Carnie, Robert Hay and Doig, Ronald Paterson (1959) 'Scottish Printers and Booksellers 1668–1775: A Supplement', *Studies in Bibliography: Papers of the Bibliographical Society of the University of Virginia* 12: 131–59.

Chard, Chloe (1986) 'Introduction and Select Bibliography' to Ann Radcliffe *The Romance of the Forest*, Oxford: Oxford University Press.

Clark, Alice (1919 [1982]) *The Working Life of Women in the Seventeenth Century*, London: Routledge & Kegan Paul.

Clinton, Katherine B. (1974–5) 'Femme et Philosophe: Enlightenment Origins of Feminism', *Eighteenth-Century Studies* 8: 283–99.

Collins, A.S. (1927 [1973]) *Authorship in the Days of Johnson: Being a Study of the Relation Between Author, Patron, Publisher and Public 1726–1780*, Clifton, N.J.: Augustus M. Kelley.

Cotton, Nancy (1980) *Women Playwrights in England c.1363–1750*, London: Associated University Presses.

Cranfield, G.A. (1962) *The Development of the Provincial Newspaper 1700–1760*, London: Oxford University Press.

Cressy, David (1980) *Literacy and the Social Order*, Cambridge: Cambridge University Press.

Davidoff, L. and Hall, C. (1987) *Family Fortunes: Men and Women of the English Middle Class 1780–1850*, London: Hutchinson.

Davin, Anna (1972) 'Women and History', in *The Body Politic: Writings from the Women's Liberation Movement in Britain, 1969–1972*, ed. Michelene Wandor, London: Stage I.

Davin, Anna and Alexander, Sally (1976) 'Feminist History', *History Workshop: A Journal of Socialist Historians* 1 (Spring): 4–6.

Davis, Natalie Z. (1976) 'Women's History in Transition: The European Case', *Feminist Studies* 3 (3–4): 83–103.

Day, Robert Adams (1966) *Told in Letters: Epistolary Fiction Before Richardson*, Ann Arbor: University of Michigan Press.

Dictionary of Anonymous and Pseudonymous English Literature (Halkett and Laing) vols 1–7 (1926–34), ed. J. Kennedy, W.A. Smith, and A.F. Johnson, London: Oliver & Boyd.

—— vol. 9 (1962), ed. Dennis Rhodes and Anna E.C. Simoni, London: Oliver & Boyd.

The Dictionary of National Biography: From the Earliest Times to 1900 (1922), ed. Sir Leslie Stephen and Sir Sidney Lee, 22 vols, London: Oxford University Press.

Dobrée, Bonamy (1959) *English Literature in the Early Eighteenth Century: 1700–1740*, vol. 7 of *The Oxford History of English Literature*, ed. F.P. Wilson and Bonamy Dobrée, London: Oxford University Press.

Donnelly, Lucy M. (1949) 'The Celebrated Mrs. Macaulay', *William and Mary Quarterly* 3rd ser. 6: 173–207.

Donnison, Jean (1977) *Midwives and Medical Men: A History of Inter-professional Rivalries and Women's Rights*, New York: Schocken Books.

Duffy, Maureen (1977) *The Passionate Shepherdess: Aphra Behn 1640–89*, London: Jonathan Cape.

Ehrenpreis, Anne Henry (1971) 'Introduction' to Charlotte Smith (1788 [1971]) *Emmeline: the orphan of the Castle*, London: Oxford University Press.

Eshleman, Dorothy H. (1949) *Elizabeth Griffith; a Biographical and Critical Study*, Ph.D. thesis 1947, Philadelphia: University of Pennsylvania.

Ferguson, Moira and Todd, Janet (1984) *Mary Wollstonecraft*, Boston: Twayne Publishers.

Fetterley, Judith (1978) *The Resisting Reader: A Feminist Approach to American Fiction*, Bloomington: Indiana University Press.

Figes, Eva (1982) *Sex and Subterfuge: Women Novelists to 1850*, London: Macmillan.

Fox-Genovese, Elizabeth (1982) 'Placing Women in History', *New Left Review* 133 (May–June): 5–29.

Fritz, Paul and Morton, Richard (eds) (1976) *Woman in the 18th Century and Other Essays*, Toronto: Samuel Stevens Hakkert.

Gagen, Jean E. (1954) *The New Woman: Her Emergence in English Drama, 1600–1730*, New York: Twayne Publishers.

Gardiner, Dorothy (1929) *English Girlhood at School: A Study of Women's Education Through Twelve Centuries*, Oxford: Oxford University Press.

George, M. Dorothy (1925 [1966]) *London Life in the Eighteenth Century*, London: Peregrine.

Gilbert, Sandra and Gubar, Susan (1979) *The Madwoman in the Attic: The Woman Writer and the Nineteenth-Century Literary Imagination*, New Haven: Yale University Press.

Goreau, Angeline (1980) *Reconstructing Aphra: A Social Biography of Aphra Behn*, New York: Dial Press.

Graham, Elspeth, Hinds, Hilary, Hobby, Elaine, and Wilcox, Helen (eds) (1989) *Her Own Life: Autobiographical Writings By Seventeenth-Century Englishwomen*, London: Routledge.

Green, Mary Elizabeth (1980) 'Elizabeth Elstob: "The Saxon Nymph" (1683–1765)', in *Female Scholars: A Tradition of Learned Women Before 1800*, ed. Jeanie R. Brink, Montreal: Eden Press Women's Publications.

Greer, Germaine (1979) *The Obstacle Race*, London: Secker & Warburg.

Habakkuk, H.J. (1950) 'Marriage Settlements in the Eighteenth Century', *Transactions of the Royal Historical Society*, 4th ser., 32: 15–30.

Halsband, Robert (1976) 'Women and Literature in 18th Century England', in *Woman in the 18th Century and Other Essays*, ed. Paul Fritz and Richard Morton, Toronto: Samuel Stevens Hakkert.

Hapgood, Kathleen (1981) 'Library Practice in the Bristol Library Society 1772–1830', *Library History* 5: 145–53.

Hardy, J.C. (c.1982) *A Catalogue of English Prose Fiction: Mainly of the Eighteenth Century from a Private Library*, Foss (Frenich, Foss [Pitlochry, Perthshire PH16 5NG]): K.D. Duval.

Hecht, J. Jean (1956) *The Domestic Servant Class in Eighteenth-Century England*, London: Routledge & Kegan Paul.

Hilbish, Florence May Anna (1941) *Charlotte Smith, Poet and Novelist (1749–1806)*, Ph.D. thesis 1936, Philadelphia: University of Pennsylvania.

Hobby, Elaine (1984) 'English Women's Writing 1649–1688', unpublished Ph.D. thesis, Birmingham University.

—— (1988) *Virtue of Necessity: English Women's Writing 1649–1688*, London: Virago.

Horner, Joyce M. (1929–30) *The English Women Novelists and their Connection with the Feminist Movement (1688–1797)*, Northampton: Smith College Studies in Modern Language 11.

Hughes, Helen Sard (1917) 'The Life and Works of Mary Mitchell Collyer', unpublished Ph.D. thesis, Chicago University.

Hull, Suzanne W. (1982) *Chaste, Silent and Obedient: English Books for Women, 1475–1640*, San Marino: Huntington Library.

Ingram, Martin (1988) 'The Reform of Popular Culture? Sex and Marriage in Early Modern England', in *Popular Culture in Seventeenth-century England*, ed. Barry Reay, London: Routledge.

Jones, M[ary] G[wladys] (1952 [1968]) *Hannah More*, New York: Greenwood Press.

Jones, Vivien (ed.) (1990) *Women in the Eighteenth Century: Constructions of Femininity*, London: Routledge.

Kamm, Josephine (1965) *Hope Deferred: Girls' Education in English History*, London: Methuen.

Kanner, Barbara (1979) 'Old and New Women's History', in *The Women of England From Anglo-Saxon times to the Present: Interpretive Bibliographical Essays*, ed. Barbara Kanner, Hamden, Conn.: Archon Books.

245

Kaufman, Paul (1960) *Borrowings from the Bristol Library, 1773–1784: A Unique Record of Reading Vogues*, Charlottesville: Bibliographical Society of the University of Virginia.

—— (1964 [1969]) 'English Book Clubs', *Libri* 14, No. 1, rpt. 'English Book Clubs and their Social Import', in P. Kaufman *Libraries and their Users: Collected Papers in Library History*, London: Library Association.

—— (1967a) 'The Community Library: A Chapter in English Social History', *Transactions of the American Philosophical Society* N.S. 57, Pt. 7.

—— (1967b [1969]) 'In Defence of Fair Readers', *A Review of English Literature* 8 (April 1967), rpt. in P. Kaufman *Libraries and their Users: Collected Papers in Library History*, London: Library Association.

Kavanagh, Julia (1862) *English Women of Letters*, 2nd edn, London: Hurst & Blackett.

Kelly, Gary (1976) *The English Jacobin Novel 1780–1805*, Oxford: Oxford University Press.

Kilpatrick, Sarah (1980) *Fanny Burney*, London: David & Charles.

Koon, Helene (1978–9) 'Eliza Haywood and *The Female Spectator*', *Huntington Library Quarterly* 42: 43–55.

Larson, Edith Sedgwick (1981) 'Early Eighteenth-Century English Women Writers: Their Lives, Fiction and Letters', unpublished Ph.D. thesis, Brandeis University.

Laslett, Peter (1977) *Family Life and Illicit Love in Earlier Generations: Essays in Historical Sociology*, Cambridge: Cambridge University Press.

Lawler, John (1898) *Book Auctions in England in the Seventeenth Century (1676–1700): With a Chronological List of the Book Auctions of the Period*, London: Elliot Stock.

Leavis, F.R. (1960) *The Great Tradition: George Eliot, Henry James, Joseph Conrad*, new edn, London: Chatto & Windus.

LeGates, Marlene (1976–7) 'The Cult of Womanhood in Eighteenth-Century Thought', *Eighteenth-Century Studies* 10: 21–39.

Lerner, Gerda (1975) 'Placing Women in History: Definitions and Challenges', *Feminist-Studies* 3 (Fall): 5–14.

Leydesdorff, Selma (1989) 'Politics, Identification and the Writing of Women's History', in *Current Issues in Women's History*, ed. A. Angerman, G. Binnema, A. Keunen, V. Poels, and J. Zirkzee, London: Routledge.

Link, Frederick (1968) *Aphra Behn*, New York: Twayne Publishers.

Littlewood, S.R. (1921) *Elizabeth Inchbald and her Circle: The Life Story of a Charming Woman (1753–1821)*, London: Daniel O'Connor.

London Stationers' Company (1913–14) *A Transcript of the Registers of the Worshipful Company of Stationers; from 1640–1708 A.D.*, ed. for the Roxburghe Club by G.E. Briscoe Eyre, entries transcribed by H.R. Plomer, 3 vols, London: Privately Printed.

Lonsdale, Roger (ed.) (1989) *Eighteenth Century Women Poets: An Oxford Anthology*, Oxford: Oxford University Press.

McBurney, William Harlin (1958) 'Edmund Curll, Mrs. Jane Barker and the English Novel', *Philological Quarterly* 37: 385–99.

—— (1959) 'Mrs Mary Davys: Forerunner of Fielding', *Publications of the Modern Language Association of America* 74: 348–55.

—— (1960) *A Check List of English Prose Fiction 1700–1739*, Cambridge, Mass.: Harvard University Press.

—— (ed.) (1964) *Four Before Richardson: Selected English Novels, 1720–1727*, Lincoln: University of Nebraska Press.

MacCarthy, B.G. (1944) *Women Writers: Their Contribution to the English Novel, 1621–1744*, vol. 1 of *The Female Pen*, Cork: Cork University Press.

—— (1947) *The Later Women Novelists: 1744–1818*, vol. 2 of *The Female Pen*, Cork: Cork University Press.

McKeon, Michael (1988) *The Origins of the English Novel 1600–1740*, London: Radius.

McKillop, Alan Dugald (1951–2) 'Charlotte Smith's Letters', *Huntington Library Quarterly* 15: 237–55.

Manners, Emily (1914) *Elizabeth Hooton First Quaker Woman Preacher (1600–1672)*, London: Headley Brothers.

Matthews, William (compiler) (1950) *British Diaries: An Annotated Bibliography of British Diaries Between 1442 and 1942*, Berkeley and Los Angeles: University of California Press.

—— (compiler) (1955) *British Autobiographies: An Annotated Bibliography of British Autobiographies Published or Written Before 1951*, Berkeley and Los Angeles: University of California Press.

Mayo, Robert D. (1962) *The English Novel in the Magazines 1740–1815: With a Catalogue of Magazine Novels and Novelettes*, London: Oxford University Press.

Moers, Ellen (1978) *Literary Women*, London: The Women's Press.

Morgan, Charlotte E. (1911 [1963]) *The Rise of the Novel of Manners: A Study of English Prose Fiction between 1600 and 1740*, New York: Russell.

Morgan, Fidelis (1981) *The Female Wits: Women Playwrights on the London Stage 1660–1720*, London: Virago.

—— (1987) *A Woman of No Character: An Autobigraphy of Mrs Manley*, London: Faber & Faber.

Morton, A.L. (1970) *The World of the Ranters: Religious Radicalism in the English Revolution*, London: Lawrence & Wishart.

Mumby, Frank Arthur and Norrie, Ian (1974) *Publishing and Bookselling*, 5th edn, London: Jonathan Cape.

Nangle, Benjamin Christie (1934) *The Monthly Review First Series, 1749–1789: Indexes of Contributors and Articles*, London: Oxford University Press.

—— (1955) *The Monthly Review Second Series, 1790–1815: Indexes of Contributors and Articles*, London: Oxford University Press.

Needham, G.B. (1948–9) 'Mary de la Rivière Manley, Tory Defender', *Huntington Library Quarterly* 12: 253–88.

Okin, Susan Moller (1982) 'Women and the Making of the Sentimental Family', *Philosophy and Public Affairs* 11 (1): 65–88.

O'Malley, Ida B. (1933) *Women in Subjection: A Study of the Lives of Englishwomen Before 1832*, London: Duckworth.

Palomo, Dolores (1978) 'A Woman Writer and the Scholars: A Review of Mary Manley's Reputation', *Women and Literature* 6: 36–45.

Perkin, Harold (1969) *The Origins of Modern English Society 1780–1880*, London: Routledge & Kegan Paul.

Perry, Ruth (1980) *Women, Letters, and the Novel*, New York: AMS Press.

Pinchbeck, Ivy (1930 [1981]) *Women Workers and the Industrial Revolution 1750–1850*, 3rd edn, London: Virago.

Pitcher, Edward N. (1976) 'Robert Mayo's the English Novel in the Magazines 1740–1815: New Facts', *The Library* 5th ser. 31: 20–30.

Plant, Marjorie (1974) *The English Book Trade: An Economic History of the Making and Sale of Books*, 3rd edn, London: Allen & Unwin.

Plomer, Henry R. (1907) *A Dictionary of the Booksellers and Printers who were at Work in England, Scotland and Ireland from 1641–1667*, London: London Bibliographical Society.

Plomer, Henry R. with the help of Aldis, H.G. [and others] (1922) *A Dictionary of the Printers and Booksellers who were at Work in England, Scotland and Ireland from 1668–1725*, ed. Arundel Esdaile, London: London Bibliographical Society.

Plomer, Henry R., Bushnall, G.H., and Dix, E.R.McC. (1932) *A Dictionary of the Printers and Booksellers who were at Work in England, Scotland and Ireland from 1726 to 1775*, London: London Bibliographical Society.

Plumb, J.H. (1971) 'Reason and Unreason in the Eighteenth Century: The English Experience', in *Some Aspects of Eighteenth Century England*, papers read at the Clark Library Seminar, 7 March 1970 by J.H. Plumb and Vinton A. Dearing, Los Angeles: William Andrews Clark Memorial Library.

—— (1975) 'The New World of Children in Eighteenth-Century England', *Past and Present* 67 (May): 64–95.

Pomerleau, Cynthia S. (1980) 'The Emergence of Women's Autobiography in England', in *Women's Autobiography: Essays in Criticism*, ed. Estelle C. Jelinek, Bloomington and London: Indiana University Press.

Porter, Roy (1982) *English Society in the Eighteenth Century*, London: Penguin.

Prochaska, F.K. (1974) 'Women in English Philanthropy 1790–1830', *International Review of Social History* 19: 426–45.

Reynolds, Myra (1920 [1964]) *The Learned Lady in England: 1650–1760*, Gloucester, Mass.: Peter Smith.

Richetti, John (1969) *Popular Fiction Before Richardson: Narrative Patterns, 1700–1739*, London: Oxford University Press.

Robinson, F.J.G. and Wallis, P.J. (1975) *Book Subscription Lists: A Revised Guide*, Newcastle-upon-Tyne: Harold Hill.

Rogers, Katharine M. (1982) *Feminism in Eighteenth-Century England*, Brighton: Harvester Press.

Rogers, Pat (1972) *Grub Street: Studies in Subculture*, London: Methuen.

Sackville-West, Vita (1927) *Aphra Behn*, London: Gerald Howe.

Sanderson, Michael (1972) 'Literacy and Social Mobility in the Industrial Revolution in England', *Past and Present* 56 (August): 75–104.

Saunders, J.W. (1964) *The Profession of English Letters*, London: Routledge & Kegan Paul.

Schofield, R.S. (1972–3) 'Dimensions of Illiteracy, 1750–1850', *Explorations in Economic History* 10: 437–54.

Schnorrenberg, Barbara B. (1976) 'Education for Women in Eighteenth Century England: An Annotated Bibliography', *Women and Literature* 4: 49–55.

Schnorrenberg, Barbara B. with Hunter, Jean E. (1979) 'The Eighteenth-Century Englishwoman', in *The Women of England from Anglo-Saxon Times to the Present: Interpretive Bibliographical Essays*, ed. B. Kanner, Hamden, Conn.: Archon Books.

Schweickart, Patrocinio P. (1989) 'Reading Ourselves: Towards a Feminist Theory of Reading', in *Speaking of Gender*, ed. Elaine Showalter, London: Routledge.

Séjourné, Philippe (1966) *Aspects généraux du roman féminin en Angleterre de 1740 à 1800*, Aix-en-Provence: Publications des Annales de la Faculté des Lettres.

Shevelow, Kathryn (1989) *Women and Print Culture: The Constructions of Femininity in the Early Periodical*, London: Routledge.

Showalter, Elaine (1977) *A Literature of Their Own: British Women Novelists from Brontë to Lessing*, Guildford: Princeton University Press.

—— (1979) 'Towards a Feminist Poetics', in *Women Writing and Writing About Women*, ed. Mary Jacobus, London: Croom Helm.

—— (1986) 'The Feminist Critical Revolution', in *The New Feminist Criticism: Essays on Women, Literature and Theory*, ed. Elaine Showalter, London: Virago Press.

—— (1989) 'Introduction: The Rise of Gender', in *Speaking of Gender*, ed. Elaine Showalter, London: Routledge.

Singer, Godfrey Frank (1933 [1963]) *The Epistolary Novel: Its Origin, Development, Decline and Residuary Influence*, New York: Russell & Russell.

Small, Miriam R. (1935) *Charlotte Ramsay Lennox: An Eighteenth Century Lady of Letters*, London: Oxford University Press.

Smith-Rosenburg, Carroll (1975) 'The New Woman and the New History', *Feminist Studies* 3 (Fall): 185–98.

Spacks, Patricia Meyer (1974–5) 'Ev'ry Woman is at Heart a Rake', *Eighteenth-Century Studies* 8: 27–46.

—— (1975) *The Female Imagination*, New York: Alfred A. Knopf.

—— (1976) *Imagining a Self: Autobiography and Novel in Eighteenth-Century England*, Cambridge, Mass.: Harvard University Press.

Spencer, Jane (1986) *The Rise of the Woman Novelist: From Aphra Behn to Jane Austen*, Oxford: Basil Blackwell.

Spender, Dale (1986) *Mothers of the Novel*, London: Pandora.

Spufford, Margaret (1981) *Small Books and Pleasant Histories: Popular Fiction and its Readership in Seventeenth Century England*, London: Methuen.

Stenton, Doris Mary (1957) *The English Woman in History*, London: Allen & Unwin.

Stevenson, Lionel (1960) *The English Novel: A Panorama*, London: Constable.

Stone, Lawrence (1969) 'Literacy and Education in England 1640–1900', *Past and Present* 42 (February): 69–139.

—— (1979) *The Family, Sex and Marriage in England 1500–1800*, abridged edn, London: Penguin.

Straus, Ralph (1927) *The Unspeakable Curll: Being Some Account of Edmund Curll Bookseller; to which is Added a Full List of his Books*, London: Chapman and Hall.

Summers, Montague (ed.) (1915) *The Works of Aphra Behn*, 6 vols, London: Heinemann.

—— (1940 [1969]) *A Gothic Bibliography (1728–1916)*, London: Fortune Press.

Sutherland, James (1969) *English Literature of the Late Seventeenth Century*, vol. 6 of *The Oxford History of English Literature*, ed. Bonamy Dobrée and Norman Davis, London: Oxford University Press.

Term Catalogues, 1668–1709 A.D.; with a Number for Easter Term, 1711 A.D., ed. Edward Arber (1903; 1905) vol. 1 *(1668–1682 A.D.)* and vol. 2 *(1683–1696 A.D.)*, London: Privately Printed.

Thomas, Keith (1959) 'The Double Standard', *Journal of the History of Ideas* 20: 195–216.

Todd, Janet (1986) *Sensibility: An Introduction*, London: Methuen.

—— (ed.) (1987) *A Dictionary of British and American Women Writers 1660–1800*, London: Methuen.

—— (1989) *The Sign of Angellica: Women, Writing, and Fiction 1660–1800*, London: Virago Press.

Tompkins, J.M.S. (1932 [1962]) *The Popular Novel in England: 1770–1800*, London: Methuen.

Turner, Cheryl L. (1985) 'The Growth of Published and Professional Fiction Writing By Women Before Jane Austen', unpublished Ph.D. thesis, Nottingham University.

Vincent, David (1989) *Literacy and Popular Culture: England 1750–1914*, Cambridge: Cambridge University Press.

Watt, Ian (1957 [1972]) *The Rise of the Novel: Studies in Defoe, Richardson and Fielding*, London: Pelican.

Whicher, George Frisbie (1915) *The Life and Romances of Mrs. Eliza Haywood*, New York: Columbia University Press.

Whitmore, Clara Helen (1910) *Women's Work in English Fiction from the Restoration to the Mid-Victorian Period*, London: G.P. Putnam's.

Wiles, R.M. (1957) *Serial Publication in England Before 1750*, Cambridge: Cambridge University Press.

—— (1968) 'Middle-Class Literacy in Eighteenth-Century England: Fresh Evidence', in *Studies in the Eighteenth Century*, ed. R.F. Brissenden, a collection of papers presented at the David Nichol Smith Memorial Seminar, Canberra, 1966, Canberra: Australian National University Press.

Wilson, Charles (1957) 'The Entrepreneur in the Industrial Revolution in Britain', *History* 42: 101–80.

Woodcock, G. (1948) *The Incomparable Aphra*, London: T.V. Boardman & Co.

INDEX